The Essential Air Fryer

Cookbook

Over 1000 Quick, Nutritious and Mouthwatering Air Fryer Recipes to Fry, Grill, Roast, and Bake with Your Air Fryer for All Occasions and Seasons

Quinn B. Leuschke

Table of Contents

Chapter 8 Vegetables and Sides 71

Chapter 9 Vegetarian Mains   82

Chapter 10 Desserts   88

Appendix 1: Measurement Conversion Chart   96

Appendix 2: Air Fryer Cooking Chart   97

INTRODUCTION

Welcome to my air fryer cookbook, a collection of mouth-watering recipes that will help you make healthy and delicious meals using your air fryer. As a professional dietitian and a food lover, I know how important it is to eat well-balanced and nutritious meals while still enjoying the foods we love. That's why I've created this cookbook specifically for air fryer users in the United States.

The Air Fryer Craze: Making Healthier Meals with Ease

Air fryers have become increasingly popular in recent years, and for good reason. They offer a healthier alternative to traditional frying methods, using hot air instead of oil to cook food. This not only reduces the amount of fat and calories in the food but also creates a crispy and delicious texture that rivals fried food. With air fryers, you can enjoy your favorite foods without sacrificing taste or health.

◊ Health Benefits of Air Frying: Eating Well Without Sacrificing Flavor

Air frying has several health benefits that make it an attractive option for health-conscious home cooks. By reducing the amount of oil used in cooking, air frying can help lower the calorie and fat content of your meals, making it easier to maintain a healthy weight. It can also reduce the risk of heart disease and other health conditions associated with a high-fat diet.

◊ Versatility of Air Fryers: From Breakfast to Dessert

Air fryers are incredibly versatile kitchen appliances that can be used to cook a wide variety of foods. From chicken wings and French fries to vegetables and even desserts, air fryers can handle it all. They can also be used to reheat leftovers and cook frozen foods, making them a convenient option for busy home cooks.

While air fryers are easy to use and maintain, it's important to follow proper usage and maintenance guidelines to ensure optimal results and safe cooking practices. Here are some tips for air fryer maintenance and cleaning:

1. Unplug the air fryer and let it cool down completely before cleaning.
2. Remove any food residue from the air fryer basket or tray using a soft sponge or cloth. Avoid
3. using abrasive materials that could damage the non-stick coating.
4. Wash the air fryer basket or tray, as well as any accessories, in warm soapy water. If they are dishwasher-safe, you can also clean them in the dishwasher.
5. Clean the inside of the air fryer using a damp cloth or sponge. Avoid using water directly on the heating element.
6. Clean the outside of the air fryer with a damp cloth or sponge. Avoid using harsh cleaners or abrasive materials that could damage the surface.
7. If your air fryer has a removable heating element, remove it and clean it separately according to the manufacturer's instructions.
8. Regularly check the air intake and exhaust vents to ensure that they are not blocked by debris or food residue. If necessary, use a soft brush or cloth to remove any buildup.

A Perfect Cookbook: Healthy, Delicious Recipes for Air Fryer Users

The purpose of this cookbook is to provide American air fryer users with a collection of healthy and delicious recipes that they can enjoy at home. From breakfast to dinner, appetizers to desserts, this cookbook has something for everyone. Each recipe is easy to follow and includes a nutrition analysis, so you know exactly what you're eating.

I hope this air fryer cookbook will inspire you to cook healthier meals and try new recipes using your air fryer. With the right ingredients and techniques, you can create delicious meals that are both healthy and satisfying. So, fire up your air fryer, and let's get cooking!

Chapter 1 Breakfasts

Drop Biscuits

Prep time: 10 minutes | Cook time: 9 to 10 minutes | Serves 5

4 cups all-purpose flour
1 tablespoon baking powder
1 tablespoon sugar (optional)
1 teaspoon salt
6 tablespoons butter, plus more

for brushing on the biscuits
(optional)
¾ cup buttermilk
1 to 2 tablespoons oil

1. In a large bowl, whisk the flour, baking powder, sugar (if using), and salt until blended. 2. Add the butter. Using a pastry cutter or 2 forks, work the dough until pea-size balls of the butter-flour mixture appear. Stir in the buttermilk until the mixture is sticky. 3. Preheat the air fryer to 330ºF (166ºC). Line the air fryer basket with parchment paper and spritz it with oil. 4. Drop the dough by the tablespoonful onto the prepared basket, leaving 1 inch between each, to form 10 biscuits. 5. Bake for 5 minutes. Flip the biscuits and cook for 4 minutes more for a light brown top, or 5 minutes more for a darker biscuit. Brush the tops with melted butter, if desired.

Cheesy Cauliflower "Hash Browns"

Prep time: 30 minutes | Cook time: 24 minutes | Makes 6 hash browns

2 ounces (57 g) 100% cheese
crisps
1 (12-ounce / 340-g) steamer
bag cauliflower, cooked
according to package

instructions
1 large egg
½ cup shredded sharp Cheddar
cheese
½ teaspoon salt

1. Let cooked cauliflower cool 10 minutes. 2. Place cheese crisps into food processor and pulse on low 30 seconds until crisps are finely ground. 3. Using a kitchen towel, wring out excess moisture from cauliflower and place into food processor. 4. Add egg to food processor and sprinkle with Cheddar and salt. Pulse five times until mixture is mostly smooth. 5. Cut two pieces of parchment to fit air fryer basket. Separate mixture into six even scoops and place three on each piece of ungreased parchment, keeping at least 2 inch of space between each scoop. Press each into a hash brown shape, about ¼ inch thick. 6. Place one batch on parchment into air fryer basket. Adjust the temperature to 375ºF (191ºC) and air fry for 12 minutes, turning hash browns halfway through cooking. Hash browns will be golden brown when done. Repeat with second batch. 7. Allow 5 minutes to cool. Serve warm.

Breakfast Meatballs

Prep time: 10 minutes | Cook time: 15 minutes | Makes 18 meatballs

1 pound (454 g) ground pork
breakfast sausage
½ teaspoon salt
¼ teaspoon ground black
pepper

½ cup shredded sharp Cheddar
cheese
1 ounce (28 g) cream cheese,
softened
1 large egg, whisked

1. Combine all ingredients in a large bowl. Form mixture into eighteen 1-inch meatballs. 2. Place meatballs into ungreased air fryer basket. Adjust the temperature to 400ºF (204ºC) and air fry for 15 minutes, shaking basket three times during cooking. Meatballs will be browned on the outside and have an internal temperature of at least 145ºF (63ºC) when completely cooked. Serve warm.

Greek Bagels

Prep time: 10 minutes | Cook time: 10 minutes | Makes 2 bagels

½ cup self-rising flour, plus
more for dusting
½ cup plain Greek yogurt
1 egg
1 tablespoon water

4 teaspoons everything bagel
spice mix
Cooking oil spray
1 tablespoon butter, melted

1. In a large bowl, using a wooden spoon, stir together the flour and yogurt until a tacky dough forms. Transfer the dough to a lightly floured work surface and roll the dough into a ball. 2. Cut the dough into 2 pieces and roll each piece into a log. Form each log into a bagel shape, pinching the ends together. 3. In a small bowl, whisk the egg and water. Brush the egg wash on the bagels. 4. Sprinkle 2 teaspoons of the spice mix on each bagel and gently press it into the dough. 5. Insert the crisper plate into the basket and the basket into the unit. Preheat the unit by selecting BAKE, setting the temperature to 330ºF (166ºC), and setting the time to 3 minutes. Select START/STOP to begin. 6. Once the unit is preheated, spray the crisper plate with cooking spray. Drizzle the bagels with the butter and place them into the basket. 7. Select BAKE, set the temperature to 330ºF (166ºC), and set the time to 10 minutes. Select START/STOP to begin. 8. When the cooking is complete, the bagels should be lightly golden on the outside. Serve warm.

Creamy Cinnamon Rolls

Prep time: 10 minutes | Cook time: 9 minutes | Serves 8

1 pound (454 g) frozen bread dough, thawed	Cream Cheese Glaze:
¼ cup butter, melted	4 ounces (113 g) cream cheese, softened
¾ cup brown sugar	2 tablespoons butter, softened
1½ tablespoons ground cinnamon	1¼ cups powdered sugar
	½ teaspoon vanilla extract

1. Let the bread dough come to room temperature on the counter. On a lightly floured surface, roll the dough into a 13-inch by 11-inch rectangle. Position the rectangle so the 13-inch side is facing you. Brush the melted butter all over the dough, leaving a 1-inch border uncovered along the edge farthest away from you. 2. Combine the brown sugar and cinnamon in a small bowl. Sprinkle the mixture evenly over the buttered dough, keeping the 1-inch border uncovered. Roll the dough into a log, starting with the edge closest to you. Roll the dough tightly, rolling evenly, and push out any air pockets. When you get to the uncovered edge of the dough, press the dough onto the roll to seal it together. 3. Cut the log into 8 pieces, slicing slowly with a sawing motion so you don't flatten the dough. Turn the slices on their sides and cover with a clean kitchen towel. Let the rolls sit in the warmest part of the kitchen for 1½ to 2 hours to rise. 4. To make the glaze, place the cream cheese and butter in a microwave-safe bowl. Soften the mixture in the microwave for 30 seconds at a time until it is easy to stir. Gradually add the powdered sugar and stir to combine. Add the vanilla extract and whisk until smooth. Set aside. 5. When the rolls have risen, preheat the air fryer to 350ºF (177ºC). 6. Transfer 4 of the rolls to the air fryer basket. Air fry for 5 minutes. Turn the rolls over and air fry for another 4 minutes. Repeat with the remaining 4 rolls. 7. Let the rolls cool for two minutes before glazing. Spread large dollops of cream cheese glaze on top of the warm cinnamon rolls, allowing some glaze to drip down the side of the rolls. Serve warm.

Butternut Squash and Ricotta Frittata

Prep time: 10 minutes | Cook time: 33 minutes | Serves 2 to 3

1 cup cubed (½-inch) butternut squash (5½ ounces / 156 g)	4 fresh sage leaves, thinly sliced
2 tablespoons olive oil	6 large eggs, lightly beaten
Kosher salt and freshly ground black pepper, to taste	½ cup ricotta cheese
	Cayenne pepper

1. In a bowl, toss the squash with the olive oil and season with salt and black pepper until evenly coated. Sprinkle the sage on the bottom of a cake pan and place the squash on top. Place the pan in the air fryer and bake at 400ºF (204ºC) for 10 minutes. Stir to incorporate the sage, then cook until the squash is tender and lightly caramelized at the edges, about 3 minutes more. 2. Pour the eggs over the squash, dollop the ricotta all over, and sprinkle with cayenne. Bake at 300ºF (149ºC) until the eggs are set and the frittata is golden brown on top, about 20 minutes. Remove the pan from the air fryer and cut the frittata into wedges to serve.

Three-Berry Dutch Pancake

Prep time: 10 minutes | Cook time: 12 to 16 minutes | Serves 4

2 egg whites	1 tablespoon unsalted butter, melted
1 egg	1 cup sliced fresh strawberries
½ cup whole-wheat pastry flour	½ cup fresh blueberries
½ cup 2% milk	½ cup fresh raspberries
1 teaspoon pure vanilla extract	

1. In a medium bowl, use an eggbeater or hand mixer to quickly mix the egg whites, egg, pastry flour, milk, and vanilla until well combined. 2. Use a pastry brush to grease the bottom of a baking pan with the melted butter. Immediately pour in the batter and put the basket back in the fryer. Bake at 330ºF (166ºC) for 12 to 16 minutes, or until the pancake is puffed and golden brown. 3. Remove the pan from the air fryer; the pancake will fall. Top with the strawberries, blueberries, and raspberries. Serve immediately.

Gyro Breakfast Patties with Tzatziki

Prep time: 10 minutes | Cook time: 20 minutes per batch | Makes 16 patties

Patties:	½ teaspoon fine sea salt
2 pounds (907 g) ground lamb or beef	½ teaspoon garlic powder, or 1 clove garlic, minced
½ cup diced red onions	¼ teaspoon dried dill weed, or 1 teaspoon finely chopped fresh dill
¼ cup sliced black olives	
2 tablespoons tomato sauce	For Garnish/Serving:
1 teaspoon dried oregano leaves	½ cup crumbled feta cheese (about 2 ounces / 57 g)
1 teaspoon Greek seasoning	
2 cloves garlic, minced	Diced red onions
1 teaspoon fine sea salt	Sliced black olives
Tzatziki:	Sliced cucumbers
1 cup full-fat sour cream	
1 small cucumber, chopped	

1. Preheat the air fryer to 350ºF (177ºC). 2. Place the ground lamb, onions, olives, tomato sauce, oregano, Greek seasoning, garlic, and salt in a large bowl. Mix well to combine the ingredients. 3. Using your hands, form the mixture into sixteen 3-inch patties. Place about 5 of the patties in the air fryer and air fry for 20 minutes, flipping halfway through. Remove the patties and place them on a serving platter. Repeat with the remaining patties. 4. While the patties cook, make the tzatziki: Place all the ingredients in a small bowl and stir well. Cover and store in the fridge until ready to serve. Garnish with ground black pepper before serving. 5. Serve the patties with a dollop of tzatziki, a sprinkle of crumbled feta cheese, diced red onions, sliced black olives, and sliced cucumbers. 6. Store leftovers in an airtight container in the refrigerator for up to 5 days or in the freezer for up to a month. Reheat the patties in a preheated 390ºF (199ºC) air fryer for a few minutes, until warmed through.

Tomato and Cheddar Rolls

Prep time: 30 minutes | Cook time: 25 minutes |
Makes 12 rolls

4 Roma tomatoes
½ clove garlic, minced
1 tablespoon olive oil
¼ teaspoon dried thyme
Salt and freshly ground black pepper, to taste
4 cups all-purpose flour
1 teaspoon active dry yeast

2 teaspoons sugar
2 teaspoons salt
1 tablespoon olive oil
1 cup grated Cheddar cheese, plus more for sprinkling at the end
1½ cups water

1. Cut the Roma tomatoes in half, remove the seeds with your fingers and transfer to a bowl. Add the garlic, olive oil, dried thyme, salt and freshly ground black pepper and toss well. 2. Preheat the air fryer to 390ºF (199ºC). 3. Place the tomatoes, cut side up in the air fryer basket and air fry for 10 minutes. The tomatoes should just start to brown. Shake the basket to redistribute the tomatoes, and air fry for another 5 to 10 minutes at 330ºF (166ºC) until the tomatoes are no longer juicy. Let the tomatoes cool and then rough chop them. 4. Combine the flour, yeast, sugar and salt in the bowl of a stand mixer. Add the olive oil, chopped roasted tomatoes and Cheddar cheese to the flour mixture and start to mix using the dough hook attachment. As you're mixing, add 1¼ cups of the water, mixing until the dough comes together. Continue to knead the dough with the dough hook for another 10 minutes, adding enough water to the dough to get it to the right consistency. 5. Transfer the dough to an oiled bowl, cover with a clean kitchen towel and let it rest and rise until it has doubled in volume, about 1 to 2 hours. Then, divide the dough into 12 equal portions. Roll each portion of dough into a ball. Lightly coat each dough ball with oil and let the dough balls rest and rise a second time, covered lightly with plastic wrap for 45 minutes. (Alternately, you can place the rolls in the refrigerator overnight and take them out 2 hours before you bake them.) 6. Preheat the air fryer to 360ºF (182ºC). 7. Spray the dough balls and the air fryer basket with a little olive oil. Place three rolls at a time in the basket and bake for 10 minutes. Add a little grated Cheddar cheese on top of the rolls for the last 2 minutes of air frying for an attractive finish.

Spinach and Bacon Roll-ups

Prep time: 5 minutes | Cook time: 8 to 9 minutes |
Serves 4

4 flour tortillas (6- or 7-inch size)
4 slices Swiss cheese
1 cup baby spinach leaves

4 slices turkey bacon
Special Equipment:
4 toothpicks, soak in water for at least 30 minutes

1. Preheat the air fryer to 390ºF (199ºC). 2. On a clean work surface, top each tortilla with one slice of cheese and ¼ cup of spinach, then tightly roll them up. 3. Wrap each tortilla with a strip of turkey bacon and secure with a toothpick. 4. Arrange the roll-ups in the air fryer basket, leaving space between each roll-up. 5. Air fry for 4 minutes. Flip the roll-ups with tongs and rearrange them for more even cooking. Air fry for another 4 to 5 minutes until the bacon is crisp. 6. Rest for 5 minutes and remove the toothpicks before serving.

Baked Egg and Mushroom Cups

Prep time: 5 minutes | Cook time: 15 minutes | Serves 6

Olive oil cooking spray
6 large eggs
1 garlic clove, minced
½ teaspoon salt
½ teaspoon black pepper
Pinch red pepper flakes

8 ounces (227 g) baby bella mushrooms, sliced
1 cup fresh baby spinach
2 scallions, white parts and green parts, diced

1. Preheat the air fryer to 320ºF (160ºC). Lightly coat the inside of six silicone muffin cups or a six-cup muffin tin with olive oil cooking spray. 2. In a large bowl, beat the eggs, garlic, salt, pepper, and red pepper flakes for 1 to 2 minutes, or until well combined. 3. Fold in the mushrooms, spinach, and scallions. 4. Divide the mixture evenly among the muffin cups. 5. Place into the air fryer and bake for 12 to 15 minutes, or until the eggs are set. 6. Remove and allow to cool for 5 minutes before serving.

Smoky Sausage Patties

Prep time: 30 minutes | Cook time: 9 minutes |
Serves 8

1 pound (454 g) ground pork
1 tablespoon coconut aminos
2 teaspoons liquid smoke
1 teaspoon dried sage
1 teaspoon sea salt

½ teaspoon fennel seeds
½ teaspoon dried thyme
½ teaspoon freshly ground black pepper
¼ teaspoon cayenne pepper

1. In a large bowl, combine the pork, coconut aminos, liquid smoke, sage, salt, fennel seeds, thyme, black pepper, and cayenne pepper. Work the meat with your hands until the seasonings are fully incorporated. 2. Shape the mixture into 8 equal-size patties. Using your thumb, make a dent in the center of each patty. Place the patties on a plate and cover with plastic wrap. Refrigerate the patties for at least 30 minutes. 3. Working in batches if necessary, place the patties in a single layer in the air fryer, being careful not to overcrowd them. 4. Set the air fryer to 400ºF (204ºC) and air fry for 5 minutes. Flip and cook for about 4 minutes more.

Onion Omelet

Prep time: 10 minutes | Cook time: 12 minutes | Serves 2

3 eggs
Salt and ground black pepper, to taste
½ teaspoons soy sauce

1 large onion, chopped
2 tablespoons grated Cheddar cheese
Cooking spray

1. Preheat the air fryer to 355ºF (179ºC). 2. In a bowl, whisk together the eggs, salt, pepper, and soy sauce. 3. Spritz a small pan with cooking spray. Spread the chopped onion across the bottom of the pan, then transfer the pan to the air fryer. 4. Bake in the preheated air fryer for 6 minutes or until the onion is translucent. 5. Add the egg mixture on top of the onions to coat well. Add the cheese on top, then continue baking for another 6 minutes. 6. Allow to cool before serving.

Bourbon Vanilla French Toast

Prep time: 15 minutes | Cook time: 6 minutes | Serves 4

2 large eggs
2 tablespoons water
⅔ cup whole or 2% milk
1 tablespoon butter, melted
2 tablespoons bourbon

1 teaspoon vanilla extract
8 (1-inch-thick) French bread slices
Cooking spray

1. Preheat the air fryer to 320ºF (160ºC). Line the air fryer basket with parchment paper and spray it with cooking spray. 2. Beat the eggs with the water in a shallow bowl until combined. Add the milk, melted butter, bourbon, and vanilla and stir to mix well. 3. Dredge 4 slices of bread in the batter, turning to coat both sides evenly. Transfer the bread slices onto the parchment paper. 4. Bake for 6 minutes until nicely browned. Flip the slices halfway through the cooking time. 5. Remove from the basket to a plate and repeat with the remaining 4 slices of bread. 6. Serve warm.

Canadian Bacon Muffin Sandwiches

Prep time: 5 minutes | Cook time: 8 minutes | Serves 4

4 English muffins, split
8 slices Canadian bacon

4 slices cheese
Cooking spray

1. Preheat the air fryer to 370ºF (188ºC). 2. Make the sandwiches: Top each of 4 muffin halves with 2 slices of Canadian bacon, 1 slice of cheese, and finish with the remaining muffin half. 3. Put the sandwiches in the air fryer basket and spritz the tops with cooking spray. 4. Bake for 4 minutes. Flip the sandwiches and bake for another 4 minutes. 5. Divide the sandwiches among four plates and serve warm.

Oat Bran Muffins

Prep time: 10 minutes | Cook time: 10 to 12 minutes per batch | Makes 8 muffins

⅔ cup oat bran
½ cup flour
¼ cup brown sugar
1 teaspoon baking powder
½ teaspoon baking soda
⅛ teaspoon salt
½ cup buttermilk

1 egg
2 tablespoons canola oil
½ cup chopped dates, raisins, or dried cranberries
24 paper muffin cups
Cooking spray

1. Preheat the air fryer to 330ºF (166ºC). 2. In a large bowl, combine the oat bran, flour, brown sugar, baking powder, baking soda, and salt. 3. In a small bowl, beat together the buttermilk, egg, and oil. 4. Pour buttermilk mixture into bowl with dry ingredients and stir just until moistened. Do not beat. 5. Gently stir in dried fruit. 6. Use triple baking cups to help muffins hold shape during baking. Spray them with cooking spray, place 4 sets of cups in air fryer basket at a time, and fill each one ¾ full of batter. 7. Cook for 10 to 12 minutes, until top springs back when lightly touched and toothpick inserted in center comes out clean. 8. Repeat for remaining muffins.

Bacon and Cheese Quiche

Prep time: 5 minutes | Cook time: 12 minutes | Serves 2

3 large eggs
2 tablespoons heavy whipping cream
¼ teaspoon salt

4 slices cooked sugar-free bacon, crumbled
½ cup shredded mild Cheddar cheese

1. In a large bowl, whisk eggs, cream, and salt together until combined. Mix in bacon and Cheddar. 2. Pour mixture evenly into two ungreased ramekins. Place into air fryer basket. Adjust the temperature to 320ºF (160ºC) and bake for 12 minutes. Quiche will be fluffy and set in the middle when done. 3. Let quiche cool in ramekins 5 minutes. Serve warm.

Savory Sweet Potato Hash

Prep time: 15 minutes | Cook time: 18 minutes | Serves 6

2 medium sweet potatoes, peeled and cut into 1-inch cubes
½ green bell pepper, diced
½ red onion, diced
4 ounces (113 g) baby bella mushrooms, diced

2 tablespoons olive oil
1 garlic clove, minced
½ teaspoon salt
½ teaspoon black pepper
½ tablespoon chopped fresh rosemary

1. Preheat the air fryer to 380ºF(193ºC). 2. In a large bowl, toss all ingredients together until the vegetables are well coated and seasonings distributed. 3. Pour the vegetables into the air fryer basket, making sure they are in a single even layer. (If using a smaller air fryer, you may need to do this in two batches.) 4. Roast for 9 minutes, then toss or flip the vegetables. Roast for 9 minutes more. 5. Transfer to a serving bowl or individual plates and enjoy.

Gluten-Free Granola Cereal

Prep time: 7 minutes | Cook time: 30 minutes | Makes 3½ cups

Oil, for spraying
1½ cups gluten-free rolled oats
½ cup chopped walnuts
½ cup chopped almonds
½ cup pumpkin seeds
¼ cup maple syrup or honey

1 tablespoon toasted sesame oil or vegetable oil
1 teaspoon ground cinnamon
½ teaspoon salt
½ cup dried cranberries

1. Preheat the air fryer to 250ºF (121ºC). Line the air fryer basket with parchment and spray lightly with oil. (Do not skip the step of lining the basket; the parchment will keep the granola from falling through the holes.) 2. In a large bowl, mix together the oats, walnuts, almonds, pumpkin seeds, maple syrup, sesame oil, cinnamon, and salt. 3. Spread the mixture in an even layer in the prepared basket. 4. Cook for 30 minutes, stirring every 10 minutes. 5. Transfer the granola to a bowl, add the dried cranberries, and toss to combine. 6. Let cool to room temperature before storing in an airtight container.

Sausage and Egg Breakfast Burrito

Prep time: 5 minutes | Cook time: 30 minutes | Serves 6

6 eggs
Salt and pepper, to taste
Cooking oil
½ cup chopped red bell pepper
½ cup chopped green bell pepper

8 ounces (227 g) ground chicken sausage
½ cup salsa
6 medium (8-inch) flour tortillas
½ cup shredded Cheddar cheese

1. In a medium bowl, whisk the eggs. Add salt and pepper to taste. 2. Place a skillet on medium-high heat. Spray with cooking oil. Add the eggs. Scramble for 2 to 3 minutes, until the eggs are fluffy. Remove the eggs from the skillet and set aside. 3. If needed, spray the skillet with more oil. Add the chopped red and green bell peppers. Cook for 2 to 3 minutes, until the peppers are soft. 4. Add the ground sausage to the skillet. Break the sausage into smaller pieces using a spatula or spoon. Cook for 3 to 4 minutes, until the sausage is brown. 5. Add the salsa and scrambled eggs. Stir to combine. Remove the skillet from heat. 6. Spoon the mixture evenly onto the tortillas. 7. To form the burritos, fold the sides of each tortilla in toward the middle and then roll up from the bottom. You can secure each burrito with a toothpick. Or you can moisten the outside edge of the tortilla with a small amount of water. I prefer to use a cooking brush, but you can also dab with your fingers. 8. Spray the burritos with cooking oil and place them in the air fryer. Do not stack. Cook the burritos in batches if they do not all fit in the basket. Air fry at 400ºF (204ºC) for 8 minutes. 9. Open the air fryer and flip the burritos. Cook for an additional 2 minutes or until crisp. 10. If necessary, repeat steps 8 and 9 for the remaining burritos. 11. Sprinkle the Cheddar cheese over the burritos. Cool before serving.

Pork Sausage Eggs with Mustard Sauce

Prep time: 20 minutes | Cook time: 12 minutes | Serves 8

1 pound (454 g) pork sausage
8 soft-boiled or hard-boiled eggs, peeled
1 large egg
2 tablespoons milk
1 cup crushed pork rinds

Smoky Mustard Sauce:
¼ cup mayonnaise
2 tablespoons sour cream
1 tablespoon Dijon mustard
1 teaspoon chipotle hot sauce

1. Preheat the air fryer to 390ºF (199ºC). 2. Divide the sausage into 8 portions. Take each portion of sausage, pat it down into a patty, and place 1 egg in the middle, gently wrapping the sausage around the egg until the egg is completely covered. (Wet your hands slightly if you find the sausage to be too sticky.) Repeat with the remaining eggs and sausage. 3. In a small shallow bowl, whisk the egg and milk until frothy. In another shallow bowl, place the crushed pork rinds. Working one at a time, dip a sausage-wrapped egg into the beaten egg and then into the pork rinds, gently rolling to coat evenly. Repeat with the remaining sausage-wrapped eggs. 4. Arrange the eggs in a single layer in the air fryer basket, and lightly spray with olive oil. Air fry for 10 to 12 minutes, pausing halfway through the baking time to turn the eggs, until the eggs are hot and the sausage is cooked through. 5. To make the sauce: In a small bowl, combine the mayonnaise, sour cream, Dijon, and hot sauce. Whisk until thoroughly combined. Serve with the Scotch eggs.

Spinach Omelet

Prep time: 5 minutes | Cook time: 12 minutes | Serves 2

4 large eggs
1½ cups chopped fresh spinach leaves
2 tablespoons peeled and chopped yellow onion

2 tablespoons salted butter, melted
½ cup shredded mild Cheddar cheese
¼ teaspoon salt

1. In an ungreased round nonstick baking dish, whisk eggs. Stir in spinach, onion, butter, Cheddar, and salt. 2. Place dish into air fryer basket. Adjust the temperature to 320ºF (160ºC) and bake for 12 minutes. Omelet will be done when browned on the top and firm in the middle. 3. Slice in half and serve warm on two medium plates.

Double-Dipped Mini Cinnamon Biscuits

Prep time: 15 minutes | Cook time: 13 minutes | Makes 8 biscuits

2 cups blanched almond flour
½ cup Swerve confectioners'-style sweetener or equivalent amount of liquid or powdered sweetener
1 teaspoon baking powder
½ teaspoon fine sea salt
¼ cup plus 2 tablespoons (¾ stick) very cold unsalted butter
¼ cup unsweetened, unflavored almond milk

1 large egg
1 teaspoon vanilla extract
3 teaspoons ground cinnamon
Glaze:
½ cup Swerve confectioners'-style sweetener or equivalent amount of powdered sweetener
¼ cup heavy cream or unsweetened, unflavored almond milk

1. Preheat the air fryer to 350ºF (177ºC). Line a pie pan that fits into your air fryer with parchment paper. 2. In a medium-sized bowl, mix together the almond flour, sweetener (if powdered; do not add liquid sweetener), baking powder, and salt. Cut the butter into ½-inch squares, then use a hand mixer to work the butter into the dry ingredients. When you are done, the mixture should still have chunks of butter. 3. In a small bowl, whisk together the almond milk, egg, and vanilla extract (if using liquid sweetener, add it as well) until blended. Using a fork, stir the wet ingredients into the dry ingredients until large clumps form. Add the cinnamon and use your hands to swirl it into the dough. 4. Form the dough into sixteen 1-inch balls and place them on the prepared pan, spacing them about ½ inch apart. (If you're using a smaller air fryer, work in batches if necessary.) Bake in the air fryer until golden, 10 to 13 minutes. Remove from the air fryer and let cool on the pan for at least 5 minutes. 5. While the biscuits bake, make the glaze: Place the powdered sweetener in a small bowl and slowly stir in the heavy cream with a fork. 6. When the biscuits have cooled somewhat, dip the tops into the glaze, allow it to dry a bit, and then dip again for a thick glaze. 7. Serve warm or at room temperature. Store unglazed biscuits in an airtight container in the refrigerator for up to 3 days or in the freezer for up to a month. Reheat in a preheated 350ºF (177ºC) air fryer for 5 minutes, or until warmed through, and dip in the glaze as instructed above.

Pita and Pepperoni Pizza

Prep time: 10 minutes | Cook time: 6 minutes | Serves 1

1 teaspoon olive oil	¼ cup grated Mozzarella cheese
1 tablespoon pizza sauce	¼ teaspoon garlic powder
1 pita bread	¼ teaspoon dried oregano
6 pepperoni slices	

1. Preheat the air fryer to 350ºF (177ºC). Grease the air fryer basket with olive oil. 2. Spread the pizza sauce on top of the pita bread. Put the pepperoni slices over the sauce, followed by the Mozzarella cheese. 3. Season with garlic powder and oregano. 4. Put the pita pizza inside the air fryer and place a trivet on top. 5. Bake in the preheated air fryer for 6 minutes and serve.

Poached Eggs on Whole Grain Avocado Toast

Prep time: 5 minutes | Cook time: 7 minutes | Serves 4

Olive oil cooking spray	4 pieces whole grain bread
4 large eggs	1 avocado
Salt	Red pepper flakes (optional)
Black pepper	

1. Preheat the air fryer to 320ºF(160ºC). Lightly coat the inside of four small oven-safe ramekins with olive oil cooking spray. 2. Crack one egg into each ramekin, and season with salt and black pepper. 3. Place the ramekins into the air fryer basket. Close and set the timer to 7 minutes. 4. While the eggs are cooking, toast the bread in a toaster. 5. Slice the avocado in half lengthwise, remove the pit, and scoop the flesh into a small bowl. Season with salt, black pepper, and red pepper flakes, if desired. Using a fork, smash the avocado lightly. 6. Spread a quarter of the smashed avocado evenly over each slice of toast. 7. Remove the eggs from the air fryer, and gently spoon one onto each slice of avocado toast before serving.

Lemon-Blueberry Muffins

Prep time: 5 minutes | Cook time: 20 to 25 minutes | Makes 6 muffins

1¼ cups almond flour	3 tablespoons melted butter
3 tablespoons Swerve	1 tablespoon almond milk
1 teaspoon baking powder	1 tablespoon fresh lemon juice
2 large eggs	½ cup fresh blueberries

1. Preheat the air fryer to 350ºF (177ºC). Lightly coat 6 silicone muffin cups with vegetable oil. Set aside. 2. In a large mixing bowl, combine the almond flour, Swerve, and baking soda. Set aside. 3. In a separate small bowl, whisk together the eggs, butter, milk, and lemon juice. Add the egg mixture to the flour mixture and stir until just combined. Fold in the blueberries and let the batter sit for 5 minutes. 4. Spoon the muffin batter into the muffin cups, about two-thirds full. Air fry for 20 to 25 minutes, or until a toothpick inserted into the center of a muffin comes out clean. 5. Remove the basket from the air fryer and let the muffins cool for about 5 minutes before transferring them to a wire rack to cool completely.

Bunless Breakfast Turkey Burgers

Prep time: 5 minutes | Cook time: 15 minutes | Serves 4

1 pound (454 g) ground turkey breakfast sausage	¼ cup seeded and chopped green bell pepper
½ teaspoon salt	2 tablespoons mayonnaise
¼ teaspoon ground black pepper	1 medium avocado, peeled, pitted, and sliced

1. In a large bowl, mix sausage with salt, black pepper, bell pepper, and mayonnaise. Form meat into four patties. 2. Place patties into ungreased air fryer basket. Adjust the temperature to 370ºF (188ºC) and air fry for 15 minutes, turning patties halfway through cooking. Burgers will be done when dark brown and they have an internal temperature of at least 165ºF (74ºC). 3. Serve burgers topped with avocado slices on four medium plates.

Sausage and Cheese Balls

Prep time: 10 minutes | Cook time: 12 minutes | Makes 16 balls

1 pound (454 g) pork breakfast sausage	1 ounce (28 g) full-fat cream cheese, softened
½ cup shredded Cheddar cheese	1 large egg

1. Mix all ingredients in a large bowl. Form into sixteen (1-inch) balls. Place the balls into the air fryer basket. 2. Adjust the temperature to 400ºF (204ºC) and air fry for 12 minutes. 3. Shake the basket two or three times during cooking. Sausage balls will be browned on the outside and have an internal temperature of at least 145ºF (63ºC) when completely cooked. 4. Serve warm.

Homemade Toaster Pastries

Prep time: 10 minutes | Cook time: 11 minutes | Makes 6 pastries

Oil, for spraying	2 cups confectioners' sugar
1 (15-ounce / 425-g) package refrigerated piecrust	3 tablespoons milk
6 tablespoons jam or preserves of choice	1 to 2 tablespoons sprinkles of choice

1. Preheat the air fryer to 350ºF (177ºC). Line the air fryer basket with parchment and spray lightly with oil. 2. Cut the piecrust into 12 rectangles, about 3 by 4 inches each. You will need to reroll the dough scraps to get 12 rectangles. 3. Spread 1 tablespoon of jam in the center of 6 rectangles, leaving ¼ inch around the edges. 4. Pour some water into a small bowl. Use your finger to moisten the edge of each rectangle. 5. Top each rectangle with another and use your fingers to press around the edges. Using the tines of a fork, seal the edges of the dough and poke a few holes in the top of each one. Place the pastries in the prepared basket. 6. Air fry for 11 minutes. Let cool completely. 7. In a medium bowl, whisk together the confectioners' sugar and milk. Spread the icing over the tops of the pastries and add sprinkles. Serve immediately

Berry Muffins

Prep time: 15 minutes | Cook time: 12 to 17 minutes | Makes 8 muffins

1⅓ cups plus 1 tablespoon all-purpose flour, divided
¼ cup granulated sugar
2 tablespoons light brown sugar
2 teaspoons baking powder
2 eggs
⅔ cup whole milk
⅓ cup safflower oil
1 cup mixed fresh berries

1. In a medium bowl, stir together 1⅓ cups of flour, the granulated sugar, brown sugar, and baking powder until mixed well. 2. In a small bowl, whisk the eggs, milk, and oil until combined. Stir the egg mixture into the dry ingredients just until combined. 3. In another small bowl, toss the mixed berries with the remaining 1 tablespoon of flour until coated. Gently stir the berries into the batter. 4. Double up 16 foil muffin cups to make 8 cups. 5. Insert the crisper plate into the basket and the basket into the unit. Preheat the unit by selecting BAKE, setting the temperature to 315°F (157°C), and setting the time to 3 minutes. Select START/STOP to begin. 6. Once the unit is preheated, place 4 cups into the basket and fill each three-quarters full with the batter. 7. Select BAKE, set the temperature to 315°F (157°C), and set the time for 17 minutes. Select START/STOP to begin. 8. After about 12 minutes, check the muffins. If they spring back when lightly touched with your finger, they are done. If not, resume cooking. 9. When the cooking is done, transfer the muffins to a wire rack to cool. 10. Repeat steps 6, 7, and 8 with the remaining muffin cups and batter. 11. Let the muffins cool for 10 minutes before serving.

Vegetable Frittata

Prep time: 10 minutes | Cook time: 19 minutes | Serves 1 to 2

½ red or green bell pepper, cut into ½-inch chunks
4 button mushrooms, sliced
½ cup diced zucchini
½ teaspoon chopped fresh oregano or thyme
1 teaspoon olive oil
3 eggs, beaten
½ cup grated Cheddar cheese
Salt and freshly ground black pepper, to taste
1 teaspoon butter
1 teaspoon chopped fresh parsley

1. Preheat the air fryer to 400°F (204°C). 2. Toss the peppers, mushrooms, zucchini and oregano with the olive oil and air fry for 6 minutes, shaking the basket once or twice during the cooking process to redistribute the ingredients. 3. While the vegetables are cooking, beat the eggs well in a bowl, stir in the Cheddar cheese and season with salt and freshly ground black pepper. Add the air-fried vegetables to this bowl when they have finished cooking. 4. Place a cake pan into the air fryer basket with the butter using an aluminum sling to lower the pan into the basket. Air fry for 1 minute at 380°F (193°C) to melt the butter. Remove the cake pan and rotate the pan to distribute the butter and grease the pan. Pour the egg mixture into the cake pan and return the pan to the air fryer, using the aluminum sling. 5. Air fry at 380°F (193°C) for 12 minutes, or until the frittata has puffed up and is lightly browned. Let the frittata sit in the air fryer for 5 minutes to cool to an edible temperature and set up. Remove the cake pan from the air fryer, sprinkle with parsley and serve immediately.

Red Pepper and Feta Frittata

Prep time: 10 minutes | Cook time: 20 minutes | Serves 4

Olive oil cooking spray
8 large eggs
1 medium red bell pepper, diced
½ teaspoon salt
½ teaspoon black pepper
1 garlic clove, minced
½ cup feta, divided

1. Preheat the air fryer to 360°F(182°C). Lightly coat the inside of a 6-inch round cake pan with olive oil cooking spray. 2. In a large bowl, beat the eggs for 1 to 2 minutes, or until well combined. 3. Add the bell pepper, salt, black pepper, and garlic to the eggs, and mix together until the bell pepper is distributed throughout. 4. Fold in ¼ cup of the feta cheese. 5. Pour the egg mixture into the prepared cake pan, and sprinkle the remaining ¼ cup of feta over the top. 6. Place into the air fryer and bake for 18 to 20 minutes, or until the eggs are set in the center. 7. Remove from the air fryer and allow to cool for 5 minutes before serving.

Cheddar Eggs

Prep time: 5 minutes | Cook time: 15 minutes | Serves 2

4 large eggs
2 tablespoons unsalted butter, melted
½ cup shredded sharp Cheddar cheese

1. Crack eggs into a round baking dish and whisk. Place dish into the air fryer basket. 2. Adjust the temperature to 400°F (204°C) and set the timer for 10 minutes. 3. After 5 minutes, stir the eggs and add the butter and cheese. Let cook 3 more minutes and stir again. 4. Allow eggs to finish cooking an additional 2 minutes or remove if they are to your desired liking. 5. Use a fork to fluff. Serve warm.

Spinach and Mushroom Mini Quiche

Prep time: 10 minutes | Cook time: 15 minutes | Serves 4

1 teaspoon olive oil, plus more for spraying
1 cup coarsely chopped mushrooms
1 cup fresh baby spinach, shredded
4 eggs, beaten
½ cup shredded Cheddar cheese
½ cup shredded Mozzarella cheese
¼ teaspoon salt
¼ teaspoon black pepper

1. Spray 4 silicone baking cups with olive oil and set aside. 2. In a medium sauté pan over medium heat, warm 1 teaspoon of olive oil. Add the mushrooms and sauté until soft, 3 to 4 minutes. 3. Add the spinach and cook until wilted, 1 to 2 minutes. Set aside. 4. In a medium bowl, whisk together the eggs, Cheddar cheese, Mozzarella cheese, salt, and pepper. 5. Gently fold the mushrooms and spinach into the egg mixture. 6. Pour ¼ of the mixture into each silicone baking cup. 7. Place the baking cups into the air fryer basket and air fry at 350°F (177°C) for 5 minutes. Stir the mixture in each ramekin slightly and air fry until the egg has set, an additional 3 to 5 minutes.

Cheddar-Ham-Corn Muffins

Prep time: 10 minutes | Cook time: 6 to 8 minutes per batch | Makes 8 muffins

¾ cup yellow cornmeal
¼ cup flour
1½ teaspoons baking powder
¼ teaspoon salt
1 egg, beaten
2 tablespoons canola oil
½ cup milk

½ cup shredded sharp Cheddar cheese
½ cup diced ham
8 foil muffin cups, liners removed and sprayed with cooking spray

1. Preheat the air fryer to 390ºF (199ºC). 2. In a medium bowl, stir together the cornmeal, flour, baking powder, and salt. 3. Add egg, oil, and milk to dry ingredients and mix well. 4. Stir in shredded cheese and diced ham. 5. Divide batter among the muffin cups. 6. Place 4 filled muffin cups in air fryer basket and bake for 5 minutes. 7. Reduce temperature to 330ºF (166ºC) and bake for 1 to 2 minutes or until toothpick inserted in center of muffin comes out clean. 8. Repeat steps 6 and 7 to cook remaining muffins.

Tomato and Mozzarella Bruschetta

Prep time: 5 minutes | Cook time: 4 minutes | Serves 1

6 small loaf slices
½ cup tomatoes, finely chopped
3 ounces (85 g) Mozzarella cheese, grated

1 tablespoon fresh basil, chopped
1 tablespoon olive oil

1. Preheat the air fryer to 350ºF (177ºC). 2. Put the loaf slices inside the air fryer and air fry for about 3 minutes. 3. Add the tomato, Mozzarella, basil, and olive oil on top. 4. Air fry for an additional minute before serving.

Baked Potato Breakfast Boats

Prep time: 10 minutes | Cook time: 20 minutes | Serves 4

2 large russet potatoes, scrubbed
Olive oil
Salt and freshly ground black pepper, to taste

4 eggs
2 tablespoons chopped, cooked bacon
1 cup shredded Cheddar cheese

1. Poke holes in the potatoes with a fork and microwave on full power for 5 minutes. 2. Turn potatoes over and cook an additional 3 to 5 minutes, or until the potatoes are fork-tender. 3. Cut the potatoes in half lengthwise and use a spoon to scoop out the inside of the potato. Be careful to leave a layer of potato so that it makes a sturdy "boat." 4. Preheat the air fryer to 350ºF (177ºC). 5. Lightly spray the air fryer basket with olive oil. Spray the skin side of the potatoes with oil and sprinkle with salt and pepper to taste. 6. Place the potato skins in the air fryer basket, skin-side down. Crack one egg into each potato skin. 7. Sprinkle ½ tablespoon of bacon pieces and ¼ cup of shredded cheese on top of each egg. Sprinkle with salt and pepper to taste. 8. Air fry until the yolk is slightly runny, 5 to 6 minutes, or until the yolk is fully cooked, 7 to 10 minutes.

Breakfast Hash

Prep time: 10 minutes | Cook time: 30 minutes | Serves 6

Oil, for spraying
3 medium russet potatoes, diced
½ yellow onion, diced
1 green bell pepper, seeded and diced

2 tablespoons olive oil
2 teaspoons granulated garlic
1 teaspoon salt
½ teaspoon freshly ground black pepper

1. Line the air fryer basket with parchment and spray lightly with oil. 2. In a large bowl, mix together the potatoes, onion, bell pepper, and olive oil. 3. Add the garlic, salt, and black pepper and stir until evenly coated. 4. Transfer the mixture to the prepared basket. 5. Air fry at 400ºF (204ºC) for 20 to 30 minutes, shaking or stirring every 10 minutes, until browned and crispy. If you spray the potatoes with a little oil each time you stir, they will get even crispier.

Mississippi Spice Muffins

Prep time: 15 minutes | Cook time: 13 minutes | Makes 12 muffins

4 cups all-purpose flour
1 tablespoon ground cinnamon
2 teaspoons baking soda
2 teaspoons allspice
1 teaspoon ground cloves
1 teaspoon salt
1 cup (2 sticks) butter, room

temperature
2 cups sugar
2 large eggs, lightly beaten
2 cups unsweetened applesauce
¼ cup chopped pecans
1 to 2 tablespoons oil

1. In a large bowl, whisk the flour, cinnamon, baking soda, allspice, cloves, and salt until blended. 2. In another large bowl, combine the butter and sugar. Using an electric mixer, beat the mixture for 2 to 3 minutes until light and fluffy. Add the beaten eggs and stir until blended. 3. Add the flour mixture and applesauce, alternating between the two and blending after each addition. Stir in the pecans. 4. Preheat the air fryer to 325ºF (163ºC). Spritz 12 silicone muffin cups with oil. 5. Pour the batter into the prepared muffin cups, filling each halfway. Place the muffins in the air fryer basket. 6. Air fry for 6 minutes. Shake the basket and air fry for 7 minutes more. The muffins are done when a toothpick inserted into the middle comes out clean.

Egg and Bacon Muffins

Prep time: 5 minutes | Cook time: 15 minutes | Serves 1

2 eggs
Salt and ground black pepper, to taste
1 tablespoon green pesto

3 ounces (85 g) shredded Cheddar cheese
5 ounces (142 g) cooked bacon
1 scallion, chopped

1. Preheat the air fryer to 350ºF (177ºC). Line a cupcake tin with parchment paper. 2. Beat the eggs with pepper, salt, and pesto in a bowl. Mix in the cheese. 3. Pour the eggs into the cupcake tin and top with the bacon and scallion. 4. Bake in the preheated air fryer for 15 minutes, or until the egg is set. 5. Serve immediately.

Cheesy Bell Pepper Eggs

Prep time: 10 minutes | Cook time: 15 minutes | Serves 4

4 medium green bell peppers	chopped
3 ounces (85 g) cooked ham,	8 large eggs
chopped	1 cup mild Cheddar cheese
¼ medium onion, peeled and	

1. Cut the tops off each bell pepper. Remove the seeds and the white membranes with a small knife. Place ham and onion into each pepper. 2. Crack 2 eggs into each pepper. Top with ¼ cup cheese per pepper. Place into the air fryer basket. 3. Adjust the temperature to 390°F (199°C) and air fry for 15 minutes. 4. When fully cooked, peppers will be tender and eggs will be firm. Serve immediately.

Honey-Apricot Granola with Greek Yogurt

Prep time: 10 minutes | Cook time: 30 minutes | Serves 6

1 cup rolled oats	1 tablespoon olive oil
¼ cup dried apricots, diced	1 teaspoon ground cinnamon
¼ cup almond slivers	¼ teaspoon ground nutmeg
¼ cup walnuts, chopped	¼ teaspoon salt
¼ cup pumpkin seeds	2 tablespoons sugar-free dark
¼ cup hemp hearts	chocolate chips (optional)
¼ to ⅓ cup raw honey, plus	3 cups nonfat plain Greek
more for drizzling	yogurt

1. Preheat the air fryer to 260°F(127°C). Line the air fryer basket with parchment paper. 2. In a large bowl, combine the oats, apricots, almonds, walnuts, pumpkin seeds, hemp hearts, honey, olive oil, cinnamon, nutmeg, and salt, mixing so that the honey, oil, and spices are well distributed. 3. Pour the mixture onto the parchment paper and spread it into an even layer. 4. Bake for 10 minutes, then shake or stir and spread back out into an even layer. Continue baking for 10 minutes more, then repeat the process of shaking or stirring the mixture. Bake for an additional 10 minutes before removing from the air fryer. 5. Allow the granola to cool completely before stirring in the chocolate chips (if using) and pouring into an airtight container for storage. 6. For each serving, top ½ cup Greek yogurt with ⅓ cup granola and a drizzle of honey, if needed.

Golden Avocado Tempura

Prep time: 5 minutes | Cook time: 10 minutes | Serves 4

½ cup bread crumbs	and sliced
½ teaspoons salt	Liquid from 1 can white beans
1 Haas avocado, pitted, peeled	

1. Preheat the air fryer to 350°F (177°C). 2. Mix the bread crumbs and salt in a shallow bowl until well-incorporated. 3. Dip the avocado slices in the bean liquid, then into the bread crumbs. 4. Put the avocados in the air fryer, taking care not to overlap any slices, and air fry for 10 minutes, giving the basket a good shake at the halfway point. 5. Serve immediately.

Bacon Hot Dogs

Prep time: 5 minutes | Cook time: 15 minutes | Serves 4

3 brazilian sausages, cut into 3	1 tablespoon Italian herbs
equal pieces	Salt and ground black pepper,
9 slices bacon	to taste

1. Preheat the air fryer to 355°F (179°C). 2. Take each slice of bacon and wrap around each piece of sausage. Sprinkle with Italian herbs, salt and pepper. 3. Air fry the sausages in the preheated air fryer for 15 minutes. 4. Serve warm.

Pancake for Two

Prep time: 5 minutes | Cook time: 30 minutes | Serves 2

1 cup blanched finely ground	melted
almond flour	1 large egg
2 tablespoons granular	⅓ cup unsweetened almond
erythritol	milk
1 tablespoon salted butter,	½ teaspoon vanilla extract

1. In a large bowl, mix all ingredients together, then pour half the batter into an ungreased round nonstick baking dish. 2. Place dish into air fryer basket. Adjust the temperature to 320°F (160°C) and bake for 15 minutes. The pancake will be golden brown on top and firm, and a toothpick inserted in the center will come out clean when done. Repeat with remaining batter. 3. Slice in half in dish and serve warm.

Egg Tarts

Prep time: 10 minutes | Cook time: 17 to 20 minutes | Makes 2 tarts

⅓ sheet frozen puff pastry,	2 eggs
thawed	¼ teaspoon salt, divided
Cooking oil spray	1 teaspoon minced fresh parsley
½ cup shredded Cheddar cheese	(optional)

1. Insert the crisper plate into the basket and the basket into the unit. Preheat the unit by selecting BAKE, setting the temperature to 390°F (199°C), and setting the time to 3 minutes. Select START/STOP to begin. 2. Lay the puff pastry sheet on a piece of parchment paper and cut it in half. 3. Once the unit is preheated, spray the crisper plate with cooking oil. Transfer the 2 squares of pastry to the basket, keeping them on the parchment paper. 4. Select BAKE, set the temperature to 390°F (199°C), and set the time to 20 minutes. Select START/STOP to begin. 5. After 10 minutes, use a metal spoon to press down the center of each pastry square to make a well. Divide the cheese equally between the baked pastries. Carefully crack an egg on top of the cheese, and sprinkle each with the salt. Resume cooking for 7 to 10 minutes. 6. When the cooking is complete, the eggs will be cooked through. Sprinkle each with parsley (if using) and serve.

Bacon, Cheese, and Avocado Melt

Prep time: 5 minutes | Cook time: 3 to 5 minutes | Serves 2

1 avocado
4 slices cooked bacon, chopped
2 tablespoons salsa

1 tablespoon heavy cream
¼ cup shredded Cheddar cheese

1. Preheat the air fryer to 400ºF (204ºC). 2. Slice the avocado in half lengthwise and remove the stone. To ensure the avocado halves do not roll in the basket, slice a thin piece of skin off the base. 3. In a small bowl, combine the bacon, salsa, and cream. Divide the mixture between the avocado halves and top with the cheese. 4. Place the avocado halves in the air fryer basket and air fry for 3 to 5 minutes until the cheese has melted and begins to brown. Serve warm.

Nutty Granola

Prep time: 5 minutes | Cook time: 1 hour | Serves 4

½ cup pecans, coarsely chopped
½ cup walnuts or almonds, coarsely chopped
¼ cup unsweetened flaked coconut
¼ cup almond flour
¼ cup ground flaxseed or chia seeds

2 tablespoons sunflower seeds
2 tablespoons melted butter
¼ cup Swerve
½ teaspoon ground cinnamon
½ teaspoon vanilla extract
¼ teaspoon ground nutmeg
¼ teaspoon salt
2 tablespoons water

1. Preheat the air fryer to 250ºF (121ºC). Cut a piece of parchment paper to fit inside the air fryer basket. 2. In a large bowl, toss the nuts, coconut, almond flour, ground flaxseed or chia seeds, sunflower seeds, butter, Swerve, cinnamon, vanilla, nutmeg, salt, and water until thoroughly combined. 3. Spread the granola on the parchment paper and flatten to an even thickness. 4. Air fry for about an hour, or until golden throughout. Remove from the air fryer and allow to fully cool. Break the granola into bite-size pieces and store in a covered container for up to a week.

Cheddar Soufflés

Prep time: 15 minutes | Cook time: 12 minutes | Serves 4

3 large eggs, whites and yolks separated
¼ teaspoon cream of tartar
½ cup shredded sharp Cheddar

cheese
3 ounces (85 g) cream cheese, softened

1. In a large bowl, beat egg whites together with cream of tartar until soft peaks form, about 2 minutes. 2. In a separate medium bowl, beat egg yolks, Cheddar, and cream cheese together until frothy, about 1 minute. Add egg yolk mixture to whites, gently folding until combined. 3. Pour mixture evenly into four ramekins greased with cooking spray. Place ramekins into air fryer basket. Adjust the temperature to 350ºF (177ºC) and bake for 12 minutes. Eggs will be browned on the top and firm in the center when done. Serve warm.

Parmesan Ranch Risotto

Prep time: 10 minutes | Cook time: 30 minutes | Serves 2

1 tablespoon olive oil
1 clove garlic, minced
1 tablespoon unsalted butter
1 onion, diced

¾ cup Arborio rice
2 cups chicken stock, boiling
½ cup Parmesan cheese, grated

1. Preheat the air fryer to 390ºF (199ºC). 2. Grease a round baking tin with olive oil and stir in the garlic, butter, and onion. 3. Transfer the tin to the air fryer and bake for 4 minutes. Add the rice and bake for 4 more minutes. 4. Turn the air fryer to 320ºF (160ºC) and pour in the chicken stock. Cover and bake for 22 minutes. 5. Scatter with cheese and serve.

Chapter 2 Family Favorites

Berry Cheesecake

Prep time: 5 minutes | Cook time: 10 minutes | Serves 4

Oil, for spraying
8 ounces (227 g) cream cheese
6 tablespoons sugar
1 tablespoon sour cream

1 large egg
½ teaspoon vanilla extract
¼ teaspoon lemon juice
½ cup fresh mixed berries

1. Preheat the air fryer to 350ºF (177ºC). Line the air fryer basket with parchment and spray lightly with oil. 2. In a blender, combine the cream cheese, sugar, sour cream, egg, vanilla, and lemon juice and blend until smooth. Pour the mixture into a 4-inch springform pan. 3. Place the pan in the prepared basket. 4. Cook for 8 to 10 minutes, or until only the very center jiggles slightly when the pan is moved. 5. Refrigerate the cheesecake in the pan for at least 2 hours. 6. Release the sides from the springform pan, top the cheesecake with the mixed berries, and serve.

Beef Jerky

Prep time: 30 minutes | Cook time: 2 hours | Serves 8

Oil, for spraying
1 pound (454 g) round steak, cut into thin, short slices
¼ cup soy sauce
3 tablespoons packed light

brown sugar
1 tablespoon minced garlic
1 teaspoon ground ginger
1 tablespoon water

1. Line the air fryer basket with parchment and spray lightly with oil. 2. Place the steak, soy sauce, brown sugar, garlic, ginger, and water in a zip-top plastic bag, seal, and shake well until evenly coated. Refrigerate for 30 minutes. 3. Place the steak in the prepared basket in a single layer. You may need to work in batches, depending on the size of your air fryer. 4. Air fry at 180ºF (82ºC) for at least 2 hours. Add more time if you like your jerky a bit tougher.

Steak Tips and Potatoes

Prep time: 10 minutes | Cook time: 20 minutes | Serves 4

Oil, for spraying
8 ounces (227 g) baby gold potatoes, cut in half
½ teaspoon salt
1 pound (454 g) steak, cut into ½-inch pieces

1 teaspoon Worcestershire sauce
1 teaspoon granulated garlic
½ teaspoon salt
½ teaspoon freshly ground black pepper

1. Line the air fryer basket with parchment and spray lightly with oil. 2. In a microwave-safe bowl, combine the potatoes and salt, then pour in about ½ inch of water. Microwave for 7 minutes, or until the potatoes are nearly tender. Drain. 3. In a large bowl, gently mix together the steak, potatoes, Worcestershire sauce, garlic, salt, and black pepper. Spread the mixture in an even layer in the prepared basket. 4. Air fry at 400ºF (204ºC) for 12 to 17 minutes, stirring after 5 to 6 minutes. The cooking time will depend on the thickness of the meat and preferred doneness.

Buffalo Cauliflower

Prep time: 15 minutes | Cook time: 5 minutes | Serves 6

1 large head cauliflower, separated into small florets
1 tablespoon olive oil
½ teaspoon garlic powder
⅓ cup low-sodium hot wing sauce

⅔ cup nonfat Greek yogurt
½ teaspoons Tabasco sauce
1 celery stalk, chopped
1 tablespoon crumbled blue cheese

1. In a large bowl, toss the cauliflower florets with the olive oil. Sprinkle with the garlic powder and toss again to coat. Put half of the cauliflower in the air fryer basket. Air fry at 380ºF (193ºC) for 5 to 7 minutes, until the cauliflower is browned, shaking the basket once during cooking. 2. Transfer to a serving bowl and toss with half of the wing sauce. Repeat with the remaining cauliflower and wing sauce. 3. In a small bowl, stir together the yogurt, Tabasco sauce, celery, and blue cheese. Serve with the cauliflower for dipping.

Steak and Vegetable Kebabs

Prep time: 15 minutes | Cook time: 5 to 7 minutes | Serves 4

2 tablespoons balsamic vinegar
2 teaspoons olive oil
½ teaspoon dried marjoram
⅛ teaspoon freshly ground black pepper

¾ pound (340 g) round steak, cut into 1-inch pieces
1 red bell pepper, sliced
16 button mushrooms
1 cup cherry tomatoes

1. In a medium bowl, stir together the balsamic vinegar, olive oil, marjoram, and black pepper. 2. Add the steak and stir to coat. Let stand for 10 minutes at room temperature. 3. Alternating items, thread the beef, red bell pepper, mushrooms, and tomatoes onto 8 bamboo or metal skewers that fit in the air fryer. 4. Air fry at 390ºF (199ºC) for 5 to 7 minutes, or until the beef is browned and reaches at least 145ºF (63ºC) on a meat thermometer. Serve immediately.

Elephant Ears

Prep time: 5 minutes | Cook time: 5 minutes | Serves 8

Oil, for spraying
1 (8-ounce / 227-g) can buttermilk biscuits
3 tablespoons sugar
1 tablespoon ground cinnamon

3 tablespoons unsalted butter, melted
8 scoops vanilla ice cream (optional)

1. Line the air fryer basket with parchment and spray lightly with oil. 2. Separate the dough. Using a rolling pin, roll out the biscuits into 6- to 8-inch circles. 3. Place the dough circles in the prepared basket and spray liberally with oil. You may need to work in batches, depending on the size of your air fryer. 4. Air fry at 350ºF (177ºC) for 5 minutes, or until lightly browned. 5. In a small bowl, mix together the sugar and cinnamon. 6. Brush the elephant ears with the melted butter and sprinkle with the cinnamon-sugar mixture. 7. Top each serving with a scoop of ice cream (if using).

Old Bay Tilapia

Prep time: 15 minutes | Cook time: 6 minutes | Serves 4

Oil, for spraying
1 cup panko bread crumbs
2 tablespoons Old Bay seasoning
2 teaspoons granulated garlic
1 teaspoon onion powder

½ teaspoon salt
¼ teaspoon freshly ground black pepper
1 large egg
4 tilapia fillets

1. Preheat the air fryer to 400ºF (204ºC). Line the air fryer basket with parchment and spray lightly with oil. 2. In a shallow bowl, mix together the bread crumbs, Old Bay, garlic, onion powder, salt, and black pepper. 3. In a small bowl, whisk the egg. 4. Coat the tilapia in the egg, then dredge in the bread crumb mixture until completely coated. 5. Place the tilapia in the prepared basket. You may need to work in batches, depending on the size of your air fryer. Spray lightly with oil. 6. Cook for 4 to 6 minutes, depending on the thickness of the fillets, until the internal temperature reaches 145ºF (63ºC). Serve immediately.

Apple Pie Egg Rolls

Prep time: 10 minutes | Cook time: 8 minutes | Makes 6 rolls

Oil, for spraying
1 (21-ounce / 595-g) can apple pie filling
1 tablespoon all-purpose flour

½ teaspoon lemon juice
¼ teaspoon ground nutmeg
¼ teaspoon ground cinnamon
6 egg roll wrappers

1. Preheat the air fryer to 400ºF (204ºC). Line the air fryer basket with parchment and spray lightly with oil. 2. In a medium bowl, mix together the pie filling, flour, lemon juice, nutmeg, and cinnamon. 3. Lay out the egg roll wrappers on a work surface and spoon a dollop of pie filling in the center of each. 4. Fill a small bowl with water. Dip your finger in the water and, working one at a time, moisten the edges of the wrappers. Fold the wrapper like an envelope: First fold one corner into the center. Fold each side corner in, and then fold over the remaining corner, making sure each corner overlaps a bit and the moistened edges stay closed. Use additional water and your fingers to seal any open edges. 5. Place the rolls in the prepared basket and spray liberally with oil. You may need to work in batches, depending on the size of your air fryer. 6. Cook for 4 minutes, flip, spray with oil, and cook for another 4 minutes, or until crispy and golden brown. Serve immediately.

Puffed Egg Tarts

Prep time: 10 minutes | Cook time: 42 minutes | Makes 4 tarts

Oil, for spraying
All-purpose flour, for dusting
1 (12-ounce / 340-g) sheet frozen puff pastry, thawed
¾ cup shredded Cheddar cheese, divided

4 large eggs
2 teaspoons chopped fresh parsley
Salt and freshly ground black pepper, to taste

1. Preheat the air fryer to 390ºF (199ºC). Line the air fryer basket with parchment and spray lightly with oil. 2. Lightly dust your work surface with flour. Unfold the puff pastry and cut it into 4 equal squares. Place 2 squares in the prepared basket. 3. Cook for 10 minutes. 4. Remove the basket. Press the center of each tart shell with a spoon to make an indentation. 5. Sprinkle 3 tablespoons of cheese into each indentation and crack 1 egg into the center of each tart shell. 6. Cook for another 7 to 11 minutes, or until the eggs are cooked to your desired doneness. 7. Repeat with the remaining puff pastry squares, cheese, and eggs. 8. Sprinkle evenly with the parsley, and season with salt and black pepper. Serve immediately.

Pecan Rolls

Prep time: 20 minutes | Cook time: 20 to 24 minutes | Makes 12 rolls

2 cups all-purpose flour, plus more for dusting
2 tablespoons granulated sugar, plus ¼ cup, divided
1 teaspoon salt
3 tablespoons butter, at room temperature

¾ cup milk, whole or 2%
¼ cup packed light brown sugar
½ cup chopped pecans, toasted
1 to 2 tablespoons oil
¼ cup confectioners' sugar (optional)

1. In a large bowl, whisk the flour, 2 tablespoons granulated sugar, and salt until blended. Stir in the butter and milk briefly until a sticky dough forms. 2. In a small bowl, stir together the brown sugar and remaining ¼ cup of granulated sugar. 3. Place a piece of parchment paper on a work surface and dust it with flour. Roll the dough on the prepared surface to ¼ inch thickness. 4. Spread the sugar mixture over the dough. Sprinkle the pecans on top. Roll up the dough jelly roll-style, pinching the ends to seal. Cut the dough into 12 rolls. 5. Preheat the air fryer to 320ºF (160ºC). 6. Line the air fryer basket with parchment paper and spritz the parchment with oil. Place 6 rolls on the prepared parchment. 7. Bake for 5 minutes. Flip the rolls and bake for 5 to 7 minutes more until lightly browned. Repeat with the remaining rolls. 8. Sprinkle with confectioners' sugar (if using).

Churro Bites

Prep time: 5 minutes | Cook time: 6 minutes | Makes
36 bites

Oil, for spraying	1 tablespoon ground cinnamon
1 (17¼-ounce / 489-g) package	½ cup confectioners' sugar
frozen puffed pastry, thawed	1 tablespoon milk
1 cup granulated sugar	

1. Preheat the air fryer to 400ºF (204ºC). Line the air fryer basket with parchment and spray lightly with oil. 2. Unfold the puff pastry onto a clean work surface. Using a sharp knife, cut the dough into 36 bite-size pieces. 3. Place the dough pieces in one layer in the prepared basket, taking care not to let the pieces touch or overlap. 4. Cook for 3 minutes, flip, and cook for another 3 minutes, or until puffed and golden. 5. In a small bowl, mix together the granulated sugar and cinnamon. 6. In another small bowl, whisk together the confectioners' sugar and milk. 7. Dredge the bites in the cinnamon-sugar mixture until evenly coated. 8. Serve with the icing on the side for dipping.

Fish and Vegetable Tacos

Prep time: 15 minutes | Cook time: 9 to 12 minutes |
Serves 4

1 pound (454 g) white fish	1 large carrot, grated
fillets, such as sole or cod	½ cup low-sodium salsa
2 teaspoons olive oil	⅓ cup low-fat Greek yogurt
3 tablespoons freshly squeezed	4 soft low-sodium whole-wheat
lemon juice, divided	tortillas
1½ cups chopped red cabbage	

1. Brush the fish with the olive oil and sprinkle with 1 tablespoon of lemon juice. Air fry in the air fryer basket at 390ºF (199ºC) for 9 to 12 minutes, or until the fish just flakes when tested with a fork. 2. Meanwhile, in a medium bowl, stir together the remaining 2 tablespoons of lemon juice, the red cabbage, carrot, salsa, and yogurt. 3. When the fish is cooked, remove it from the air fryer basket and break it up into large pieces. 4. Offer the fish, tortillas, and the cabbage mixture, and let each person assemble a taco.

Pork Stuffing Meatballs

Prep time: 10 minutes | Cook time: 12 minutes |
Makes 35 meatballs

Oil, for spraying	1 tablespoon dried thyme
1½ pounds (680 g) ground pork	1 teaspoon salt
1 cup bread crumbs	1 teaspoon freshly ground black
½ cup milk	pepper
¼ cup minced onion	1 teaspoon finely chopped fresh
1 large egg	parsley
1 tablespoon dried rosemary	

1. Line the air fryer basket with parchment and spray lightly with oil. 2. In a large bowl, mix together the ground pork, bread crumbs, milk, onion, egg, rosemary, thyme, salt, black pepper, and parsley. 3. Roll about 2 tablespoons of the mixture into a ball. Repeat with the rest of the mixture. You should have 30 to 35 meatballs. 4. Place the meatballs in the prepared basket in a single layer, leaving space between each one. You may need to work in batches, depending on the size of your air fryer. 5. Air fry at 390ºF (199ºC) for 10 to 12 minutes, flipping after 5 minutes, or until golden brown and the internal temperature reaches 160ºF (71ºC).

Pork Burgers with Red Cabbage Salad

Prep time: 20 minutes | Cook time: 7 to 9 minutes |
Serves 4

½ cup Greek yogurt	pork
2 tablespoons low-sodium	½ teaspoon paprika
mustard, divided	1 cup mixed baby lettuce greens
1 tablespoon lemon juice	2 small tomatoes, sliced
¼ cup sliced red cabbage	8 small low-sodium whole-
¼ cup grated carrots	wheat sandwich buns, cut in
1 pound (454 g) lean ground	half

1. In a small bowl, combine the yogurt, 1 tablespoon mustard, lemon juice, cabbage, and carrots; mix and refrigerate. 2. In a medium bowl, combine the pork, remaining 1 tablespoon mustard, and paprika. Form into 8 small patties. 3. Put the sliders into the air fryer basket. Air fry at 400ºF (204ºC) for 7 to 9 minutes, or until the sliders register 165ºF (74ºC) as tested with a meat thermometer. 4. Assemble the burgers by placing some of the lettuce greens on a bun bottom. Top with a tomato slice, the burgers, and the cabbage mixture. Add the bun top and serve immediately.

Meatball Subs

Prep time: 15 minutes | Cook time: 19 minutes | Serves 6

Oil, for spraying	1 teaspoon salt
1 pound (454 g) 85% lean	1 teaspoon freshly ground black
ground beef	pepper
½ cup Italian bread crumbs	6 hoagie rolls
1 tablespoon dried minced	1 (18-ounce / 510-g) jar
onion	marinara sauce
1 tablespoon minced garlic	1½ cups shredded Mozzarella
1 large egg	cheese

1. Line the air fryer basket with parchment and spray lightly with oil. 2. In a large bowl, mix together the ground beef, bread crumbs, onion, garlic, egg, salt, and black pepper. Roll the mixture into 18 meatballs. 3. Place the meatballs in the prepared basket. 4. Air fry at 390ºF (199ºC) for 15 minutes. 5. Place 3 meatballs in each hoagie roll. Top with marinara and Mozzarella cheese. 6. Place the loaded rolls in the air fryer and cook for 3 to 4 minutes, or until the cheese is melted. You may need to work in batches, depending on the size of your air fryer. Serve immediately.

Chinese-Inspired Spareribs

Prep time: 30 minutes | Cook time: 8 minutes | Serves 4

Oil, for spraying
12 ounces (340 g) boneless pork spareribs, cut into 3-inch-long pieces
1 cup soy sauce
¾ cup sugar
½ cup beef or chicken stock
¼ cup honey
2 tablespoons minced garlic
1 teaspoon ground ginger
2 drops red food coloring (optional)

1. Line the air fryer basket with parchment and spray lightly with oil. 2. Combine the ribs, soy sauce, sugar, beef stock, honey, garlic, ginger, and food coloring (if using) in a large zip-top plastic bag, seal, and shake well until completely coated. Refrigerate for at least 30 minutes. 3. Place the ribs in the prepared basket. 4. Air fry at 375ºF (191ºC) for 8 minutes, or until the internal temperature reaches 165ºF (74ºC).

Fried Green Tomatoes

Prep time: 15 minutes | Cook time: 6 to 8 minutes | Serves 4

4 medium green tomatoes
⅓ cup all-purpose flour
2 egg whites
¼ cup almond milk
1 cup ground almonds
½ cup panko bread crumbs
2 teaspoons olive oil
1 teaspoon paprika
1 clove garlic, minced

1. Rinse the tomatoes and pat dry. Cut the tomatoes into ½-inch slices, discarding the thinner ends. 2. Put the flour on a plate. In a shallow bowl, beat the egg whites with the almond milk until frothy. And on another plate, combine the almonds, bread crumbs, olive oil, paprika, and garlic and mix well. 3. Dip the tomato slices into the flour, then into the egg white mixture, then into the almond mixture to coat. 4. Place four of the coated tomato slices in the air fryer basket. Air fry at 400ºF (204ºC) for 6 to 8 minutes or until the tomato coating is crisp and golden brown. Repeat with remaining tomato slices and serve immediately.

Scallops with Green Vegetables

Prep time: 15 minutes | Cook time: 8 to 11 minutes | Serves 4

1 cup green beans
1 cup frozen peas
1 cup frozen chopped broccoli
2 teaspoons olive oil
½ teaspoon dried basil
½ teaspoon dried oregano
12 ounces (340 g) sea scallops

1. In a large bowl, toss the green beans, peas, and broccoli with the olive oil. Place in the air fryer basket. Air fry at 400ºF (204ºC) for 4 to 6 minutes, or until the vegetables are crisp-tender. 2. Remove the vegetables from the air fryer basket and sprinkle with the herbs. Set aside. 3. In the air fryer basket, put the scallops and air fry for 4 to 5 minutes, or until the scallops are firm and reach an internal temperature of just 145ºF (63ºC) on a meat thermometer. 4. Toss scallops with the vegetables and serve immediately.

Veggie Tuna Melts

Prep time: 15 minutes | Cook time: 7 to 11 minutes | Serves 4

2 low-sodium whole-wheat English muffins, split
1 (6-ounce / 170-g) can chunk light low-sodium tuna, drained
1 cup shredded carrot
⅓ cup chopped mushrooms
2 scallions, white and green parts, sliced
⅓ cup nonfat Greek yogurt
2 tablespoons low-sodium stone-ground mustard
2 slices low-sodium low-fat Swiss cheese, halved

1. Place the English muffin halves in the air fryer basket. Air fry at 340ºF (171ºC) for 3 to 4 minutes, or until crisp. Remove from the basket and set aside. 2. In a medium bowl, thoroughly mix the tuna, carrot, mushrooms, scallions, yogurt, and mustard. Top each half of the muffins with one-fourth of the tuna mixture and a half slice of Swiss cheese. 3. Air fry for 4 to 7 minutes, or until the tuna mixture is hot and the cheese melts and starts to brown. Serve immediately.

Cajun Shrimp

Prep time: 15 minutes | Cook time: 9 minutes | Serves 4

Oil, for spraying
1 pound (454 g) jumbo raw shrimp, peeled and deveined
1 tablespoon Cajun seasoning
6 ounces (170 g) cooked kielbasa, cut into thick slices
½ medium zucchini, cut into
¼-inch-thick slices
½ medium yellow squash, cut into ¼-inch-thick slices
1 green bell pepper, seeded and cut into 1-inch pieces
2 tablespoons olive oil
½ teaspoon salt

1. Preheat the air fryer to 400ºF (204ºC). Line the air fryer basket with parchment and spray lightly with oil. 2. In a large bowl, toss together the shrimp and Cajun seasoning. Add the kielbasa, zucchini, squash, bell pepper, olive oil, and salt and mix well. 3. Transfer the mixture to the prepared basket, taking care not to overcrowd. You may need to work in batches, depending on the size of your air fryer. 4. Cook for 9 minutes, shaking and stirring every 3 minutes. Serve immediately.

Chapter 3 Fast and Easy Everyday Favorites

Classic Poutine

Prep time: 15 minutes | Cook time: 25 minutes | Serves 2

2 russet potatoes, scrubbed and cut into ½-inch sticks	1 teaspoon tomato paste
2 teaspoons vegetable oil	1½ cups beef stock
2 tablespoons butter	2 teaspoons Worcestershire sauce
¼ onion, minced	Salt and freshly ground black pepper, to taste
¼ teaspoon dried thyme	
1 clove garlic, smashed	⅔ cup chopped string cheese
3 tablespoons all-purpose flour	

1. Bring a pot of water to a boil, then put in the potato sticks and blanch for 4 minutes. 2. Preheat the air fryer to 400ºF (204ºC). 3. Drain the potato sticks and rinse under running cold water, then pat dry with paper towels. 4. Transfer the sticks in a large bowl and drizzle with vegetable oil. Toss to coat well. 5. Place the potato sticks in the preheated air fryer. Air fry for 25 minutes or until the sticks are golden brown. Shake the basket at least three times during the frying. 6. Meanwhile, make the gravy: Heat the butter in a saucepan over medium heat until melted. 7. Add the onion, thyme, and garlic and sauté for 5 minutes or until the onion is translucent. 8. Add the flour and sauté for an additional 2 minutes. Pour in the tomato paste and beef stock and cook for 1 more minute or until lightly thickened. 9. Drizzle the gravy with Worcestershire sauce and sprinkle with salt and ground black pepper. Reduce the heat to low to keep the gravy warm until ready to serve. 10. Transfer the fried potato sticks onto a plate, then sprinkle with salt and ground black pepper. Scatter with string cheese and pour the gravy over. Serve warm.

Easy Cinnamon Toast

Prep time: 5 minutes | Cook time: 20 minutes | Serves 6

1½ teaspoons cinnamon	pepper
1½ teaspoons vanilla extract	2 tablespoons melted coconut oil
½ cup sugar	
2 teaspoons ground black	12 slices whole wheat bread

1. Preheat the air fryer to 400ºF (204ºC). 2. Combine all the ingredients, except for the bread, in a large bowl. Stir to mix well. 3. Dunk the bread in the bowl of mixture gently to coat and infuse well. Shake the excess off. 4. Arrange the bread slices in the preheated air fryer. Air fry for 5 minutes or until golden brown. Flip the bread halfway through. You may need to cook in batches to avoid overcrowding. 5. Remove the bread slices from the air fryer and slice to serve.

Baked Chorizo Scotch Eggs

Prep time: 5 minutes | Cook time: 15 to 20 minutes |
Makes 4 eggs

1 pound (454 g) Mexican chorizo or other seasoned sausage meat	1 tablespoon water
	½ cup all-purpose flour
	1 cup panko bread crumbs
4 soft-boiled eggs plus 1 raw egg	Cooking spray

1. Divide the chorizo into 4 equal portions. Flatten each portion into a disc. Place a soft-boiled egg in the center of each disc. Wrap the chorizo around the egg, encasing it completely. Place the encased eggs on a plate and chill for at least 30 minutes. 2. Preheat the air fryer to 360ºF (182ºC). 3. Beat the raw egg with 1 tablespoon of water. Place the flour on a small plate and the panko on a second plate. Working with 1 egg at a time, roll the encased egg in the flour, then dip it in the egg mixture. Dredge the egg in the panko and place on a plate. Repeat with the remaining eggs. 4. Spray the eggs with oil and place in the air fryer basket. Bake for 10 minutes. Turn and bake for an additional 5 to 10 minutes, or until browned and crisp on all sides. 5. Serve immediately.

Sweet Corn and Carrot Fritters

Prep time: 10 minutes | Cook time: 8 to 11 minutes |
Serves 4

1 medium-sized carrot, grated	1 medium-sized egg, whisked
1 yellow onion, finely chopped	2 tablespoons plain milk
4 ounces (113 g) canned sweet corn kernels, drained	1 cup grated Parmesan cheese
	¼ cup flour
1 teaspoon sea salt flakes	⅓ teaspoon baking powder
1 tablespoon chopped fresh cilantro	⅓ teaspoon sugar
	Cooking spray

1. Preheat the air fryer to 350ºF (177ºC). 2. Place the grated carrot in a colander and press down to squeeze out any excess moisture. Dry it with a paper towel. 3. Combine the carrots with the remaining ingredients. 4. Mold 1 tablespoon of the mixture into a ball and press it down with your hand or a spoon to flatten it. Repeat until the rest of the mixture is used up. 5. Spritz the balls with cooking spray. 6. Arrange in the air fryer basket, taking care not to overlap any balls. Bake for 8 to 11 minutes, or until they're firm. 7. Serve warm.

Cheesy Jalapeño Cornbread

Prep time: 10 minutes | Cook time: 20 minutes | Serves 8

⅔ cup cornmeal
⅓ cup all-purpose flour
¾ teaspoon baking powder
2 tablespoons buttery spread, melted
½ teaspoon kosher salt
1 tablespoon granulated sugar

¾ cup whole milk
1 large egg, beaten
1 jalapeño pepper, thinly sliced
⅓ cup shredded sharp Cheddar cheese
Cooking spray

1. Preheat the air fryer to 300°F (149°C). Spritz the air fryer basket with cooking spray. 2. Combine all the ingredients in a large bowl. Stir to mix well. Pour the mixture in a baking pan. 3. Arrange the pan in the preheated air fryer. Bake for 20 minutes or until a toothpick inserted in the center of the bread comes out clean. 4. When the cooking is complete, remove the baking pan from the air fryer and allow the bread to cool for a few minutes before slicing to serve.

Crispy Potato Chips with Lemony Cream Dip

Prep time: 20 minutes | Cook time: 15 minutes | Serves 2 to 4

2 large russet potatoes, sliced into ⅛-inch slices, rinsed
Sea salt and freshly ground black pepper, to taste
Cooking spray
Lemony Cream Dip:
½ cup sour cream

¼ teaspoon lemon juice
2 scallions, white part only, minced
1 tablespoon olive oil
¼ teaspoon salt
Freshly ground black pepper, to taste

1. Soak the potato slices in water for 10 minutes, then pat dry with paper towels. 2. Preheat the air fryer to 300°F (149°C). 3. Transfer the potato slices in the preheated air fryer. Spritz the slices with cooking spray. You may need to work in batches to avoid overcrowding. 4. Air fry for 15 minutes or until crispy and golden brown. Shake the basket periodically. Sprinkle with salt and ground black pepper in the last minute. 5. Meanwhile, combine the ingredients for the dip in a small bowl. Stir to mix well. 6. Serve the potato chips immediately with the dip.

Air Fried Shishito Peppers

Prep time: 5 minutes | Cook time: 5 minutes | Serves 4

½ pound (227 g) shishito peppers (about 24)
1 tablespoon olive oil

Coarse sea salt, to taste
Lemon wedges, for serving
Cooking spray

1. Preheat the air fryer to 400°F (204°C). Spritz the air fryer basket with cooking spray. 2. Toss the peppers with olive oil in a large bowl to coat well. 3. Arrange the peppers in the preheated air fryer. 4. Air fryer for 5 minutes or until blistered and lightly charred. Shake the basket and sprinkle the peppers with salt halfway through the cooking time. 5. Transfer the peppers onto a plate and squeeze the lemon wedges on top before serving.

Indian-Style Sweet Potato Fries

Prep time: 5 minutes | Cook time: 8 minutes | Makes 20 fries

Seasoning Mixture:
¾ teaspoon ground coriander
½ teaspoon garam masala
½ teaspoon garlic powder
½ teaspoon ground cumin

¼ teaspoon ground cayenne pepper
Fries:
2 large sweet potatoes, peeled
2 teaspoons olive oil

1. Preheat the air fryer to 400°F (204°C). 2. In a small bowl, combine the coriander, garam masala, garlic powder, cumin, and cayenne pepper. 3. Slice the sweet potatoes into ¼-inch-thick fries. 4. In a large bowl, toss the sliced sweet potatoes with the olive oil and the seasoning mixture. 5. Transfer the seasoned sweet potatoes to the air fryer basket and fry for 8 minutes, until crispy. 6. Serve warm.

Honey Bartlett Pears with Lemony Ricotta

Prep time: 10 minutes | Cook time: 8 minutes | Serves 4

2 large Bartlett pears, peeled, cut in half, cored
3 tablespoons melted butter
½ teaspoon ground ginger
¼ teaspoon ground cardamom
3 tablespoons brown sugar

½ cup whole-milk ricotta cheese
1 teaspoon pure lemon extract
1 teaspoon pure almond extract
1 tablespoon honey, plus additional for drizzling

1. Preheat the air fryer to 375°F (191°C). 2. Toss the pears with butter, ginger, cardamom, and sugar in a large bowl. Toss to coat well. 3. Arrange the pears in the preheated air fryer, cut side down. Air fry for 5 minutes, then flip the pears and air fry for 3 more minutes or until the pears are soft and browned. 4. In the meantime, combine the remaining ingredients in a separate bowl. Whip for 1 minute with a hand mixer until the mixture is puffed. 5. Divide the mixture into four bowls, then put the pears over the mixture and drizzle with more honey to serve.

Corn Fritters

Prep time: 15 minutes | Cook time: 8 minutes | Serves 6

1 cup self-rising flour
1 tablespoon sugar
1 teaspoon salt
1 large egg, lightly beaten

¼ cup buttermilk
¾ cup corn kernels
¼ cup minced onion
Cooking spray

1. Preheat the air fryer to 350°F (177°C). Line the air fryer basket with parchment paper. 2. In a medium bowl, whisk the flour, sugar, and salt until blended. Stir in the egg and buttermilk. Add the corn and minced onion. Mix well. Shape the corn fritter batter into 12 balls. 3. Place the fritters on the parchment and spritz with oil. Bake for 4 minutes. Flip the fritters, spritz them with oil, and bake for 4 minutes more until firm and lightly browned. 4. Serve immediately.

Easy Roasted Asparagus

Prep time: 5 minutes | Cook time: 6 minutes | Serves 4

1 pound (454 g) asparagus, trimmed and halved crosswise
1 teaspoon extra-virgin olive oil
Salt and pepper, to taste
Lemon wedges, for serving

1. Preheat the air fryer to 400°F (204°C). 2. Toss the asparagus with the oil, ⅛ teaspoon salt, and ⅛ teaspoon pepper in bowl. Transfer to air fryer basket. 3. Place the basket in air fryer and roast for 6 to 8 minutes, or until tender and bright green, tossing halfway through cooking. 4. Season with salt and pepper and serve with lemon wedges.

Easy Devils on Horseback

Prep time: 5 minutes | Cook time: 7 minutes | Serves 12

24 petite pitted prunes (4½ ounces / 128 g)
¼ cup crumbled blue cheese, divided
8 slices center-cut bacon, cut crosswise into thirds

1. Preheat the air fryer to 400°F (204°C). 2. Halve the prunes lengthwise, but don't cut them all the way through. Place ½ teaspoon of cheese in the center of each prune. Wrap a piece of bacon around each prune and secure the bacon with a toothpick. 3. Working in batches, arrange a single layer of the prunes in the air fryer basket. Air fry for about 7 minutes, flipping halfway, until the bacon is cooked through and crisp. 4. Let cool slightly and serve warm.

Beery and Crunchy Onion Rings

Prep time: 10 minutes | Cook time: 16 minutes |
Serves 2 to 4

⅔ cup all-purpose flour
1 teaspoon paprika
½ teaspoon baking soda
1 teaspoon salt
½ teaspoon freshly ground black pepper
1 egg, beaten
¾ cup beer
1½ cups breadcrumbs
1 tablespoons olive oil
1 large Vidalia onion, peeled and sliced into ½-inch rings
Cooking spray

1. Preheat the air fryer to 360°F (182°C). Spritz the air fryer basket with cooking spray. 2. Combine the flour, paprika, baking soda, salt, and ground black pepper in a bowl. Stir to mix well. 3. Combine the egg and beer in a separate bowl. Stir to mix well. 4. Make a well in the center of the flour mixture, then pour the egg mixture in the well. Stir to mix everything well. 5. Pour the breadcrumbs and olive oil in a shallow plate. Stir to mix well. 6. Dredge the onion rings gently into the flour and egg mixture, then shake the excess off and put into the plate of breadcrumbs. Flip to coat the both sides well. 7. Arrange the onion rings in the preheated air fryer. Air fry in batches for 16 minutes or until golden brown and crunchy. Flip the rings and put the bottom rings to the top halfway through. 8. Serve immediately.

Classic Latkes

Prep time: 15 minutes | Cook time: 10 minutes |
Makes 4 latkes

1 egg
2 tablespoons all-purpose flour
2 medium potatoes, peeled and shredded, rinsed and drained
¼ teaspoon granulated garlic
½ teaspoon salt
Cooking spray

1. Preheat the air fryer to 380°F (193°C). Spritz the air fryer basket with cooking spray. 2. Whisk together the egg, flour, potatoes, garlic, and salt in a large bowl. Stir to mix well. 3. Divide the mixture into four parts, then flatten them into four circles. Arrange the circles into the preheated air fryer. 4. Spritz the circles with cooking spray, then air fry for 10 minutes or until golden brown and crispy. Flip the latkes halfway through. 5. Serve immediately.

Parsnip Fries with Garlic-Yogurt Dip

Prep time: 10 minutes | Cook time: 10 minutes | Serves 4

3 medium parsnips, peeled, cut into sticks
¼ teaspoon kosher salt
1 teaspoon olive oil
1 garlic clove, unpeeled
Cooking spray
Dip:
¼ cup plain Greek yogurt
⅛ teaspoon garlic powder
1 tablespoon sour cream
¼ teaspoon kosher salt
Freshly ground black pepper, to taste

1. Preheat the air fryer to 360°F (182°C). Spritz the air fryer basket with cooking spray. 2. Put the parsnip sticks in a large bowl, then sprinkle with salt and drizzle with olive oil. 3. Transfer the parsnip into the preheated air fryer and add the garlic. 4. Air fry for 5 minutes, then remove the garlic from the air fryer and shake the basket. Air fry for 5 more minutes or until the parsnip sticks are crisp. 5. Meanwhile, peel the garlic and crush it. Combine the crushed garlic with the ingredients for the dip. Stir to mix well. 6. When the frying is complete, remove the parsnip fries from the air fryer and serve with the dipping sauce.

Simple Pea Delight

Prep time: 5 minutes | Cook time: 15 minutes |
Serves 2 to 4

1 cup flour
1 teaspoon baking powder
3 eggs
1 cup coconut milk
1 cup cream cheese
3 tablespoons pea protein
½ cup chicken or turkey strips
Pinch of sea salt
1 cup Mozzarella cheese

1. Preheat the air fryer to 390°F (199°C). 2. In a large bowl, mix all ingredients together using a large wooden spoon. 3. Spoon equal amounts of the mixture into muffin cups and bake for 15 minutes. 4. Serve immediately.

Simple Cheesy Shrimps

Prep time: 10 minutes | Cook time: 16 minutes | Serves 4 to 6

⅔ cup grated Parmesan cheese
4 minced garlic cloves
1 teaspoon onion powder
½ teaspoon oregano
1 teaspoon basil
1 teaspoon ground black pepper
2 tablespoons olive oil
2 pounds (907 g) cooked large shrimps, peeled and deveined
Lemon wedges, for topping
Cooking spray

1. Preheat the air fryer to 350°F (177°C). Spritz the air fryer basket with cooking spray. 2. Combine all the ingredients, except for the shrimps, in a large bowl. Stir to mix well. 3. Dunk the shrimps in the mixture and toss to coat well. Shake the excess off. 4. Arrange the shrimps in the preheated air fryer. Air fry for 8 minutes or until opaque. Flip the shrimps halfway through. You may need to work in batches to avoid overcrowding. 5. Transfer the cooked shrimps on a large plate and squeeze the lemon wedges over before serving.

Air Fried Butternut Squash with Chopped Hazelnuts

Prep time: 10 minutes | Cook time: 20 minutes | Makes 3 cups

2 tablespoons whole hazelnuts
3 cups butternut squash, peeled, deseeded, and cubed
¼ teaspoon kosher salt
¼ teaspoon freshly ground black pepper
2 teaspoons olive oil
Cooking spray

1. Preheat the air fryer to 300°F (149°C). Spritz the air fryer basket with cooking spray. 2. Arrange the hazelnuts in the preheated air fryer. Air fry for 3 minutes or until soft. 3. Chopped the hazelnuts roughly and transfer to a small bowl. Set aside. 4. Set the air fryer temperature to 360°F (182°C). Spritz with cooking spray. 5. Put the butternut squash in a large bowl, then sprinkle with salt and pepper and drizzle with olive oil. Toss to coat well. 6. Transfer the squash in the air fryer. Air fry for 20 minutes or until the squash is soft. Shake the basket halfway through the frying time. 7. When the frying is complete, transfer the squash onto a plate and sprinkle with chopped hazelnuts before serving.

Easy Air Fried Edamame

Prep time: 5 minutes | Cook time: 7 minutes | Serves 6

1½ pounds (680 g) unshelled edamame
2 tablespoons olive oil
1 teaspoon sea salt

1. Preheat the air fryer to 400°F (204°C). 2. Place the edamame in a large bowl, then drizzle with olive oil. Toss to coat well. 3. Transfer the edamame to the preheated air fryer. Cook for 7 minutes or until tender and warmed through. Shake the basket at least three times during the cooking. 4. Transfer the cooked edamame onto a plate and sprinkle with salt. Toss to combine well and set aside for 3 minutes to infuse before serving.

Southwest Corn and Bell Pepper Roast

Prep time: 10 minutes | Cook time: 10 minutes | Serves 4

For the Corn:
1½ cups thawed frozen corn kernels
1 cup mixed diced bell peppers
1 jalapeño, diced
1 cup diced yellow onion
½ teaspoon ancho chile powder
1 tablespoon fresh lemon juice
1 teaspoon ground cumin
½ teaspoon kosher salt
Cooking spray
For Serving:
¼ cup feta cheese
¼ cup chopped fresh cilantro
1 tablespoon fresh lemon juice

1. Preheat the air fryer to 375°F (191°C). Spritz the air fryer with cooking spray. 2. Combine the ingredients for the corn in a large bowl. Stir to mix well. 3. Pout the mixture into the air fryer. Air fry for 10 minutes or until the corn and bell peppers are soft. Shake the basket halfway through the cooking time. 4. Transfer them onto a large plate, then spread with feta cheese and cilantro. Drizzle with lemon juice and serve.

Scalloped Veggie Mix

Prep time: 10 minutes | Cook time: 15 minutes | Serves 4

1 Yukon Gold potato, thinly sliced
1 small sweet potato, peeled and thinly sliced
1 medium carrot, thinly sliced
¼ cup minced onion
3 garlic cloves, minced
¾ cup 2 percent milk
2 tablespoons cornstarch
½ teaspoon dried thyme

1. Preheat the air fryer to 380°F (193°C). 2. In a baking pan, layer the potato, sweet potato, carrot, onion, and garlic. 3. In a small bowl, whisk the milk, cornstarch, and thyme until blended. Pour the milk mixture evenly over the vegetables in the pan. 4. Bake for 15 minutes. Check the casserole—it should be golden brown on top, and the vegetables should be tender. 5. Serve immediately.

Cheesy Baked Grits

Prep time: 10 minutes | Cook time: 12 minutes | Serves 6

¾ cup hot water
2 (1-ounce / 28-g) packages instant grits
1 large egg, beaten
1 tablespoon butter, melted
2 cloves garlic, minced
½ to 1 teaspoon red pepper flakes
1 cup shredded Cheddar cheese or jalapeño Jack cheese

1. Preheat the air fryer to 400°F (204°C). 2. In a baking pan, combine the water, grits, egg, butter, garlic, and red pepper flakes. Stir until well combined. Stir in the shredded cheese. 3. Place the pan in the air fryer basket and air fry for 12 minutes, or until the grits have cooked through and a knife inserted near the center comes out clean. 4. Let stand for 5 minutes before serving.

Simple and Easy Croutons

Prep time: 5 minutes | Cook time: 8 minutes | Serves 4

2 slices friendly bread
1 tablespoon olive oil

Hot soup, for serving

1. Preheat the air fryer to 390°F (199°C). 2. Cut the slices of bread into medium-size chunks. 3. Brush the air fryer basket with the oil. 4. Place the chunks inside and air fry for at least 8 minutes. 5. Serve with hot soup.

Frico

Prep time: 5 minutes | Cook time: 5 minutes | Serves 2

1 cup shredded aged Manchego cheese
1 teaspoon all-purpose flour

½ teaspoon cumin seeds
¼ teaspoon cracked black pepper

1. Preheat the air fryer to 375°F (191°C). Line the air fryer basket with parchment paper. 2. Combine the cheese and flour in a bowl. Stir to mix well. Spread the mixture in the basket into a 4-inch round. 3. Combine the cumin and black pepper in a small bowl. Stir to mix well. Sprinkle the cumin mixture over the cheese round. 4. Air fry 5 minutes or until the cheese is lightly browned and frothy. 5. Use tongs to transfer the cheese wafer onto a plate and slice to serve.

Lemony and Garlicky Asparagus

Prep time: 5 minutes | Cook time: 10 minutes |
Makes 10 spears

10 spears asparagus (about ½ pound / 227 g in total), snap the ends off
1 tablespoon lemon juice
2 teaspoons minced garlic

½ teaspoon salt
¼ teaspoon ground black pepper
Cooking spray

1. Preheat the air fryer to 400°F (204°C). Line a parchment paper in the air fryer basket. 2. Put the asparagus spears in a large bowl. Drizzle with lemon juice and sprinkle with minced garlic, salt, and ground black pepper. Toss to coat well. 3. Transfer the asparagus in the preheated air fryer and spritz with cooking spray. Air fryer for 10 minutes or until wilted and soft. Flip the asparagus halfway through. 4. Serve immediately.

Buttery Sweet Potatoes

Prep time: 5 minutes | Cook time: 10 minutes | Serves 4

2 tablespoons butter, melted
1 tablespoon light brown sugar
2 sweet potatoes, peeled and cut

into ½-inch cubes
Cooking spray

1. Preheat the air fryer to 400°F (204°C). Line the air fryer basket with parchment paper. 2. In a medium bowl, stir together the melted butter and brown sugar until blended. Toss the sweet potatoes in the butter mixture until coated. 3. Place the sweet potatoes on the parchment and spritz with oil. 4. Air fry for 5 minutes. Shake the basket, spritz the sweet potatoes with oil, and air fry for 5 minutes more until they're soft enough to cut with a fork. 5. Serve immediately.

Air Fried Tortilla Chips

Prep time: 5 minutes | Cook time: 10 minutes | Serves 4

4 six-inch corn tortillas, cut in half and slice into thirds
1 tablespoon canola oil

¼ teaspoon kosher salt
Cooking spray

1. Preheat the air fryer to 360°F (182°C). Spritz the air fryer basket with cooking spray. 2. On a clean work surface, brush the tortilla chips with canola oil, then transfer the chips in the preheated air fryer. 3. Air fry for 10 minutes or until crunchy and lightly browned. Shake the basket and sprinkle with salt halfway through the cooking time. 4. Transfer the chips onto a plate lined with paper towels. Serve immediately.

Rosemary and Orange Roasted Chickpeas

Prep time: 5 minutes | Cook time: 10 to 12 minutes |
Makes 4 cups

4 cups cooked chickpeas
2 tablespoons vegetable oil
1 teaspoon kosher salt
1 teaspoon cumin

1 teaspoon paprika
Zest of 1 orange
1 tablespoon chopped fresh rosemary

1. Preheat the air fryer to 400°F (204°C). 2. Make sure the chickpeas are completely dry prior to roasting. In a medium bowl, toss the chickpeas with oil, salt, cumin, and paprika. 3. Working in batches, spread the chickpeas in a single layer in the air fryer basket. Air fry for 10 to 12 minutes until crisp, shaking once halfway through. 4. Return the warm chickpeas to the bowl and toss with the orange zest and rosemary. Allow to cool completely. 5. Serve.

Peppery Brown Rice Fritters

Prep time: 10 minutes | Cook time: 8 to 10 minutes |
Serves 4

1 (10-ounce / 284-g) bag frozen cooked brown rice, thawed
1 egg
3 tablespoons brown rice flour
⅓ cup finely grated carrots
⅓ cup minced red bell pepper

2 tablespoons minced fresh basil
3 tablespoons grated Parmesan cheese
2 teaspoons olive oil

1. Preheat the air fryer to 380°F (193°C). 2. In a small bowl, combine the thawed rice, egg, and flour and mix to blend. 3. Stir in the carrots, bell pepper, basil, and Parmesan cheese. 4. Form the mixture into 8 fritters and drizzle with the olive oil. 5. Put the fritters carefully into the air fryer basket. Air fry for 8 to 10 minutes, or until the fritters are golden brown and cooked through. 6. Serve immediately.

Prep time: 5 minutes | Cook time: 20 minutes | Serves 4

¼ teaspoon salt
⅛ teaspoon ground black pepper
1 tablespoon extra-virgin olive oil

1 pound (454 g) Brussels sprouts, trimmed and halved
Lemon wedges, for garnish

1. Preheat the air fryer to 350ºF (177ºC). 2. Combine the salt, black pepper, and olive oil in a large bowl. Stir to mix well. 3. Add the Brussels sprouts to the bowl of mixture and toss to coat well. 4. Arrange the Brussels sprouts in the preheated air fryer. Air fry for 20 minutes or until lightly browned and wilted. Shake the basket two times during the air frying. 5. Transfer the cooked Brussels sprouts to a large plate and squeeze the lemon wedges on top to serve.

Chapter 4 Poultry

Barbecue Chicken

Prep time: 10 minutes | Cook time: 18 to 20 minutes | Serves 4

⅓ cup no-salt-added tomato sauce
2 tablespoons low-sodium grainy mustard
2 tablespoons apple cider vinegar
1 tablespoon honey

2 garlic cloves, minced
1 jalapeño pepper, minced
3 tablespoons minced onion
4 (5-ounce / 142-g) low-sodium boneless, skinless chicken breasts

1. Preheat the air fryer to 370°F (188°C). 2. In a small bowl, stir together the tomato sauce, mustard, cider vinegar, honey, garlic, jalapeño, and onion. 3. Brush the chicken breasts with some sauce and air fry for 10 minutes. 4. Remove the air fryer basket and turn the chicken; brush with more sauce. Air fry for 5 minutes more. 5. Remove the air fryer basket and turn the chicken again; brush with more sauce. Air fry for 3 to 5 minutes more, or until the chicken reaches an internal temperature of 165°F (74°C) on a meat thermometer. Discard any remaining sauce. Serve immediately.

Chicken Hand Pies

Prep time: 30 minutes | Cook time: 10 minutes per batch | Makes 8 pies

¾ cup chicken broth
¾ cup frozen mixed peas and carrots
1 cup cooked chicken, chopped
1 tablespoon cornstarch

1 tablespoon milk
Salt and pepper, to taste
1 (8-count) can organic flaky biscuits
Oil for misting or cooking spray

1. In a medium saucepan, bring chicken broth to a boil. Stir in the frozen peas and carrots and cook for 5 minutes over medium heat. Stir in chicken. 2. Mix the cornstarch into the milk until it dissolves. Stir it into the simmering chicken broth mixture and cook just until thickened. 3. Remove from heat, add salt and pepper to taste, and let cool slightly. 4. Lay biscuits out on wax paper. Peel each biscuit apart in the middle to make 2 rounds so you have 16 rounds total. Using your hands or a rolling pin, flatten each biscuit round slightly to make it larger and thinner. 5. Divide chicken filling among 8 of the biscuit rounds. Place remaining biscuit rounds on top and press edges all around. Use the tines of a fork to crimp biscuit edges and make sure they are sealed well. 6. Spray both sides lightly with oil or cooking spray. 7. Cook in a single layer, 4 at a time, at 330°F (166°C) for 10 minutes or until biscuit dough is cooked through and golden brown.

Chipotle Drumsticks

Prep time: 5 minutes | Cook time: 25 minutes | Serves 4

1 tablespoon tomato paste
½ teaspoon chipotle powder
¼ teaspoon apple cider vinegar
¼ teaspoon garlic powder

8 chicken drumsticks
½ teaspoon salt
⅛ teaspoon ground black pepper

1. In a small bowl, combine tomato paste, chipotle powder, vinegar, and garlic powder. 2. Sprinkle drumsticks with salt and pepper, then place into a large bowl and pour in tomato paste mixture. Toss or stir to evenly coat all drumsticks in mixture. 3. Place drumsticks into ungreased air fryer basket. Adjust the temperature to 400°F (204°C) and air fry for 25 minutes, turning drumsticks halfway through cooking. Drumsticks will be dark red with an internal temperature of at least 165°F (74°C) when done. Serve warm.

Chicken and Broccoli Casserole

Prep time: 5 minutes | Cook time: 20 to 25 minutes | Serves 4

½ pound (227 g) broccoli, chopped into florets
2 cups shredded cooked chicken
4 ounces (113 g) cream cheese
⅓ cup heavy cream
1½ teaspoons Dijon mustard

½ teaspoon garlic powder
Salt and freshly ground black pepper, to taste
2 tablespoons chopped fresh basil
1 cup shredded Cheddar cheese

1. Preheat the air fryer to 390°F (199°C). Lightly coat a casserole dish that will fit in air fryer, with olive oil and set aside. 2. Place the broccoli in a large glass bowl with 1 tablespoon of water and cover with a microwavable plate. Microwave on high for 2 to 3 minutes until the broccoli is bright green but not mushy. Drain if necessary and add to another large bowl along with the shredded chicken. 3. In the same glass bowl used to microwave the broccoli, combine the cream cheese and cream. Microwave for 30 seconds to 1 minute on high and stir until smooth. Add the mustard and garlic powder and season to taste with salt and freshly ground black pepper. Whisk until the sauce is smooth. 4. Pour the warm sauce over the broccoli and chicken mixture and then add the basil. Using a silicone spatula, gently fold the mixture until thoroughly combined. 5. Transfer the chicken mixture to the prepared casserole dish and top with the cheese. Air fry for 20 to 25 minutes until warmed through and the cheese has browned.

Pecan Turkey Cutlets

Prep time: 10 minutes | Cook time: 10 to 12 minutes per batch | Serves 4

¾ cup panko bread crumbs
¼ teaspoon salt
¼ teaspoon pepper
¼ teaspoon dry mustard
¼ teaspoon poultry seasoning
½ cup pecans

¼ cup cornstarch
1 egg, beaten
1 pound (454 g) turkey cutlets, ½-inch thick
Salt and pepper, to taste
Oil for misting or cooking spray

1. Place the panko crumbs, ¼ teaspoon salt, ¼ teaspoon pepper, mustard, and poultry seasoning in food processor. Process until crumbs are finely crushed. Add pecans and process in short pulses just until nuts are finely chopped. Go easy so you don't overdo it! 2. Preheat the air fryer to 360ºF (182ºC). 3. Place cornstarch in one shallow dish and beaten egg in another. Transfer coating mixture from food processor into a third shallow dish. 4. Sprinkle turkey cutlets with salt and pepper to taste. 5. Dip cutlets in cornstarch and shake off excess. Then dip in beaten egg and roll in crumbs, pressing to coat well. Spray both sides with oil or cooking spray. 6. Place 2 cutlets in air fryer basket in a single layer and cook for 10 to 12 minutes or until juices run clear. 7. Repeat step 6 to cook remaining cutlets.

Teriyaki Chicken Thighs with Lemony Snow Peas

Prep time: 30 minutes | Cook time: 34 minutes | Serves 4

¼ cup chicken broth
½ teaspoon grated fresh ginger
⅛ teaspoon red pepper flakes
1½ tablespoons soy sauce
4 (5-ounce / 142-g) bone-in chicken thighs, trimmed
1 tablespoon mirin
½ teaspoon cornstarch

1 tablespoon sugar
6 ounces (170 g) snow peas, strings removed
⅛ teaspoon lemon zest
1 garlic clove, minced
¼ teaspoon salt
Ground black pepper, to taste
½ teaspoon lemon juice

1. Combine the broth, ginger, pepper flakes, and soy sauce in a large bowl. Stir to mix well. 2. Pierce 10 to 15 holes into the chicken skin. Put the chicken in the broth mixture and toss to coat well. Let sit for 10 minutes to marinate. 3. Preheat the air fryer to 400ºF (205ºC). 4. Transfer the marinated chicken on a plate and pat dry with paper towels. 5. Scoop 2 tablespoons of marinade in a microwave-safe bowl and combine with mirin, cornstarch and sugar. Stir to mix well. Microwave for 1 minute or until frothy and has a thick consistency. Set aside. 6. Arrange the chicken in the preheated air fryer, skin side up, and air fry for 25 minutes or until the internal temperature of the chicken reaches at least 165ºF (74ºC). Gently turn the chicken over halfway through. 7. When the frying is complete, brush the chicken skin with marinade mixture. Air fryer the chicken for 5 more minutes or until glazed. 8. Remove the chicken from the air fryer and reserve ½ teaspoon of chicken fat remains in the air fryer. Allow the chicken to cool for 10 minutes. 9. Meanwhile, combine the reserved chicken fat, snow peas, lemon zest, garlic, salt, and ground black pepper in a small bowl. Toss to coat well. 10. Transfer the snow peas in the air fryer and air fry for 3 minutes or until soft. Remove the peas from the air fryer and toss with lemon juice. 11. Serve the chicken with lemony snow peas.

Porchetta-Style Chicken Breasts

Prep time: 10 minutes | Cook time: 15 minutes | Serves 4

½ cup fresh parsley leaves
¼ cup roughly chopped fresh chives
4 cloves garlic, peeled
2 tablespoons lemon juice
3 teaspoons fine sea salt
1 teaspoon dried rubbed sage
1 teaspoon fresh rosemary leaves

1 teaspoon ground fennel
½ teaspoon red pepper flakes
4 (4-ounce / 113-g) boneless, skinless chicken breasts, pounded to ¼ inch thick
8 slices bacon
Sprigs of fresh rosemary, for garnish (optional)

1. Spray the air fryer basket with avocado oil. Preheat the air fryer to 340ºF (171ºC). 2. Place the parsley, chives, garlic, lemon juice, salt, sage, rosemary, fennel, and red pepper flakes in a food processor and purée until a smooth paste forms. 3. Place the chicken breasts on a cutting board and rub the paste all over the tops. With a short end facing you, roll each breast up like a jelly roll to make a log and secure it with toothpicks. 4. Wrap 2 slices of bacon around each chicken breast log to cover the entire breast. Secure the bacon with toothpicks. 5. Place the chicken breast logs in the air fryer basket and air fry for 5 minutes, flip the logs over, and cook for another 5 minutes. Increase the heat to 390ºF (199ºC) and cook until the bacon is crisp, about 5 minutes more. 6. Remove the toothpicks and garnish with fresh rosemary sprigs, if desired, before serving. Store leftovers in an airtight container in the refrigerator for up to 4 days or in the freezer for up to a month. Reheat in a preheated 350ºF (177ºC) air fryer for 5 minutes, then increase the heat to 390ºF (199ºC) and cook for 2 minutes to crisp the bacon.

Fajita-Stuffed Chicken Breast

Prep time: 15 minutes | Cook time: 25 minutes | Serves 4

2 (6-ounce / 170-g) boneless, skinless chicken breasts
¼ medium white onion, peeled and sliced
1 medium green bell pepper,

seeded and sliced
1 tablespoon coconut oil
2 teaspoons chili powder
1 teaspoon ground cumin
½ teaspoon garlic powder

1. Slice each chicken breast completely in half lengthwise into two even pieces. Using a meat tenderizer, pound out the chicken until it's about ¼-inch thickness. 2. Lay each slice of chicken out and place three slices of onion and four slices of green pepper on the end closest to you. Begin rolling the peppers and onions tightly into the chicken. Secure the roll with either toothpicks or a couple pieces of butcher's twine. 3. Drizzle coconut oil over chicken. Sprinkle each side with chili powder, cumin, and garlic powder. Place each roll into the air fryer basket. 4. Adjust the temperature to 350ºF (177ºC) and air fry for 25 minutes. 5. Serve warm.

Chicken Nuggets

Prep time: 10 minutes | Cook time: 15 minutes | Serves 4

1 pound (454 g) ground chicken thighs	1 large egg, whisked
½ cup shredded Mozzarella cheese	½ teaspoon salt
	¼ teaspoon dried oregano
	¼ teaspoon garlic powder

1. In a large bowl, combine all ingredients. Form mixture into twenty nugget shapes, about 2 tablespoons each. 2. Place nuggets into ungreased air fryer basket, working in batches if needed. Adjust the temperature to 375°F (191°C) and air fry for 15 minutes, turning nuggets halfway through cooking. Let cool 5 minutes before serving.

Sriracha-Honey Chicken Nuggets

Prep time: 15 minutes | Cook time: 19 minutes | Serves 6

Oil, for spraying	½ teaspoon freshly ground
1 large egg	black pepper
¾ cup milk	2 boneless, skinless chicken
1 cup all-purpose flour	breasts, cut into bite-size pieces
2 tablespoons confectioners' sugar	½ cup barbecue sauce
½ teaspoon paprika	2 tablespoons honey
½ teaspoon salt	1 tablespoon Sriracha

1. Line the air fryer basket with parchment and spray lightly with oil. 2. In a small bowl, whisk together the egg and milk. 3. In a medium bowl, combine the flour, confectioners' sugar, paprika, salt, and black pepper and stir. 4. Coat the chicken in the egg mixture, then dredge in the flour mixture until evenly coated. 5. Place the chicken in the prepared basket and spray liberally with oil. 6. Air fry at 390°F (199°C) for 8 minutes, flip, spray with more oil, and cook for another 6 to 8 minutes, or until the internal temperature reaches 165°F (74°C) and the juices run clear. 7. In a large bowl, mix together the barbecue sauce, honey, and Sriracha. 8. Transfer the chicken to the bowl and toss until well coated with the barbecue sauce mixture. 9. Line the air fryer basket with fresh parchment, return the chicken to the basket, and cook for another 2 to 3 minutes, until browned and crispy.

Pork Rind Fried Chicken

Prep time: 30 minutes | Cook time: 20 minutes | Serves 4

¼ cup buffalo sauce	¼ teaspoon ground black
4 (4-ounce / 113-g) boneless, skinless chicken breasts	pepper
½ teaspoon paprika	2 ounces (57 g) plain pork rinds, finely crushed
½ teaspoon garlic powder	

1. Pour buffalo sauce into a large sealable bowl or bag. Add chicken and toss to coat. Place sealed bowl or bag into refrigerator and let marinate at least 30 minutes up to overnight. 2. Remove chicken from marinade but do not shake excess sauce off chicken. Sprinkle both sides of thighs with paprika, garlic powder, and pepper. 3. Place pork rinds into a large bowl and press each chicken breast into pork rinds to coat evenly on both sides. 4. Place chicken into ungreased air fryer basket. Adjust the temperature to 400°F (204°C) and roast for 20 minutes, turning chicken halfway through cooking. Chicken will be golden and have an internal temperature of at least 165°F (74°C) when done. Serve warm.

Bacon-Wrapped Stuffed Chicken Breasts

Prep time: 15 minutes | Cook time: 30 minutes | Serves 4

½ cup chopped frozen spinach, thawed and squeezed dry	2 large boneless, skinless chicken breasts, butterflied and pounded to ½-inch thickness
¼ cup cream cheese, softened	
¼ cup grated Parmesan cheese	4 teaspoons salt-free Cajun seasoning
1 jalapeño, seeded and chopped	
½ teaspoon kosher salt	6 slices bacon
1 teaspoon black pepper	

1. In a small bowl, combine the spinach, cream cheese, Parmesan cheese, jalapeño, salt, and pepper. Stir until well combined. 2. Place the butterflied chicken breasts on a flat surface. Spread the cream cheese mixture evenly across each piece of chicken. Starting with the narrow end, roll up each chicken breast, ensuring the filling stays inside. Season chicken with the Cajun seasoning, patting it in to ensure it sticks to the meat. 3. Wrap each breast in 3 slices of bacon. Place in the air fryer basket. Set the air fryer to 350°F (177°C) for 30 minutes. Use a meat thermometer to ensure the chicken has reached an internal temperature of 165°F (74°C). 4. Let the chicken stand 5 minutes before slicing each rolled-up breast in half to serve.

Ham Chicken with Cheese

Prep time: 15 minutes | Cook time: 25 minutes | Serves 4

¼ cup unsalted butter, softened	¼ cup water
4 ounces (113 g) cream cheese, softened	2 cups shredded cooked chicken
	¼ pound (113 g) ham, chopped
1½ teaspoons Dijon mustard	4 ounces (113 g) sliced Swiss
2 tablespoons white wine vinegar	or Provolone cheese

1. Preheat the air fryer to 380°F (193°C). Lightly coat a casserole dish that will fit in the air fryer, such as an 8-inch round pan, with olive oil and set aside. 2. In a large bowl and using an electric mixer, combine the butter, cream cheese, Dijon mustard, and vinegar. With the motor running at low speed, slowly add the water and beat until smooth. Set aside. 3. Arrange an even layer of chicken in the bottom of the prepared pan, followed by the ham. Spread the butter and cream cheese mixture on top of the ham, followed by the cheese slices on the top layer. Air fry for 20 to 25 minutes until warmed through and the cheese has browned.

Cheese-Encrusted Chicken Tenderloins with Peanuts

Prep time: 10 minutes | Cook time: 25 minutes | Serves 4

½ cup grated Parmesan cheese
½ teaspoon garlic powder
1 teaspoon red pepper flakes
Sea salt and ground black pepper, to taste
2 tablespoons peanut oil

1½ pounds (680 g) chicken tenderloins
2 tablespoons peanuts, roasted and roughly chopped
Cooking spray

1. Preheat the air fryer to 360°F (182°C). Spritz the air fryer basket with cooking spray. 2. Combine the Parmesan cheese, garlic powder, red pepper flakes, salt, black pepper, and peanut oil in a large bow. Stir to mix well. 3. Dip the chicken tenderloins in the cheese mixture, then press to coat well. Shake the excess off. 4. Transfer the chicken tenderloins in the air fryer basket. Air fry for 12 minutes or until well browned. Flip the tenderloin halfway through. You may need to work in batches to avoid overcrowding. 5. Transfer the chicken tenderloins on a large plate and top with roasted peanuts before serving.

Teriyaki Chicken Legs

Prep time: 12 minutes | Cook time: 18 to 20 minutes | Serves 2

4 tablespoons teriyaki sauce
1 tablespoon orange juice
1 teaspoon smoked paprika

4 chicken legs
Cooking spray

1. Mix together the teriyaki sauce, orange juice, and smoked paprika. Brush on all sides of chicken legs. 2. Spray the air fryer basket with nonstick cooking spray and place chicken in basket. 3. Air fry at 360°F (182°C) for 6 minutes. Turn and baste with sauce. Cook for 6 more minutes, turn and baste. Cook for 6 to 8 minutes more, until juices run clear when chicken is pierced with a fork.

Air Fried Chicken Wings with Buffalo Sauce

Prep time: 10 minutes | Cook time: 20 minutes | Serves 6

16 chicken drumettes (party wings)
Chicken seasoning or rub, to taste

1 teaspoon garlic powder
Ground black pepper, to taste
¼ cup buffalo wings sauce
Cooking spray

1. Preheat the air fryer to 400°F (204°C). Spritz the air fryer basket with cooking spray. 2. Rub the chicken wings with chicken seasoning, garlic powder, and ground black pepper on a clean work surface. 3. Arrange the chicken wings in the preheated air fryer. Spritz with cooking spray. Air fry for 10 minutes or until lightly browned. Shake the basket halfway through. 4. Transfer the chicken wings in a large bowl, then pour in the buffalo wings sauce and toss to coat well. 5. Put the wings back to the air fryer and cook for an additional 7 minutes. 6. Serve immediately.

Ginger Turmeric Chicken Thighs

Prep time: 5 minutes | Cook time: 25 minutes | Serves 4

4 (4-ounce / 113-g) boneless, skin-on chicken thighs
2 tablespoons coconut oil, melted
½ teaspoon ground turmeric

½ teaspoon salt
½ teaspoon garlic powder
½ teaspoon ground ginger
¼ teaspoon ground black pepper

1. Place chicken thighs in a large bowl and drizzle with coconut oil. Sprinkle with remaining ingredients and toss to coat both sides of thighs. 2. Place thighs skin side up into ungreased air fryer basket. Adjust the temperature to 400°F (204°C) and air fry for 25 minutes. After 10 minutes, turn thighs. When 5 minutes remain, flip thighs once more. Chicken will be done when skin is golden brown and the internal temperature is at least 165°F (74°C). Serve warm.

French Garlic Chicken

Prep time: 30 minutes | Cook time: 27 minutes | Serves 4

2 tablespoon extra-virgin olive oil
1 tablespoon Dijon mustard
1 tablespoon apple cider vinegar
3 cloves garlic, minced
2 teaspoons herbes de Provence
½ teaspoon kosher salt

1 teaspoon black pepper
1 pound (454 g) boneless, skinless chicken thighs, halved crosswise
2 tablespoons butter
8 cloves garlic, chopped
¼ cup heavy whipping cream

1. In a small bowl, combine the olive oil, mustard, vinegar, minced garlic, herbes de Provence, salt, and pepper. Use a wire whisk to emulsify the mixture. 2. Pierce the chicken all over with a fork to allow the marinade to penetrate better. Place the chicken in a resealable plastic bag, pour the marinade over, and seal. Massage until the chicken is well coated. Marinate at room temperature for 30 minutes or in the refrigerator for up to 24 hours. 3. When you are ready to cook, place the butter and chopped garlic in a baking pan and place it in the air fryer basket. Set the air fryer to 400°F (204°C) for 5 minutes, or until the butter has melted and the garlic is sizzling. 4. Add the chicken and the marinade to the seasoned butter. Set the air fryer to 350°F (177°C) for 15 minutes. Use a meat thermometer to ensure the chicken has reached an internal temperature of 165°F (74°C). Transfer the chicken to a plate and cover lightly with foil to keep warm. 5. Add the cream to the pan, stirring to combine with the garlic, butter, and cooking juices. Place the pan in the air fryer basket. Set the air fryer to 350°F (177°C) for 7 minutes. 6. Pour the thickened sauce over the chicken and serve.

Thai Game Hens with Cucumber and Chile Salad

Prep time: 25 minutes | Cook time: 25 minutes | Serves 6

2 (1¼-pound / 567-g) Cornish game hens, giblets discarded
1 tablespoon fish sauce
6 tablespoons chopped fresh cilantro
2 teaspoons lime zest
1 teaspoon ground coriander
2 garlic cloves, minced
2 tablespoons packed light brown sugar
2 teaspoons vegetable oil
Salt and ground black pepper,
to taste
1 English cucumber, halved lengthwise and sliced thin
1 Thai chile, stemmed, deseeded, and minced
2 tablespoons chopped dry-roasted peanuts
1 small shallot, sliced thinly
1 tablespoon lime juice
Lime wedges, for serving
Cooking spray

1. Arrange a game hen on a clean work surface, remove the backbone with kitchen shears, then pound the hen breast to flat. Cut the breast in half. Repeat with the remaining game hen. 2. Loose the breast and thigh skin with your fingers, then pat the game hens dry and pierce about 10 holes into the fat deposits of the hens. Tuck the wings under the hens. 3. Combine 2 teaspoons of fish sauce, ¼ cup of cilantro, lime zest, coriander, garlic, 4 teaspoons of sugar, 1 teaspoon of vegetable oil, ½ teaspoon of salt, and ⅛ teaspoon of ground black pepper in a small bowl. Stir to mix well. 4. Rub the fish sauce mixture under the breast and thigh skin of the game hens, then let sit for 10 minutes to marinate. 5. Preheat the air fryer to 400°F (204°C). Spritz the air fryer basket with cooking spray. 6. Arrange the marinated game hens in the preheated air fryer, skin side down. 7. Air fry for 15 minutes, then gently turn the game hens over and air fry for 10 more minutes or until the skin is golden brown and the internal temperature of the hens reads at least 165°F (74°C). 8. Meanwhile, combine all the remaining ingredients, except for the lime wedges, in a large bowl and sprinkle with salt and black pepper. Toss to mix well. 9. Transfer the fried hens on a large plate, then sit the salad aside and squeeze the lime wedges over before serving.

Celery Chicken

Prep time: 10 minutes | Cook time: 15 minutes | Serves 4

½ cup soy sauce
2 tablespoons hoisin sauce
4 teaspoons minced garlic
1 teaspoon freshly ground black pepper
8 boneless, skinless chicken tenderloins
1 cup chopped celery
1 medium red bell pepper, diced
Olive oil spray

1. Preheat the air fryer to 375°F (191°C). Spray the air fryer basket lightly with olive oil spray. 2. In a large bowl, mix together the soy sauce, hoisin sauce, garlic, and black pepper to make a marinade. Add the chicken, celery, and bell pepper and toss to coat. 3. Shake the excess marinade off the chicken, place it and the vegetables in the air fryer basket, and lightly spray with olive oil spray. You may need to cook them in batches. Reserve the remaining marinade. 4. Air fry for 8 minutes. Turn the chicken over and brush with some of the remaining marinade. Air fry for an additional 5 to 7 minutes, or until the chicken reaches an internal temperature of at least 165°F (74°C). Serve.

Chicken Croquettes with Creole Sauce

Prep time: 30 minutes | Cook time: 10 minutes | Serves 4

2 cups shredded cooked chicken
½ cup shredded Cheddar cheese
2 eggs
¼ cup finely chopped onion
¼ cup almond meal
1 tablespoon poultry seasoning
Olive oil
Creole Sauce:
¼ cup mayonnaise
¼ cup sour cream
1½ teaspoons Dijon mustard
1½ teaspoons fresh lemon juice
½ teaspoon garlic powder
½ teaspoon Creole seasoning

1. In a large bowl, combine the chicken, Cheddar, eggs, onion, almond meal, and poultry seasoning. Stir gently until thoroughly combined. Cover and refrigerate for 30 minutes. 2. Meanwhile, to make the Creole sauce: In a small bowl, whisk together the mayonnaise, sour cream, Dijon mustard, lemon juice, garlic powder, and Creole seasoning until thoroughly combined. Cover and refrigerate until ready to serve. 3. Preheat the air fryer to 400°F (204°C). Divide the chicken mixture into 8 portions and shape into patties. 4. Working in batches if necessary, arrange the patties in a single layer in the air fryer basket and coat both sides lightly with olive oil. Pausing halfway through the cooking time to flip the patties, air fry for 10 minutes, or until lightly browned and the cheese is melted. Serve with the Creole sauce.

Harissa-Rubbed Cornish Game Hens

Prep time: 30 minutes | Cook time: 21 minutes | Serves 4

Harissa:
½ cup olive oil
6 cloves garlic, minced
2 tablespoons smoked paprika
1 tablespoon ground coriander
1 tablespoon ground cumin
1 teaspoon ground caraway
1 teaspoon kosher salt
½ to 1 teaspoon cayenne pepper
Hens:
½ cup yogurt
2 Cornish game hens, any giblets removed, split in half lengthwise

1. For the harissa: In a medium microwave-safe bowl, combine the oil, garlic, paprika, coriander, cumin, caraway, salt, and cayenne. Microwave on high for 1 minute, stirring halfway through the cooking time. (You can also heat this on the stovetop until the oil is hot and bubbling. Or, if you must use your air fryer for everything, cook it in the air fryer at 350°F (177°C) for 5 to 6 minutes, or until the paste is heated through.) 2. For the hens: In a small bowl, combine 1 to 2 tablespoons harissa and the yogurt. Whisk until well combined. Place the hen halves in a resealable plastic bag and pour the marinade over. Seal the bag and massage until all of the pieces are thoroughly coated. Marinate at room temperature for 30 minutes or in the refrigerator for up to 24 hours. 3. Arrange the hen halves in a single layer in the air fryer basket. (If you have a smaller air fryer, you may have to cook this in two batches.) Set the air fryer to 400°F (204°C) for 20 minutes. Use a meat thermometer to ensure the game hens have reached an internal temperature of 165°F (74°C).

Tandoori Chicken

Prep time: 30 minutes | Cook time: 15 minutes | Serves 4

1 pound (454 g) chicken tenders, halved crosswise	1 teaspoon ground turmeric
¼ cup plain Greek yogurt	1 teaspoon garam masala
1 tablespoon minced fresh ginger	1 teaspoon sweet smoked paprika
1 tablespoon minced garlic	1 tablespoon vegetable oil or melted ghee
¼ cup chopped fresh cilantro or parsley	2 teaspoons fresh lemon juice
1 teaspoon kosher salt	2 tablespoons chopped fresh cilantro
½ to 1 teaspoon cayenne pepper	

1. In a large glass bowl, toss together the chicken, yogurt, ginger, garlic, cilantro, salt, cayenne, turmeric, garam masala, and paprika to coat. Marinate at room temperature for 30 minutes, or cover and refrigerate for up to 24 hours. 2. Place the chicken in a single layer in the air fryer basket. (Discard remaining marinade.) Spray the chicken with oil. Set the air fryer to 350ºF (177ºC) for 15 minutes. Halfway through the cooking time, spray the chicken with more vegetable oil spray, and toss gently to coat. Cook for 5 minutes more. 3. Transfer the chicken to a serving platter. Sprinkle with lemon juice and toss to coat. Sprinkle with the cilantro and serve.

Chicken Wellington

Prep time: 30 minutes | Cook time: 31 minutes | Serves 2

2 (5-ounce / 142-g) boneless, skinless chicken breasts	2 tablespoons White Worcestershire sauce (or white wine)
½ cup White Worcestershire sauce	Salt and freshly ground black pepper, to taste
3 tablespoons butter	1 tablespoon chopped fresh tarragon
½ cup finely diced onion (about ½ onion)	2 sheets puff pastry, thawed
8 ounces (227 g) button mushrooms, finely chopped	1 egg, beaten
¼ cup chicken stock	Vegetable oil

1. Place the chicken breasts in a shallow dish. Pour the White Worcestershire sauce over the chicken coating both sides and marinate for 30 minutes. 2. While the chicken is marinating, melt the butter in a large skillet over medium-high heat on the stovetop. Add the onion and sauté for a few minutes, until it starts to soften. Add the mushrooms and sauté for 3 to 5 minutes until the vegetables are brown and soft. Deglaze the skillet with the chicken stock, scraping up any bits from the bottom of the pan. Add the White Worcestershire sauce and simmer for 2 to 3 minutes until the mixture reduces and starts to thicken. Season with salt and freshly ground black pepper. Remove the mushroom mixture from the heat and stir in the fresh tarragon. Let the mushroom mixture cool. 3. Preheat the air fryer to 360ºF (182ºC). 4. Remove the chicken from the marinade and transfer it to the air fryer basket. Tuck the small end of the chicken breast under the thicker part to shape it into a circle rather than an oval. Pour the marinade over the chicken and air fry for 10 minutes. 5. Roll out the puff pastry and cut out two 6-inch squares. Brush the perimeter of each square with the egg wash. Place half of the mushroom mixture in the center of each puff pastry square. Place the chicken breasts, top side down on the mushroom mixture. Starting with one corner of puff pastry and working in one direction, pull the pastry up over the chicken to enclose it and press the ends of the pastry together in the middle. Brush the pastry with the egg wash to seal the edges. Turn the Wellingtons over and set aside. 6. Make a decorative design with the remaining puff pastry, cut out four 10-inch strips. For each Wellington, twist two of the strips together, place them over the chicken breast wrapped in puff pastry, and tuck the ends underneath to seal it. Brush the entire top and sides of the Wellingtons with the egg wash. 7. Preheat the air fryer to 350ºF (177ºC). 8. Spray or brush the air fryer basket with vegetable oil. Air fry the chicken Wellingtons for 13 minutes. Carefully turn the Wellingtons over. Air fry for another 8 minutes. Transfer to serving plates, light a candle and enjoy!

Almond-Crusted Chicken

Prep time: 15 minutes | Cook time: 25 minutes | Serves 4

¼ cup slivered almonds	2 tablespoons full-fat mayonnaise
2 (6-ounce / 170-g) boneless, skinless chicken breasts	1 tablespoon Dijon mustard

1. Pulse the almonds in a food processor or chop until finely chopped. Place almonds evenly on a plate and set aside. 2. Completely slice each chicken breast in half lengthwise. 3. Mix the mayonnaise and mustard in a small bowl and then coat chicken with the mixture. 4. Lay each piece of chicken in the chopped almonds to fully coat. Carefully move the pieces into the air fryer basket. 5. Adjust the temperature to 350ºF (177ºC) and air fry for 25 minutes. 6. Chicken will be done when it has reached an internal temperature of 165ºF (74ºC) or more. Serve warm.

Sweet and Spicy Turkey Meatballs

Prep time: 15 minutes | Cook time: 15 minutes | Serves 6

Olive oil	¼ cup plus 1 tablespoon hoisin sauce, divided
1 pound (454 g) lean ground turkey	2 teaspoons minced garlic
½ cup whole-wheat panko bread crumbs	⅛ teaspoon salt
1 egg, beaten	⅛ teaspoon freshly ground black pepper
1 tablespoon soy sauce	1 teaspoon Sriracha

1. Spray the air fryer basket lightly with olive oil. 2. In a large bowl, mix together the turkey, panko bread crumbs, egg, soy sauce, 1 tablespoon of hoisin sauce, garlic, salt, and black pepper. 3. Using a tablespoon, form 24 meatballs. 4. In a small bowl, combine the remaining ¼ cup of hoisin sauce and Sriracha to make a glaze and set aside. 5. Place the meatballs in the air fryer basket in a single layer. You may need to cook them in batches. 6. Air fry at 350ºF (177ºC) for 8 minutes. Brush the meatballs generously with the glaze and cook until cooked through, an additional 4 to 7 minutes.

Tex-Mex Turkey Burgers

Prep time: 10 minutes | Cook time: 14 to 16 minutes

| Serves 4

⅓ cup finely crushed corn tortilla chips	Pinch salt
1 egg, beaten	Freshly ground black pepper, to taste
¼ cup salsa	1 pound (454 g) ground turkey
⅓ cup shredded pepper Jack cheese	1 tablespoon olive oil
	1 teaspoon paprika

1. Preheat the air fryer to 330°F (166°C). 2. In a medium bowl, combine the tortilla chips, egg, salsa, cheese, salt, and pepper, and mix well. 3. Add the turkey and mix gently but thoroughly with clean hands. 4. Form the meat mixture into patties about ½ inch thick. Make an indentation in the center of each patty with your thumb so the burgers don't puff up while cooking. 5. Brush the patties on both sides with the olive oil and sprinkle with paprika. 6. Put in the air fryer basket and air fry for 14 to 16 minutes or until the meat registers at least 165°F (74°C). 7. Let sit for 5 minutes before serving.

Garlic Soy Chicken Thighs

Prep time: 10 minutes | Cook time: 30 minutes |

Serves 1 to 2

2 tablespoons chicken stock	2 large scallions, cut into 2- to
2 tablespoons reduced-sodium soy sauce	3-inch batons, plus more, thinly sliced, for garnish
1½ tablespoons sugar	2 bone-in, skin-on chicken
4 garlic cloves, smashed and peeled	thighs (7 to 8 ounces / 198 to 227 g each)

1. Preheat the air fryer to 375°F (191°C). 2. In a metal cake pan, combine the chicken stock, soy sauce, and sugar and stir until the sugar dissolves. Add the garlic cloves, scallions, and chicken thighs, turning the thighs to coat them in the marinade, then resting them skin-side up. Place the pan in the air fryer and bake, flipping the thighs every 5 minutes after the first 10 minutes, until the chicken is cooked through and the marinade is reduced to a sticky glaze over the chicken, about 30 minutes. 3. Remove the pan from the air fryer and serve the chicken thighs warm, with any remaining glaze spooned over top and sprinkled with more sliced scallions.

Chicken Pesto Pizzas

Prep time: 10 minutes | Cook time: 12 minutes | Serves 4

1 pound (454 g) ground chicken thighs	¼ cup basil pesto
¼ teaspoon salt	1 cup shredded Mozzarella cheese
⅛ teaspoon ground black pepper	4 grape tomatoes, sliced

1. Cut four squares of parchment paper to fit into your air fryer basket. 2. Place ground chicken in a large bowl and mix with salt and pepper. Divide mixture into four equal sections. 3. Wet your hands with water to prevent sticking, then press each section into a 6-inch circle onto a piece of ungreased parchment. Place each chicken crust into air fryer basket, working in batches if needed. 4. Adjust the temperature to 350°F (177°C) and air fry for 10 minutes, turning crusts halfway through cooking. 5. Spread 1 tablespoon pesto across the top of each crust, then sprinkle with ¼ cup Mozzarella and top with 1 sliced tomato. Continue cooking at 350°F (177°C) for 2 minutes. Cheese will be melted and brown when done. Serve warm.

Fried Chicken Breasts

Prep time: 30 minutes | Cook time: 12 to 14 minutes

| Serves 4

1 pound (454 g) boneless, skinless chicken breasts	cheese
¾ cup dill pickle juice	½ teaspoon sea salt
¾ cup finely ground blanched almond flour	½ teaspoon freshly ground black pepper
¾ cup finely grated Parmesan	2 large eggs
	Avocado oil spray

1. Place the chicken breasts in a zip-top bag or between two pieces of plastic wrap. Using a meat mallet or heavy skillet, pound the chicken to a uniform ½-inch thickness. 2. Place the chicken in a large bowl with the pickle juice. Cover and allow to brine in the refrigerator for up to 2 hours. 3. In a shallow dish, combine the almond flour, Parmesan cheese, salt, and pepper. In a separate, shallow bowl, beat the eggs. 4. Drain the chicken and pat it dry with paper towels. Dip in the eggs and then in the flour mixture, making sure to press the coating into the chicken. Spray both sides of the coated breasts with oil. 5. Spray the air fryer basket with oil and put the chicken inside. Set the temperature to 400°F (204°C) and air fry for 6 to 7 minutes. 6. Carefully flip the breasts with a spatula. Spray the breasts again with oil and continue cooking for 6 to 7 minutes more, until golden and crispy.

Chicken with Bacon and Tomato

Prep time: 25 minutes | Cook time: 10 minutes | Serves 4

4 medium-sized skin-on chicken drumsticks	2 tablespoons olive oil
1½ teaspoons herbs de Provence	2 garlic cloves, crushed
	12 ounces (340 g) crushed canned tomatoes
Salt and pepper, to taste	1 small-size leek, thinly sliced
1 tablespoon rice vinegar	2 slices smoked bacon, chopped

1. Sprinkle the chicken drumsticks with herbs de Provence, salt and pepper; then, drizzle them with rice vinegar and olive oil. 2. Cook in the baking pan at 360°F (182°C) for 8 to 10 minutes. Pause the air fryer; stir in the remaining ingredients and continue to cook for 15 minutes longer; make sure to check them periodically. Bon appétit!

Chicken and Vegetable Fajitas

Prep time: 15 minutes | Cook time: 23 minutes | Serves 6

Chicken:
1 pound (454 g) boneless, skinless chicken thighs, cut crosswise into thirds
1 tablespoon vegetable oil
4½ teaspoons taco seasoning
Vegetables:
1 cup sliced onion
1 cup sliced bell pepper
1 or 2 jalapeños, quartered
lengthwise
1 tablespoon vegetable oil
½ teaspoon kosher salt
½ teaspoon ground cumin
For Serving:
Tortillas
Sour cream
Shredded cheese
Guacamole
Salsa

1. For the chicken: In a medium bowl, toss together the chicken, vegetable oil, and taco seasoning to coat. 2. For the vegetables: In a separate bowl, toss together the onion, bell pepper, jalapeño(s), vegetable oil, salt, and cumin to coat. 3. Place the chicken in the air fryer basket. Set the air fryer to 375ºF (191ºC) for 10 minutes. Add the vegetables to the basket, toss everything together to blend the seasonings, and set the air fryer for 13 minutes more. Use a meat thermometer to ensure the chicken has reached an internal temperature of 165ºF (74ºC). 4. Transfer the chicken and vegetables to a serving platter. Serve with tortillas and the desired fajita fixings.

Italian Chicken with Sauce

Prep time: 15 minutes | Cook time: 20 minutes | Serves 4

2 large skinless chicken breasts (about 1¼ pounds / 567 g)
Salt and freshly ground black pepper
½ cup almond meal
½ cup grated Parmesan cheese
2 teaspoons Italian seasoning
1 egg, lightly beaten
1 tablespoon olive oil
1 cup no-sugar-added marinara sauce
4 slices Mozzarella cheese or ½ cup shredded Mozzarella

1. Preheat the air fryer to 360ºF (182ºC). 2. Slice the chicken breasts in half horizontally to create 4 thinner chicken breasts. Working with one piece at a time, place the chicken between two pieces of parchment paper and pound with a meat mallet or rolling pin to flatten to an even thickness. Season both sides with salt and freshly ground black pepper. 3. In a large shallow bowl, combine the almond meal, Parmesan, and Italian seasoning; stir until thoroughly combined. Place the egg in another large shallow bowl. 4. Dip the chicken in the egg, followed by the almond meal mixture, pressing the mixture firmly into the chicken to create an even coating. 5. Working in batches if necessary, arrange the chicken breasts in a single layer in the air fryer basket and coat both sides lightly with olive oil. Pausing halfway through the cooking time to flip the chicken, air fry for 15 minutes, or until a thermometer inserted into the thickest part registers 165ºF (74ºC). 6. Spoon the marinara sauce over each piece of chicken and top with the Mozzarella cheese. Air fry for an additional 3 to 5 minutes until the cheese is melted.

Nacho Chicken Fries

Prep time: 20 minutes | Cook time: 6 to 7 minutes per batch | Serves 4 to 6

1 pound (454 g) chicken tenders
Salt, to taste
¼ cup flour
2 eggs
¾ cup panko bread crumbs
¾ cup crushed organic nacho cheese tortilla chips
Oil for misting or cooking spray
Seasoning Mix:
1 tablespoon chili powder
1 teaspoon ground cumin
½ teaspoon garlic powder
½ teaspoon onion powder

1. Stir together all seasonings in a small cup and set aside. 2. Cut chicken tenders in half crosswise, then cut into strips no wider than about ½ inch. 3. Preheat the air fryer to 390ºF (199ºC). 4. Salt chicken to taste. Place strips in large bowl and sprinkle with 1 tablespoon of the seasoning mix. Stir well to distribute seasonings. 5. Add flour to chicken and stir well to coat all sides. 6. Beat eggs together in a shallow dish. 7. In a second shallow dish, combine the panko, crushed chips, and the remaining 2 teaspoons of seasoning mix. 8. Dip chicken strips in eggs, then roll in crumbs. Mist with oil or cooking spray. 9. Chicken strips will cook best if done in two batches. They can be crowded and overlapping a little but not stacked in double or triple layers. 10. Cook for 4 minutes. Shake basket, mist with oil, and cook 2 to 3 more minutes, until chicken juices run clear and outside is crispy. 11. Repeat step 10 to cook remaining chicken fries.

Stuffed Chicken Florentine

Prep time: 10 minutes | Cook time: 20 minutes | Serves 4

3 tablespoons pine nuts
¾ cup frozen spinach, thawed and squeezed dry
⅓ cup ricotta cheese
2 tablespoons grated Parmesan cheese
3 cloves garlic, minced
Salt and freshly ground black pepper, to taste
4 small boneless, skinless chicken breast halves (about 1½ pounds / 680 g)
8 slices bacon

1. Place the pine nuts in a small pan and set in the air fryer basket. Set the air fryer to 400ºF (204ºC) and air fry for 2 to 3 minutes until toasted. Remove the pine nuts to a mixing bowl and continue preheating the air fryer. 2. In a large bowl, combine the spinach, ricotta, Parmesan, and garlic. Season to taste with salt and pepper and stir well until thoroughly combined. 3. Using a sharp knife, cut into the chicken breasts, slicing them across and opening them up like a book, but be careful not to cut them all the way through. Sprinkle the chicken with salt and pepper. 4. Spoon equal amounts of the spinach mixture into the chicken, then fold the top of the chicken breast back over the top of the stuffing. Wrap each chicken breast with 2 slices of bacon. 5. Working in batches if necessary, air fry the chicken for 18 to 20 minutes until the bacon is crisp and a thermometer inserted into the thickest part of the chicken registers 165ºF (74ºC).

Blackened Chicken

Prep time: 10 minutes | Cook time: 20 minutes | Serves 4

1 large egg, beaten	chicken breasts (about 1 pound
¾ cup Blackened seasoning	/ 454 g each), halved
2 whole boneless, skinless	1 to 2 tablespoons oil

1. Place the beaten egg in one shallow bowl and the Blackened seasoning in another shallow bowl. 2. One at a time, dip the chicken pieces in the beaten egg and the Blackened seasoning, coating thoroughly. 3. Preheat the air fryer to 360ºF (182ºC). Line the air fryer basket with parchment paper. 4. Place the chicken pieces on the parchment and spritz with oil. 5. Cook for 10 minutes. Flip the chicken, spritz it with oil, and cook for 10 minutes more until the internal temperature reaches 165ºF (74ºC) and the chicken is no longer pink inside. Let sit for 5 minutes before serving.

Peachy Chicken Chunks with Cherries

Prep time: 8 minutes | Cook time: 14 to 16 minutes |

Serves 4

⅓ cup peach preserves	chicken breasts, cut in 1½-inch
1 teaspoon ground rosemary	chunks
½ teaspoon black pepper	Oil for misting or cooking spray
½ teaspoon salt	1 (10-ounce / 283-g) package
½ teaspoon marjoram	frozen unsweetened dark
1 teaspoon light olive oil	cherries, thawed and drained
1 pound (454 g) boneless	

1. In a medium bowl, mix together peach preserves, rosemary, pepper, salt, marjoram, and olive oil. 2. Stir in chicken chunks and toss to coat well with the preserve mixture. 3. Spray the air fryer basket with oil or cooking spray and lay chicken chunks in basket. 4. Air fry at 390ºF (199ºC) for 7 minutes. Stir. Cook for 6 to 8 more minutes or until chicken juices run clear. 5. When chicken has cooked through, scatter the cherries over and cook for additional minute to heat cherries.

Lemon-Dijon Boneless Chicken

Prep time: 30 minutes | Cook time: 13 to 16 minutes

| Serves 6

½ cup sugar-free mayonnaise	½ teaspoon freshly ground
1 tablespoon Dijon mustard	black pepper
1 tablespoon freshly squeezed	¼ teaspoon cayenne pepper
lemon juice (optional)	1½ pounds (680 g) boneless,
1 tablespoon coconut aminos	skinless chicken breasts or
1 teaspoon Italian seasoning	thighs
1 teaspoon sea salt	

1. In a small bowl, combine the mayonnaise, mustard, lemon juice (if using), coconut aminos, Italian seasoning, salt, black pepper, and cayenne pepper. 2. Place the chicken in a shallow dish or large zip-top plastic bag. Add the marinade, making sure all the pieces are coated. Cover and refrigerate for at least 30 minutes or up to 4

hours. 3. Set the air fryer to 400ºF (204ºC). Arrange the chicken in a single layer in the air fryer basket, working in batches if necessary. Air fry for 7 minutes. Flip the chicken and continue cooking for 6 to 9 minutes more, until an instant-read thermometer reads 160ºF (71ºC).

Gochujang Chicken Wings

Prep time: 15 minutes | Cook time: 25 minutes | Serves 4

Wings:	1 tablespoon minced fresh
2 pounds (907 g) chicken wings	ginger
1 teaspoon kosher salt	1 tablespoon minced garlic
1 teaspoon black pepper or	1 teaspoon sugar
gochugaru (Korean red pepper)	1 teaspoon agave nectar or
Sauce:	honey
2 tablespoons gochujang	For Serving
(Korean chile paste)	1 teaspoon sesame seeds
1 tablespoon mayonnaise	¼ cup chopped scallions
1 tablespoon toasted sesame oil	

1. For the wings: Season the wings with the salt and pepper and place in the air fryer basket. Set the air fryer to 400ºF (204ºC) for 20 minutes, turning the wings halfway through the cooking time. 2. Meanwhile, for the sauce: In a small bowl, combine the gochujang, mayonnaise, sesame oil, ginger, garlic, sugar, and agave; set aside. 3. As you near the 20-minute mark, use a meat thermometer to check the meat. When the wings reach 160ºF (71ºC), transfer them to a large bowl. Pour about half the sauce on the wings; toss to coat (serve the remaining sauce as a dip). 4. Return the wings to the air fryer basket and cook for 5 minutes, until the sauce has glazed. 5. Transfer the wings to a serving platter. Sprinkle with the sesame seeds and scallions. Serve with the reserved sauce on the side for dipping.

Apricot-Glazed Chicken Drumsticks

Prep time: 15 minutes | Cook time: 30 minutes |

Makes 6 drumsticks

For the Glaze:	6 chicken drumsticks
½ cup apricot preserves	½ teaspoon seasoning salt
½ teaspoon tamari	1 teaspoon salt
¼ teaspoon chili powder	½ teaspoon ground black
2 teaspoons Dijon mustard	pepper
For the Chicken:	Cooking spray

Make the glaze: 1. Combine the ingredients for the glaze in a saucepan, then heat over low heat for 10 minutes or until thickened. 2. Turn off the heat and sit until ready to use. Make the Chicken: 1. Preheat the air fryer to 370ºF (188ºC). Spritz the air fryer basket with cooking spray. 2. Combine the seasoning salt, salt, and pepper in a small bowl. Stir to mix well. 3. Place the chicken drumsticks in the preheated air fryer. Spritz with cooking spray and sprinkle with the salt mixture on both sides. 4. Air fry for 20 minutes or until well browned. Flip the chicken halfway through. 5. Baste the chicken with the glaze and air fryer for 2 more minutes or until the chicken tenderloin is glossy. 6. Serve immediately.

Simply Terrific Turkey Meatballs

Prep time: 10 minutes | Cook time: 7 to 10 minutes |
Serves 4

1 red bell pepper, seeded and coarsely chopped	ground turkey
2 cloves garlic, coarsely chopped	1 egg, lightly beaten
	½ cup grated Parmesan cheese
¼ cup chopped fresh parsley	1 teaspoon salt
1½ pounds (680 g) 85% lean	½ teaspoon freshly ground black pepper

1. Preheat the air fryer to 400ºF (204ºC). 2. In a food processor fitted with a metal blade, combine the bell pepper, garlic, and parsley. Pulse until finely chopped. Transfer the vegetables to a large mixing bowl. 3. Add the turkey, egg, Parmesan, salt, and black pepper. Mix gently until thoroughly combined. Shape the mixture into 1¼-inch meatballs. 4. Working in batches if necessary, arrange the meatballs in a single layer in the air fryer basket; coat lightly with olive oil spray. Pausing halfway through the cooking time to shake the basket, air fry for 7 to 10 minutes, until lightly browned and a thermometer inserted into the center of a meatball registers 165ºF (74ºC).

Pecan-Crusted Chicken Tenders

Prep time: 10 minutes | Cook time: 12 minutes | Serves 4

2 tablespoons mayonnaise	¼ teaspoon ground black pepper
1 teaspoon Dijon mustard	
1 pound (454 g) boneless, skinless chicken tenders	½ cup chopped roasted pecans, finely ground
½ teaspoon salt	

1. In a small bowl, whisk mayonnaise and mustard until combined. Brush mixture onto chicken tenders on both sides, then sprinkle tenders with salt and pepper. 2. Place pecans in a medium bowl and press each tender into pecans to coat each side. 3. Place tenders into ungreased air fryer basket in a single layer, working in batches if needed. Adjust the temperature to 375ºF (191ºC) and roast for 12 minutes, turning tenders halfway through cooking. Tenders will be golden brown and have an internal temperature of at least 165ºF (74ºC) when done. Serve warm.

Chicken Cordon Bleu

Prep time: 20 minutes | Cook time: 15 to 20 minutes | Serves 4

4 small boneless, skinless chicken breasts	3 to 4 inches square)
	2 tablespoons olive oil
Salt and pepper, to taste	2 teaspoons marjoram
4 slices deli ham	¼ teaspoon paprika
4 slices deli Swiss cheese (about	

1. Split each chicken breast horizontally almost in two, leaving one edge intact. 2. Lay breasts open flat and sprinkle with salt and pepper to taste. 3. Place a ham slice on top of each chicken breast. 4. Cut cheese slices in half and place one half atop each breast. Set aside remaining halves of cheese slices. 5. Roll up chicken breasts to enclose cheese and ham and secure with toothpicks. 6. Mix together the olive oil, marjoram, and paprika. Rub all over outsides of chicken breasts. 7. Place chicken in air fryer basket and air fry at 360ºF (182ºC) for 15 to 20 minutes, until well done and juices run clear. 8. Remove all toothpicks. To avoid burns, place chicken breasts on a plate to remove toothpicks, then immediately return them to the air fryer basket. 9. Place a half cheese slice on top of each chicken breast and cook for a minute or so just to melt cheese.

Easy Chicken Fingers

Prep time: 20 minutes | Cook time: 30 minutes |
Makes 12 chicken fingers

½ cup all-purpose flour	breasts, each cut into 4 strips
2 cups panko breadcrumbs	Kosher salt and freshly ground black pepper, to taste
2 tablespoons canola oil	
1 large egg	Cooking spray
3 boneless and skinless chicken	

1. Preheat the air fryer to 360ºF (182ºC). Spritz the air fryer basket with cooking spray. 2. Pour the flour in a large bowl. Combine the panko and canola oil on a shallow dish. Whisk the egg in a separate bowl. 3. Rub the chicken strips with salt and ground black pepper on a clean work surface, then dip the chicken in the bowl of flour. Shake the excess off and dunk the chicken strips in the bowl of whisked egg, then roll the strips over the panko to coat well. 4. Arrange 4 strips in the air fryer basket each time and air fry for 10 minutes or until crunchy and lightly browned. Flip the strips halfway through. Repeat with remaining ingredients. 5. Serve immediately.

Ethiopian Chicken with Cauliflower

Prep time: 15 minutes | Cook time: 28 minutes | Serves 6

2 handful fresh Italian parsley, roughly chopped	⅓ teaspoon porcini powder
½ cup fresh chopped chives	1½ teaspoons berbere spice
2 sprigs thyme	⅓ teaspoon sweet paprika
6 chicken drumsticks	½ teaspoon shallot powder
1½ small-sized head cauliflower, broken into large-sized florets	1 teaspoon granulated garlic
	1 teaspoon freshly cracked pink peppercorns
2 teaspoons mustard powder	½ teaspoon sea salt

1. Simply combine all items for the berbere spice rub mix. After that, coat the chicken drumsticks with this rub mix on all sides. Transfer them to the baking dish. 2. Now, lower the cauliflower onto the chicken drumsticks. Add thyme, chives and Italian parsley and spritz everything with a pan spray. Transfer the baking dish to the preheated air fryer. 3. Next step, set the timer for 28 minutes; roast at 355ºF (179ºC), turning occasionally. Bon appétit!

Korean Flavor Glazed Chicken Wings

Prep time: 10 minutes | Cook time: 25 minutes | Serves 4

Wings:
2 pounds (907 g) chicken wings
1 teaspoon salt
1 teaspoon ground black pepper
Sauce:
2 tablespoons gochujang
1 tablespoon mayonnaise
1 tablespoon minced ginger

1 tablespoon minced garlic
1 teaspoon agave nectar
2 packets Splenda
1 tablespoon sesame oil
For Garnish:
2 teaspoons sesame seeds
¼ cup chopped green onions

1. Preheat the air fryer to 400ºF (204ºC). Line a baking pan with aluminum foil, then arrange the rack on the pan. 2. On a clean work surface, rub the chicken wings with salt and ground black pepper, then arrange the seasoned wings on the rack. 3. Air fry for 20 minutes or until the wings are well browned. Flip the wings halfway through. You may need to work in batches to avoid overcrowding. 4. Meanwhile, combine the ingredients for the sauce in a small bowl. Stir to mix well. Reserve half of the sauce in a separate bowl until ready to serve. 5. Remove the air fried chicken wings from the air fryer and toss with remaining half of the sauce to coat well. 6. Place the wings back to the air fryer and air fry for 5 more minutes or until the internal temperature of the wings reaches at least 165ºF (74ºC). 7. Remove the wings from the air fryer and place on a large plate. Sprinkle with sesame seeds and green onions. Serve with reserved sauce.

Italian Flavor Chicken Breasts with Roma Tomatoes

Prep time: 10 minutes | Cook time: 60 minutes | Serves 8

3 pounds (1.4 kg) chicken breasts, bone-in
1 teaspoon minced fresh basil
1 teaspoon minced fresh rosemary
2 tablespoons minced fresh parsley

1 teaspoon cayenne pepper
½ teaspoon salt
½ teaspoon freshly ground black pepper
4 medium Roma tomatoes, halved
Cooking spray

1. Preheat the air fryer to 370ºF (188ºC). Spritz the air fryer basket with cooking spray. 2. Combine all the ingredients, except for the chicken breasts and tomatoes, in a large bowl. Stir to mix well. 3. Dunk the chicken breasts in the mixture and press to coat well. 4. Transfer the chicken breasts in the preheated air fryer. You may need to work in batches to avoid overcrowding. 5. Air fry for 25 minutes or until the internal temperature of the thickest part of the breasts reaches at least 165ºF (74ºC). Flip the breasts halfway through the cooking time. 6. Remove the cooked chicken breasts from the basket and adjust the temperature to 350ºF (177ºC). 7. Place the tomatoes in the air fryer and spritz with cooking spray. Sprinkle with a touch of salt and cook for 10 minutes or until tender. Shake the basket halfway through the cooking time. 8. Serve the tomatoes with chicken breasts on a large serving plate.

Israeli Chicken Schnitzel

Prep time: 5 minutes | Cook time: 10 minutes | Serves 4

2 large boneless, skinless chicken breasts, each weighing about 1 pound (454 g)
1 cup all-purpose flour
2 teaspoons garlic powder
2 teaspoons kosher salt
1 teaspoon black pepper

1 teaspoon paprika
2 eggs beaten with 2 tablespoons water
2 cups panko bread crumbs
Vegetable oil spray
Lemon juice, for serving

1. Preheat the air fryer to 375ºF (191ºC). 2. Place 1 chicken breast between 2 pieces of plastic wrap. Use a mallet or a rolling pin to pound the chicken until it is ¼ inch thick. Set aside. Repeat with the second breast. Whisk together the flour, garlic powder, salt, pepper, and paprika on a large plate. Place the panko in a separate shallow bowl or pie plate. 3. Dredge 1 chicken breast in the flour, shaking off any excess, then dip it in the egg mixture. Dredge the chicken breast in the panko, making sure to coat it completely. Shake off any excess panko. Place the battered chicken breast on a plate. Repeat with the second chicken breast. 4. Spray the air fryer basket with oil spray. Place 1 of the battered chicken breasts in the basket and spray the top with oil spray. Air fry until the top is browned, about 5 minutes. Flip the chicken and spray the second side with oil spray. Air fry until the second side is browned and crispy and the internal temperature reaches 165ºF (74ºC). Remove the first chicken breast from the air fryer and repeat with the second chicken breast. 5. Serve hot with lemon juice.

Herbed Roast Chicken Breast

Prep time: 10 minutes | Cook time: 25 minutes | Serves 2 to 4

2 tablespoons salted butter or ghee, at room temperature
1 teaspoon dried Italian seasoning, crushed
½ teaspoon kosher salt
½ teaspoon smoked paprika

¼ teaspoon black pepper
2 bone-in, skin-on chicken breast halves (about 10 ounces / 283 g each)
Lemon wedges, for serving

1. In a small bowl, stir together the butter, Italian seasoning, salt, paprika, and pepper until thoroughly combined. 2. Using a small sharp knife, carefully loosen the skin on each chicken breast half, starting at the thin end of each. Very carefully separate the skin from the flesh, leaving the skin attached at the thick end of each breast. Divide the herb butter into quarters. Rub one-quarter of the butter onto the flesh of each breast. Fold and lightly press the skin back onto each breast. Rub the remaining butter onto the skin of each breast. 3. Place the chicken in the air fryer basket. Set the air fryer to 375ºF (191ºC) for 25 minutes. Use a meat thermometer to ensure the chicken breasts have reached an internal temperature of 165ºF (74ºC). 4. Transfer the chicken to a cutting board. Lightly cover with aluminum foil and let rest for 5 to 10 minutes. 5. Serve with lemon wedges.

Prep time: 5 minutes | Cook time: 40 minutes | Serves 5

1 tablespoon olive oil
10 chicken drumsticks
Chicken seasoning or rub, to taste

Salt and ground black pepper, to taste
1 cup barbecue sauce
¼ cup honey

1. Preheat the air fryer to 390°F (199°C). Grease the air fryer basket with olive oil. 2. Rub the chicken drumsticks with chicken seasoning or rub, salt and ground black pepper on a clean work surface. 3. Arrange the chicken drumsticks in a single layer in the air fryer, then air fry for 18 minutes or until lightly browned. Flip the drumsticks halfway through. You may need to work in batches to avoid overcrowding. 4. Meanwhile, combine the barbecue sauce and honey in a small bowl. Stir to mix well. 5. Remove the drumsticks from the air fryer and baste with the sauce mixture to serve.

Chapter 5 Beef, Pork, and Lamb

Bulgogi Burgers

Prep time: 30 minutes | Cook time: 10 minutes | Serves 4

Burgers:
1 pound (454 g) 85% lean
ground beef
¼ cup chopped scallions
2 tablespoons gochujang
(Korean red chile paste)
1 tablespoon dark soy sauce
2 teaspoons minced garlic
2 teaspoons minced fresh ginger
2 teaspoons sugar

1 tablespoon toasted sesame oil
½ teaspoon kosher salt
Gochujang Mayonnaise:
¼ cup mayonnaise
¼ cup chopped scallions
1 tablespoon gochujang (Korean
red chile paste)
1 tablespoon toasted sesame oil
2 teaspoons sesame seeds
4 hamburger buns

1. For the burgers: In a large bowl, mix the ground beef, scallions, gochujang, soy sauce, garlic, ginger, sugar, sesame oil, and salt. Marinate at room temperature for 30 minutes, or cover and refrigerate for up to 24 hours. 2. Divide the meat into four portions and form them into round patties. Make a slight depression in the middle of each patty with your thumb to prevent them from puffing up into a dome shape while cooking. 3. Place the patties in a single layer in the air fryer basket. Set the air fryer to 350ºF (177ºC) for 10 minutes. 4. Meanwhile, for the gochujang mayonnaise: Stir together the mayonnaise, scallions, gochujang, sesame oil, and sesame seeds. 5. At the end of the cooking time, use a meat thermometer to ensure the burgers have reached an internal temperature of 160ºF / 71ºC (medium). 6. To serve, place the burgers on the buns and top with the mayonnaise.

Sausage and Cauliflower Arancini

Prep time: 30 minutes | Cook time: 28 to 32 minutes | Serves 6

Avocado oil spray
6 ounces (170 g) Italian
sausage, casings removed
¼ cup diced onion
1 teaspoon minced garlic
1 teaspoon dried thyme
Sea salt and freshly ground
black pepper, to taste
2½ cups cauliflower rice
3 ounces (85 g) cream cheese

4 ounces (113 g) Cheddar
cheese, shredded
1 large egg
½ cup finely ground blanched
almond flour
¼ cup finely grated Parmesan
cheese
Keto-friendly marinara sauce,
for serving

1. Spray a large skillet with oil and place it over medium-high heat. Once the skillet is hot, put the sausage in the skillet and cook for 7 minutes, breaking up the meat with the back of a spoon. 2. Reduce the heat to medium and add the onion. Cook for 5 minutes, then add the garlic, thyme, and salt and pepper to taste. Cook for 1 minute more. 3. Add the cauliflower rice and cream cheese to the skillet. Cook for 7 minutes, stirring frequently, until the cream cheese melts and the cauliflower is tender. 4. Remove the skillet from the heat and stir in the Cheddar cheese. Using a cookie scoop, form the mixture into 1½-inch balls. Place the balls on a parchment paper-lined baking sheet. Freeze for 30 minutes. 5. Place the egg in a shallow bowl and beat it with a fork. In a separate bowl, stir together the almond flour and Parmesan cheese. 6. Dip the cauliflower balls into the egg, then coat them with the almond flour mixture, gently pressing the mixture to the balls to adhere. 7. Set the air fryer to 400ºF (204ºC). Spray the cauliflower rice balls with oil, and arrange them in a single layer in the air fryer basket, working in batches if necessary. Air fry for 5 minutes. Flip the rice balls and spray them with more oil. Air fry for 3 to 7 minutes longer, until the balls are golden brown. 8. Serve warm with marinara sauce.

Chicken Fried Steak with Cream Gravy

Prep time: 5 minutes | Cook time: 10 minutes | Serves 4

4 small thin cube steaks (about
1 pound / 454 g)
½ teaspoon salt
½ teaspoon freshly ground
black pepper
¼ teaspoon garlic powder
1 egg, lightly beaten
1 cup crushed pork rinds (about
3 ounces / 85 g)

Cream Gravy:
½ cup heavy cream
2 ounces (57 g) cream cheese
¼ cup bacon grease
2 to 3 tablespoons water
2 to 3 dashes Worcestershire
sauce
Salt and freshly ground black
pepper, to taste

1. Preheat the air fryer to 400ºF (204ºC). 2. Working one at a time, place the steak between two sheets of parchment paper and use a meat mallet to pound to an even thickness. 3. In a small bowl, combine the salt, pepper, and garlic power. Season both sides of each steak with the mixture. 4. Place the egg in a small shallow dish and the pork rinds in another small shallow dish. Dip each steak first in the egg wash, followed by the pork rinds, pressing lightly to form an even coating. Working in batches if necessary, arrange the steaks in a single layer in the air fryer basket. Air fry for 10 minutes until crispy and cooked through. 5. To make the cream gravy: In a heavy-bottomed pot, warm the cream, cream cheese, and bacon grease over medium heat, whisking until smooth. Lower the heat if the mixture begins to boil. Continue whisking as you slowly add the water, 1 tablespoon at a time, until the sauce reaches the desired consistency. Season with the Worcestershire sauce and salt and pepper to taste. Serve over the chicken fried steaks.

Southern Chili

Prep time: 20 minutes | Cook time: 25 minutes | Serves 4

1 pound (454 g) ground beef (85% lean)
1 cup minced onion
1 (28-ounce / 794-g) can tomato purée
1 (15-ounce / 425-g) can diced

tomatoes with green chilies
1 (15-ounce / 425-g) can light red kidney beans, rinsed and drained
¼ cup Chili seasoning

1. Preheat the air fryer to 400ºF (204ºC). 2. In a baking pan, mix the ground beef and onion. Place the pan in the air fryer. 3. Cook for 4 minutes. Stir and cook for 4 minutes more until browned. Remove the pan from the fryer. Drain the meat and transfer to a large bowl. 4. Reduce the air fryer temperature to 350ºF (177ºC). 5. To the bowl with the meat, add in the tomato purée, diced tomatoes and green chilies, kidney beans, and Chili seasoning. Mix well. Pour the mixture into the baking pan. 6. Cook for 25 minutes, stirring every 10 minutes, until thickened.

Apple Cornbread Stuffed Pork Loin

Prep time: 15 minutes | Cook time: 1 hour | Serves 4 to 6

4 strips of bacon, chopped
1 Granny Smith apple, peeled, cored and finely chopped
2 teaspoons fresh thyme leaves
¼ cup chopped fresh parsley
2 cups cubed cornbread
½ cup chicken stock
Salt and freshly ground black pepper, to taste
1 (2-pound / 907-g) boneless pork loin

Apple Gravy:
2 tablespoons butter
1 shallot, minced
1 Granny Smith apple, peeled, cored and finely chopped
3 sprigs fresh thyme
2 tablespoons flour
1 cup chicken stock
½ cup apple cider
Salt and freshly ground black pepper, to taste

1. Preheat the air fryer to 400ºF (204ºC). 2. Add the bacon to the air fryer and air fry for 6 to 8 minutes until crispy. While the bacon is cooking, combine the apple, fresh thyme, parsley and cornbread in a bowl and toss well. Moisten the mixture with the chicken stock and season to taste with salt and freshly ground black pepper. Add the cooked bacon to the mixture. 3. Butterfly the pork loin by holding it flat on the cutting board with one hand, while slicing into the pork loin parallel to the cutting board with the other. Slice into the longest side of the pork loin, but stop before you cut all the way through. You should then be able to open the pork loin up like a book, making it twice as wide as it was when you started. Season the inside of the pork with salt and freshly ground black pepper. 4. Spread the cornbread mixture onto the butterflied pork loin, leaving a one-inch border around the edge of the pork. Roll the pork loin up around the stuffing to enclose the stuffing, and tie the rolled pork in several places with kitchen twine or secure with toothpicks. Try to replace any stuffing that falls out of the roast as you roll it, by stuffing it into the ends of the rolled pork. Season the outside of the pork with salt and freshly ground black pepper. 5. Preheat the air fryer to 360ºF (182ºC). 6. Place the stuffed pork loin into the air fryer, seam side down. Air fry the pork loin for 15 minutes at 360ºF (182ºC). Turn the pork loin over and air fry for an additional 15 minutes. Turn the pork loin a quarter turn and air fry for an additional 15 minutes. Turn the pork loin over again to expose the fourth side, and air fry for an additional 10 minutes. The pork loin should register 155ºF (68ºC) on an instant read thermometer when it is finished. 7. While the pork is cooking, make the apple gravy. Preheat a saucepan over medium heat on the stovetop and melt the butter. Add the shallot, apple and thyme sprigs and sauté until the apple starts to soften and brown a little. Add the flour and stir for a minute or two. Whisk in the stock and apple cider vigorously to prevent the flour from forming lumps. Bring the mixture to a boil to thicken and season to taste with salt and pepper. 8. Transfer the pork loin to a resting plate and loosely tent with foil, letting the pork rest for at least 5 minutes before slicing and serving with the apple gravy poured over the top.

Parmesan-Crusted Pork Chops

Prep time: 5 minutes | Cook time: 12 minutes | Serves 4

1 large egg
½ cup grated Parmesan cheese
4 (4-ounce / 113-g) boneless pork chops

½ teaspoon salt
¼ teaspoon ground black pepper

1. Whisk egg in a medium bowl and place Parmesan in a separate medium bowl. 2. Sprinkle pork chops on both sides with salt and pepper. Dip each pork chop into egg, then press both sides into Parmesan. 3. Place pork chops into ungreased air fryer basket. Adjust the temperature to 400ºF (204ºC) and air fry for 12 minutes, turning chops halfway through cooking. Pork chops will be golden and have an internal temperature of at least 145ºF (63ºC) when done. Serve warm.

Nigerian Peanut-Crusted Flank Steak

Prep time: 30 minutes | Cook time: 8 minutes | Serves 4

Suya Spice Mix:
¼ cup dry-roasted peanuts
1 teaspoon cumin seeds
1 teaspoon garlic powder
1 teaspoon smoked paprika
½ teaspoon ground ginger

1 teaspoon kosher salt
½ teaspoon cayenne pepper
Steak:
1 pound (454 g) flank steak
2 tablespoons vegetable oil

1. For the spice mix: In a clean coffee grinder or spice mill, combine the peanuts and cumin seeds. Process until you get a coarse powder. (Do not overprocess or you will wind up with peanut butter! Alternatively, you can grind the cumin with ⅓ cup ready-made peanut powder, such as PB2, instead of the peanuts.) 2. Pour the peanut mixture into a small bowl, add the garlic powder, paprika, ginger, salt, and cayenne, and stir to combine. This recipe makes about ½ cup suya spice mix. Store leftovers in an airtight container in a cool, dry place for up to 1 month. 3. For the steak: Cut the flank steak into ½-inch-thick slices, cutting against the grain and at a slight angle. Place the beef strips in a resealable plastic bag and add the oil and 2½ to 3 tablespoons of the spice mixture. Seal the bag and massage to coat all of the meat with the oil and spice mixture. Marinate at room temperature for 30 minutes or in the refrigerator for up to 24 hours. 4. Place the beef strips in the air fryer basket. Set the air fryer to 400ºF (204ºC) for 8 minutes, turning the strips halfway through the cooking time. 5. Transfer the meat to a serving platter. Sprinkle with additional spice mix, if desired.

Sausage and Peppers

Prep time: 7 minutes | Cook time: 35 minutes | Serves 4

Oil, for spraying
2 pounds (907 g) hot or sweet Italian sausage links, cut into thick slices
4 large bell peppers of any color, seeded and cut into slices
1 onion, thinly sliced

1 tablespoon olive oil
1 tablespoon chopped fresh parsley
1 teaspoon dried oregano
1 teaspoon dried basil
1 teaspoon balsamic vinegar

1. Line the air fryer basket with parchment and spray lightly with oil. 2. In a large bowl, combine the sausage, bell peppers, and onion. 3. In a small bowl, whisk together the olive oil, parsley, oregano, basil, and balsamic vinegar. Pour the mixture over the sausage and peppers and toss until evenly coated. 4. Using a slotted spoon, transfer the mixture to the prepared basket, taking care to drain out as much excess liquid as possible. 5. Air fry at 350°F (177°C) for 20 minutes, stir, and cook for another 15 minutes, or until the sausage is browned and the juices run clear.

Beef Burger

Prep time: 20 minutes | Cook time: 12 minutes | Serves 4

1¼ pounds (567 g) lean ground beef
1 tablespoon coconut aminos
1 teaspoon Dijon mustard
A few dashes of liquid smoke
1 teaspoon shallot powder
1 clove garlic, minced

½ teaspoon cumin powder
¼ cup scallions, minced
⅓ teaspoon sea salt flakes
⅓ teaspoon freshly cracked mixed peppercorns
1 teaspoon celery seeds
1 teaspoon parsley flakes

1. Mix all of the above ingredients in a bowl; knead until everything is well incorporated. 2. Shape the mixture into four patties. Next, make a shallow dip in the center of each patty to prevent them puffing up during air frying. 3. Spritz the patties on all sides using nonstick cooking spray. Cook approximately 12 minutes at 360°F (182°C). 4. Check for doneness, an instant-read thermometer should read 160°F (71°C). Bon appétit!

Bacon and Cheese Stuffed Pork Chops

Prep time: 10 minutes | Cook time: 12 minutes | Serves 4

½ ounce (14 g) plain pork rinds, finely crushed
½ cup shredded sharp Cheddar cheese
4 slices cooked sugar-free bacon, crumbled

4 (4-ounce / 113-g) boneless pork chops
½ teaspoon salt
¼ teaspoon ground black pepper

1. In a small bowl, mix pork rinds, Cheddar, and bacon. 2. Make a 3-inch slit in the side of each pork chop and stuff with ¼ pork rind mixture. Sprinkle each side of pork chops with salt and pepper. 3. Place pork chops into ungreased air fryer basket, stuffed side up. Adjust the temperature to 400°F (204°C) and air fry for 12 minutes. Pork chops will be browned and have an internal temperature of at least 145°F (63°C) when done. Serve warm.

Currywurst

Prep time: 15 minutes | Cook time: 12 minutes | Serves 4

1 cup tomato sauce
2 tablespoons cider vinegar
2 teaspoons curry powder
2 teaspoons sweet paprika
1 teaspoon sugar

¼ teaspoon cayenne pepper
1 small onion, diced
1 pound (454 g) bratwurst, sliced diagonally into 1-inch pieces

1. In a large bowl, combine the tomato sauce, vinegar, curry powder, paprika, sugar, and cayenne. Whisk until well combined. Stir in the onion and bratwurst. 2. Transfer the mixture to a baking pan. Place the pan in the air fryer basket. Set the air fryer to 400°F (204°C) for 12 minutes, or until the sausage is heated through and the sauce is bubbling.

Greek Lamb Rack

Prep time: 5 minutes | Cook time: 10 minutes | Serves 4

¼ cup freshly squeezed lemon juice
1 teaspoon oregano
2 teaspoons minced fresh rosemary
1 teaspoon minced fresh thyme

2 tablespoons minced garlic
Salt and freshly ground black pepper, to taste
2 to 4 tablespoons olive oil
1 lamb rib rack (7 to 8 ribs)

1. Preheat the air fryer to 360°F (182°C). 2. In a small mixing bowl, combine the lemon juice, oregano, rosemary, thyme, garlic, salt, pepper, and olive oil and mix well. 3. Rub the mixture over the lamb, covering all the meat. Put the rack of lamb in the air fryer. Roast for 10 minutes. Flip the rack halfway through. 4. After 10 minutes, measure the internal temperature of the rack of lamb reaches at least 145°F (63°C). 5. Serve immediately.

Beef and Goat Cheese Stuffed Peppers

Prep time: 10 minutes | Cook time: 30 minutes | Serves 4

1 pound (454 g) lean ground beef
½ cup cooked brown rice
2 Roma tomatoes, diced
3 garlic cloves, minced
½ yellow onion, diced
2 tablespoons fresh oregano, chopped

1 teaspoon salt
½ teaspoon black pepper
¼ teaspoon ground allspice
2 bell peppers, halved and seeded
4 ounces (113 g) goat cheese
¼ cup fresh parsley, chopped

1. Preheat the air fryer to 360°F (182°C). 2. In a large bowl, combine the ground beef, rice, tomatoes, garlic, onion, oregano, salt, pepper, and allspice. Mix well. 3. Divide the beef mixture equally into the halved bell peppers and top each with about 1 ounce (28 g a quarter of the total) of the goat cheese. 4. Place the peppers into the air fryer basket in a single layer, making sure that they don't touch each other. Bake for 30 minutes. 5. Remove the peppers from the air fryer and top with fresh parsley before serving.

Greek-Style Meatloaf

Prep time: 5 minutes | Cook time: 25 minutes | Serves 6

1 pound (454 g) lean ground beef	1 teaspoon dried thyme
2 eggs	1 teaspoon salt
2 Roma tomatoes, diced	1 teaspoon black pepper
½ white onion, diced	2 ounces (57 g) mozzarella cheese, shredded
½ cup whole wheat bread crumbs	1 tablespoon olive oil
1 teaspoon garlic powder	Fresh chopped parsley, for garnish
1 teaspoon dried oregano	

1. Preheat the oven to 380°F(193°C). 2. In a large bowl, mix together the ground beef, eggs, tomatoes, onion, bread crumbs, garlic powder, oregano, thyme, salt, pepper, and cheese. 3. Form into a loaf, flattening to 1-inch thick. 4. Brush the top with olive oil, then place the meatloaf into the air fryer basket and cook for 25 minutes. 5. Remove from the air fryer and allow to rest for 5 minutes, before slicing and serving with a sprinkle of parsley.

Ritzy Skirt Steak Fajitas

Prep time: 15 minutes | Cook time: 30 minutes | Serves 4

2 tablespoons olive oil	1 green pepper, sliced
¼ cup lime juice	Salt and freshly ground black pepper, to taste
1 clove garlic, minced	8 flour tortillas
½ teaspoon ground cumin	Toppings:
½ teaspoon hot sauce	Shredded lettuce
½ teaspoon salt	Crumbled Queso Fresco (or grated Cheddar cheese)
2 tablespoons chopped fresh cilantro	Sliced black olives
1 pound (454 g) skirt steak	Diced tomatoes
1 onion, sliced	Sour cream
1 teaspoon chili powder	Guacamole
1 red pepper, sliced	

1. Combine the olive oil, lime juice, garlic, cumin, hot sauce, salt and cilantro in a shallow dish. Add the skirt steak and turn it over several times to coat all sides. Pierce the steak with a needle-style meat tenderizer or paring knife. Marinate the steak in the refrigerator for at least 3 hours, or overnight. When you are ready to cook, remove the steak from the refrigerator and let it sit at room temperature for 30 minutes. 2. Preheat the air fryer to 400°F (204°C). 3. Toss the onion slices with the chili powder and a little olive oil and transfer them to the air fryer basket. Air fry for 5 minutes. Add the red and green peppers to the air fryer basket with the onions, season with salt and pepper and air fry for 8 more minutes, until the onions and peppers are soft. Transfer the vegetables to a dish and cover with aluminum foil to keep warm. 4. Put the skirt steak in the air fryer basket and pour the marinade over the top. Air fry at 400°F (204°C) for 12 minutes. Flip the steak over and air fry for an additional 5 minutes. Transfer the cooked steak to a cutting board and let the steak rest for a few minutes. If the peppers and onions need to be heated, return them to the air fryer for just 1 to 2 minutes. 5. Thinly slice the steak at an angle, cutting against the grain of the steak. Serve the steak with the onions and peppers, the warm tortillas and the fajita toppings on the side.

Rack of Lamb with Pistachio Crust

Prep time: 10 minutes | Cook time: 19 minutes | Serves 2

½ cup finely chopped pistachios	Salt and freshly ground black pepper, to taste
3 tablespoons panko bread crumbs	1 tablespoon olive oil
1 teaspoon chopped fresh rosemary	1 rack of lamb, bones trimmed of fat and frenched
2 teaspoons chopped fresh oregano	1 tablespoon Dijon mustard

1. Preheat the air fryer to 380°F (193°C). 2. Combine the pistachios, bread crumbs, rosemary, oregano, salt and pepper in a small bowl. (This is a good job for your food processor if you have one.) Drizzle in the olive oil and stir to combine. 3. Season the rack of lamb with salt and pepper on all sides and transfer it to the air fryer basket with the fat side facing up. Air fry the lamb for 12 minutes. Remove the lamb from the air fryer and brush the fat side of the lamb rack with the Dijon mustard. Coat the rack with the pistachio mixture, pressing the bread crumbs onto the lamb with your hands and rolling the bottom of the rack in any of the crumbs that fall off. 4. Return the rack of lamb to the air fryer and air fry for another 3 to 7 minutes or until an instant read thermometer reads 140°F (60°C) for medium. Add or subtract a couple of minutes for lamb that is more or less well cooked. (Your time will vary depending on how big the rack of lamb is.) 5. Let the lamb rest for at least 5 minutes. Then, slice into chops and serve.

Pork Cutlets with Aloha Salsa

Prep time: 20 minutes | Cook time: 7 to 9 minutes | Serves 4

Aloha Salsa:	2 eggs
1 cup fresh pineapple, chopped in small pieces	2 tablespoons milk
¼ cup red onion, finely chopped	¼ cup flour
¼ cup green or red bell pepper, chopped	¼ cup panko bread crumbs
½ teaspoon ground cinnamon	4 teaspoons sesame seeds
1 teaspoon low-sodium soy sauce	1 pound (454 g) boneless, thin pork cutlets (⅜- to ½-inch thick)
⅛ teaspoon crushed red pepper	lemon pepper and salt
⅛ teaspoon ground black pepper	¼ cup cornstarch
	Oil for misting or cooking spray

1. In a medium bowl, stir together all ingredients for salsa. Cover and refrigerate while cooking pork. 2. Preheat the air fryer to 390°F (199°C). 3. Beat together eggs and milk in shallow dish. 4. In another shallow dish, mix together the flour, panko, and sesame seeds. 5. Sprinkle pork cutlets with lemon pepper and salt to taste. Most lemon pepper seasoning contains salt, so go easy adding extra. 6. Dip pork cutlets in cornstarch, egg mixture, and then panko coating. Spray both sides with oil or cooking spray. 7. Cook cutlets for 3 minutes. Turn cutlets over, spraying both sides, and continue cooking for 4 to 6 minutes or until well done. 8. Serve fried cutlets with salsa on the side.

Savory Sausage Cobbler

Prep time: 15 minutes | Cook time: 34 minutes | Serves 4

Filling:
1 pound (454 g) ground Italian sausage
1 cup sliced mushrooms
1 teaspoon fine sea salt
2 cups marinara sauce
Biscuits:
3 large egg whites

¾ cup blanched almond flour
1 teaspoon baking powder
¼ teaspoon fine sea salt
2½ tablespoons very cold unsalted butter, cut into ¼-inch pieces
Fresh basil leaves, for garnish

1. Preheat the air fryer to 400ºF (204ºC). 2. Place the sausage in a pie pan (or a pan that fits into your air fryer). Use your hands to break up the sausage and spread it evenly on the bottom of the pan. Place the pan in the air fryer and air fry for 5 minutes. 3. Remove the pan from the air fryer and use a fork or metal spatula to crumble the sausage more. Season the mushrooms with the salt and add them to the pie pan. Stir to combine the mushrooms and sausage, then return the pan to the air fryer and air fry for 4 minutes, or until the mushrooms are soft and the sausage is cooked through. 4. Remove the pan from the air fryer. Add the marinara sauce and stir well. Set aside. 5. Make the biscuits: Place the egg whites in a large mixing bowl or the bowl of a stand mixer. Using a hand mixer or stand mixer, whip the egg whites until stiff peaks form. 6. In a medium-sized bowl, whisk together the almond flour, baking powder, and salt, then cut in the butter. Gently fold the flour mixture into the egg whites with a rubber spatula. 7. Using a large spoon or ice cream scoop, spoon one-quarter of the dough on top of the sausage mixture, making sure the butter stays in separate clumps. Repeat with the remaining dough, spacing the biscuits about 1 inch apart. 8. Place the pan in the air fryer and cook for 5 minutes, then lower the heat to 325ºF (163ºC) and bake for another 15 to 20 minutes, until the biscuits are golden brown. Serve garnished with fresh basil leaves. 9. Store leftovers in an airtight container in the refrigerator for up to 3 days. Reheat in a preheated 350ºF (177ºC) air fryer for 5 minutes, or until warmed through.

Deconstructed Chicago Dogs

Prep time: 10 minutes | Cook time: 7 minutes | Serves 4

4 hot dogs
2 large dill pickles
¼ cup diced onions
1 tomato, cut into ½-inch dice
4 pickled sport peppers, diced

For Garnish (Optional):
Brown mustard
Celery salt
Poppy seeds

1. Spray the air fryer basket with avocado oil. Preheat the air fryer to 400ºF (204ºC). 2. Place the hot dogs in the air fryer basket and air fry for 5 to 7 minutes, until hot and slightly crispy. 3. While the hot dogs cook, quarter one of the dill pickles lengthwise, so that you have 4 pickle spears. Finely dice the other pickle. 4. When the hot dogs are done, transfer them to a serving platter and arrange them in a row, alternating with the pickle spears. Top with the diced pickles, onions, tomato, and sport peppers. Drizzle brown mustard on top and garnish with celery salt and poppy seeds, if desired. 5. Best served fresh. Store leftover hot dogs in an airtight container in the refrigerator for up to 3 days. Reheat in a preheated 390ºF (199ºC) air fryer for 2 minutes, or until warmed through.

Cheeseburger Casserole

Prep time: 5 minutes | Cook time: 50 minutes | Serves 4

¼ pound (113 g) reduced-sodium bacon
1 pound (454 g) 85% lean ground beef
1 clove garlic, minced
¼ teaspoon onion powder
4 eggs
¼ cup heavy cream

¼ cup tomato paste
2 tablespoons dill pickle relish
¼ teaspoon salt
¼ teaspoon freshly ground black pepper
1½ cups grated Cheddar cheese, divided

1. Lightly coat a casserole dish that will fit in air fryer, with olive oil and set aside. 2. Arrange the bacon in a single layer in the air fryer basket (it's OK if the bacon sits a bit on the sides). Set the air fryer to 350ºF (177ºC) and air fry for 10 minutes. Check for crispiness and air fry for 2 to 3 minutes longer if needed. Transfer the bacon to a plate lined with paper towels and let cool. Drain the grease. 3. Set the air fryer to 400ºF (204ºC). Crumble the beef into a single layer in the air fryer basket. Scatter the garlic on top and sprinkle with the onion powder. Air fry for 15 to 20 minutes until the beef is browned and cooked through. 4. While the beef is baking, in a bowl whisk together the eggs, cream, tomato paste, pickle relish, salt, and pepper. Stir in 1 cup of the cheese. Set aside. 5. When the beef is done, transfer it to the prepared pan. Use the side of a spoon to break up any large pieces of beef. 6. Drain the grease and, when cool enough to handle, wash the air fryer basket. Set the air fryer to 350ºF (177ºC). 7. Crumble the bacon and add it to the beef, spreading the meats into an even layer. Pour the egg mixture over the beef mixture and top with the remaining ½ cup of cheese. Air fry for 20 to 25 minutes until the eggs are set and the top is golden brown.

Meat and Rice Stuffed Bell Peppers

Prep time: 20 minutes | Cook time: 18 minutes | Serves 4

¾ pound (340 g) lean ground beef
4 ounces (113 g) lean ground pork
¼ cup onion, minced
1 (15-ounce / 425-g) can crushed tomatoes
1 teaspoon Worcestershire sauce
1 teaspoon barbecue seasoning

1 teaspoon honey
½ teaspoon dried basil
½ cup cooked brown rice
½ teaspoon garlic powder
½ teaspoon oregano
½ teaspoon salt
2 small bell peppers, cut in half, stems removed, deseeded
Cooking spray

1. Preheat the air fryer to 360ºF (182ºC) and spritz a baking pan with cooking spray. 2. Arrange the beef, pork, and onion in the baking pan and bake in the preheated air fryer for 8 minutes. Break the ground meat into chunks halfway through the cooking. 3. Meanwhile, combine the tomatoes, Worcestershire sauce, barbecue seasoning, honey, and basil in a saucepan. Stir to mix well. 4. Transfer the cooked meat mixture to a large bowl and add the cooked rice, garlic powder, oregano, salt, and ¼ cup of the tomato mixture. Stir to mix well. 5. Stuff the pepper halves with the mixture, then arrange the pepper halves in the air fryer and air fry for 10 minutes or until the peppers are lightly charred. 6. Serve the stuffed peppers with the remaining tomato sauce on top.

Spicy Flank Steak with Zhoug

Prep time: 30 minutes | Cook time: 8 minutes | Serves 4

Marinade and Steak:
½ cup dark beer or orange juice
¼ cup fresh lemon juice
3 cloves garlic, minced
2 tablespoons extra-virgin olive oil
2 tablespoons Sriracha
2 tablespoons brown sugar
2 teaspoons ground cumin
2 teaspoons smoked paprika
1 tablespoon kosher salt
1 teaspoon black pepper
1½ pounds (680 g) flank steak,
trimmed and cut into 3 pieces
Zhoug:
1 cup packed fresh cilantro leaves
2 cloves garlic, peeled
2 jalapeño or serrano chiles, stemmed and coarsely chopped
½ teaspoon ground cumin
¼ teaspoon ground coriander
¼ teaspoon kosher salt
2 to 4 tablespoons extra-virgin olive oil

1. For the marinade and steak: In a small bowl, whisk together the beer, lemon juice, garlic, olive oil, Sriracha, brown sugar, cumin, paprika, salt, and pepper. Place the steak in a large resealable plastic bag. Pour the marinade over the steak, seal the bag, and massage the steak to coat. Marinate in the refrigerator for 1 hour or up to 24 hours, turning the bag occasionally. 2. Meanwhile, for the zhoug: In a food processor, combine the cilantro, garlic, jalapeños, cumin, coriander, and salt. Process until finely chopped. Add 2 tablespoons olive oil and pulse to form a loose paste, adding up to 2 tablespoons more olive oil if needed. Transfer the zhoug to a glass container. Cover and store in the refrigerator until 30 minutes before serving if marinating more than 1 hour. 3. Remove the steak from the marinade and discard the marinade. Place the steak in the air fryer basket and set the air fryer to 400°F (204°C) for 8 minutes. Use a meat thermometer to ensure the steak has reached an internal temperature of 150°F / 66°C (for medium). 4. Transfer the steak to a cutting board and let rest for 5 minutes. Slice the steak across the grain and serve with the zhoug.

Fajita Meatball Lettuce Wraps

Prep time: 10 minutes | Cook time: 10 minutes | Serves 4

1 pound (454 g) ground beef (85% lean)
½ cup salsa, plus more for serving if desired
¼ cup chopped onions
¼ cup diced green or red bell peppers
1 large egg, beaten
1 teaspoon fine sea salt
½ teaspoon chili powder
½ teaspoon ground cumin
1 clove garlic, minced
For Serving (Optional):
8 leaves Boston lettuce
Pico de gallo or salsa
Lime slices

1. Spray the air fryer basket with avocado oil. Preheat the air fryer to 350°F (177°C). 2. In a large bowl, mix together all the ingredients until well combined. 3. Shape the meat mixture into eight 1-inch balls. Place the meatballs in the air fryer basket, leaving a little space between them. Air fry for 10 minutes, or until cooked through and no longer pink inside and the internal temperature reaches 145°F (63°C). 4. Serve each meatball on a lettuce leaf, topped with pico de gallo or salsa, if desired. Serve with lime slices if desired. 5. Store leftovers in an airtight container in the fridge for 3 days or in the freezer for up to a month. Reheat in a preheated 350°F (177°C) air fryer for 4 minutes, or until heated through.

Beef Chuck Cheeseburgers

Prep time: 10 minutes | Cook time: 15 minutes | Serves 4

¾ pound (340 g) ground beef chuck
1 envelope onion soup mix
Kosher salt and freshly ground
black pepper, to taste
1 teaspoon paprika
4 slices Monterey Jack cheese
4 ciabatta rolls

1. In a bowl, stir together the ground chuck, onion soup mix, salt, black pepper, and paprika to combine well. 2. Preheat the air fryer to 385°F (196°C). 3. Take four equal portions of the mixture and mold each one into a patty. Transfer to the air fryer and air fry for 10 minutes. 4. Put the slices of cheese on the top of the burgers. 5. Air fry for another minute before serving on ciabatta rolls.

Vietnamese Grilled Pork

Prep time: 30 minutes | Cook time: 20 minutes | Serves 6

¼ cup minced yellow onion
2 tablespoons sugar
2 tablespoons vegetable oil
1 tablespoon minced garlic
1 tablespoon fish sauce
1 tablespoon minced fresh lemongrass
2 teaspoons dark soy sauce
½ teaspoon black pepper
1½ pounds (680 g) boneless pork shoulder, cut into ½-inch-thick slices
¼ cup chopped salted roasted peanuts
2 tablespoons chopped fresh cilantro or parsley

1. In a large bowl, combine the onion, sugar, vegetable oil, garlic, fish sauce, lemongrass, soy sauce, and pepper. Add the pork and toss to coat. Marinate at room temperature for 30 minutes, or cover and refrigerate for up to 24 hours. 2. Arrange the pork slices in the air fryer basket; discard the marinade. Set the air fryer to 400°F (204°C) for 20 minutes, turning the pork halfway through the cooking time. 3. Transfer the pork to a serving platter. Sprinkle with the peanuts and cilantro and serve.

Mexican-Style Shredded Beef

Prep time: 5 minutes | Cook time: 35 minutes | Serves 6

1 (2-pound / 907-g) beef chuck roast, cut into 2-inch cubes
1 teaspoon salt
½ teaspoon ground black
pepper
½ cup no-sugar-added chipotle sauce

1. In a large bowl, sprinkle beef cubes with salt and pepper and toss to coat. Place beef into ungreased air fryer basket. Adjust the temperature to 400°F (204°C) and air fry for 30 minutes, shaking the basket halfway through cooking. Beef will be done when internal temperature is at least 160°F (71°C). 2. Place cooked beef into a large bowl and shred with two forks. Pour in chipotle sauce and toss to coat. 3. Return beef to air fryer basket for an additional 5 minutes at 400°F (204°C) to crisp with sauce. Serve warm.

Buttery Pork Chops

Prep time: 5 minutes | Cook time: 12 minutes | Serves 4

4 (4-ounce / 113-g) boneless
pork chops
½ teaspoon salt
¼ teaspoon ground black

pepper
2 tablespoons salted butter,
softened

1. Sprinkle pork chops on all sides with salt and pepper. Place chops into ungreased air fryer basket in a single layer. Adjust the temperature to 400°F (204°C) and air fry for 12 minutes. Pork chops will be golden and have an internal temperature of at least 145°F (63°C) when done. 2. Use tongs to remove cooked pork chops from air fryer and place onto a large plate. Top each chop with ½ tablespoon butter and let sit 2 minutes to melt. Serve warm.

Zesty London Broil

Prep time: 30 minutes | Cook time: 20 to 28 minutes | Serves 4 to 6

⅔ cup ketchup
¼ cup honey
¼ cup olive oil
2 tablespoons apple cider
vinegar
2 tablespoons Worcestershire
sauce
2 tablespoons minced onion

½ teaspoon paprika
1 teaspoon salt
1 teaspoon freshly ground black
pepper
2 pounds (907 g) London broil,
top round or flank steak (about
1-inch thick)

1. Combine the ketchup, honey, olive oil, apple cider vinegar, Worcestershire sauce, minced onion, paprika, salt and pepper in a small bowl and whisk together. 2. Generously pierce both sides of the meat with a fork or meat tenderizer and place it in a shallow dish. Pour the marinade mixture over the steak, making sure all sides of the meat get coated with the marinade. Cover and refrigerate overnight. 3. Preheat the air fryer to 400°F (204°C). 4. Transfer the London broil to the air fryer basket and air fry for 20 to 28 minutes, depending on how rare or well done you like your steak. Flip the steak over halfway through the cooking time. 5. Remove the London broil from the air fryer and let it rest for five minutes on a cutting board. To serve, thinly slice the meat against the grain and transfer to a serving platter.

Lamb Chops with Horseradish Sauce

Prep time: 30 minutes | Cook time: 13 minutes | Serves 4

Lamb:
4 lamb loin chops
2 tablespoons vegetable oil
1 clove garlic, minced
½ teaspoon kosher salt
½ teaspoon black pepper
Horseradish Cream Sauce:

½ cup mayonnaise
1 tablespoon Dijon mustard
1 to 1½ tablespoons prepared
horseradish
2 teaspoons sugar
Vegetable oil spray

1. For the lamb: Brush the lamb chops with the oil, rub with the garlic, and sprinkle with the salt and pepper. Marinate at room temperature for 30 minutes. 2. Meanwhile, for the sauce: In a medium bowl, combine the mayonnaise, mustard, horseradish, and sugar. Stir until well combined. Set aside half of the sauce for serving. 3. Spray the air fryer basket with vegetable oil spray and place the chops in the basket. Set the air fryer to 325°F (163°C) for 10 minutes, turning the chops halfway through the cooking time. 4. Remove the chops from the air fryer and add to the bowl with the horseradish sauce, turning to coat with the sauce. Place the chops back in the air fryer basket. Set the air fryer to 400°F (204°C) for 3 minutes. Use a meat thermometer to ensure the meat has reached an internal temperature of 145°F (63°C) (for medium-rare). 5. Serve the chops with the reserved horseradish sauce.

Easy Lamb Chops with Asparagus

Prep time: 10 minutes | Cook time: 15 minutes | Serves 4

4 asparagus spears, trimmed
2 tablespoons olive oil, divided
1 pound (454 g) lamb chops
1 garlic clove, minced

2 teaspoons chopped fresh
thyme, for serving
Salt and ground black pepper,
to taste

1. Preheat the air fryer to 400°F (204°C). Spritz the air fryer basket with cooking spray. 2. On a large plate, brush the asparagus with 1 tablespoon olive oil, then sprinkle with salt. Set aside. 3. On a separate plate, brush the lamb chops with remaining olive oil and sprinkle with salt and ground black pepper. 4. Arrange the lamb chops in the preheated air fryer. Air fry for 10 minutes. 5. Flip the lamb chops and add the asparagus and garlic. Air fry for 5 more minutes or until the lamb is well browned and the asparagus is tender. 6. Serve them on a plate with thyme on top.

Pork Butt with Garlicky Coriander-Parsley Sauce

Prep time: 1 hour 15 minutes | Cook time: 30 minutes | Serves 4

1 teaspoon golden flaxseed
meal
1 egg white, well whisked
1 tablespoon soy sauce
1 teaspoon lemon juice,
preferably freshly squeezed
1 tablespoon olive oil
1 pound (454 g) pork butt, cut
into pieces 2-inches long
Salt and ground black pepper,

to taste
Garlicky Coriander-Parsley
Sauce:
3 garlic cloves, minced
⅓ cup fresh coriander leaves
⅓ cup fresh parsley leaves
1 teaspoon lemon juice
½ tablespoon salt
⅓ cup extra-virgin olive oil

1. Combine the flaxseed meal, egg white, soy sauce, lemon juice, salt, black pepper, and olive oil in a large bowl. Dunk the pork strips in and press to submerge. 2. Wrap the bowl in plastic and refrigerate to marinate for at least an hour. 3. Preheat the air fryer to 380°F (193°C). 4. Arrange the marinated pork strips in the preheated air fryer and air fry for 30 minutes or until cooked through and well browned. Flip the strips halfway through. 5. Meanwhile, combine the ingredients for the sauce in a small bowl. Stir to mix well. Arrange the bowl in the refrigerator to chill until ready to serve. 6. Serve the air fried pork strips with the chilled sauce.

Beef Loin with Thyme and Parsley

Prep time: 5 minutes | Cook time: 15 minutes | Serves 4

1 tablespoon butter, melted	¼ teaspoon dried parsley
¼ dried thyme	1 pound (454 g) beef loin
1 teaspoon garlic salt	

1. Preheat the air fryer to 400ºF (204ºC). 2. In a bowl, combine the melted butter, thyme, garlic salt, and parsley. 3. Cut the beef loin into slices and generously apply the seasoned butter using a brush. Transfer to the air fryer basket. 4. Air fry the beef for 15 minutes. 5. Take care when removing it and serve hot.

Onion Pork Kebabs

Prep time: 22 minutes | Cook time: 18 minutes | Serves 3

2 tablespoons tomato purée	3 cloves garlic, peeled and
½ fresh serrano, minced	finely minced
⅓ teaspoon paprika	1 teaspoon ground black
1 pound (454 g) pork, ground	pepper, or more to taste
½ cup green onions, finely chopped	1 teaspoon salt, or more to taste

1. Thoroughly combine all ingredients in a mixing dish. Then form your mixture into sausage shapes. 2. Cook for 18 minutes at 355ºF (179ºC). Mound salad on a serving platter, top with air-fried kebabs and serve warm. Bon appétit!

Beef Steak Fingers

Prep time: 5 minutes | Cook time: 8 minutes | Serves 4

4 small beef cube steaks	½ cup flour
Salt and ground black pepper, to taste	Cooking spray

1. Preheat the air fryer to 390ºF (199ºC). 2. Cut cube steaks into 1-inch-wide strips. 3. Sprinkle lightly with salt and pepper to taste. 4. Roll in flour to coat all sides. 5. Spritz air fryer basket with cooking spray. 6. Put steak strips in air fryer basket in a single layer. Spritz top of steak strips with cooking spray. 7. Air fry for 4 minutes, turn strips over, and spritz with cooking spray. 8. Air fry 4 more minutes and test with fork for doneness. Steak fingers should be crispy outside with no red juices inside. 9. Repeat steps 5 through 7 to air fry remaining strips. 10. Serve immediately.

Italian Lamb Chops with Avocado Mayo

Prep time: 5 minutes | Cook time: 12 minutes | Serves 2

2 lamp chops	½ cup mayonnaise
2 teaspoons Italian herbs	1 tablespoon lemon juice
2 avocados	

1. Season the lamb chops with the Italian herbs, then set aside for 5 minutes. 2. Preheat the air fryer to 400ºF (204ºC) and place the rack inside. 3. Put the chops on the rack and air fry for 12 minutes. 4. In the meantime, halve the avocados and open to remove the pits.

Spoon the flesh into a blender. 5. Add the mayonnaise and lemon juice and pulse until a smooth consistency is achieved. 6. Take care when removing the chops from the air fryer, then plate up and serve with the avocado mayo.

Blackened Cajun Pork Roast

Prep time: 20 minutes | Cook time: 33 minutes | Serves 4

2 pounds (907 g) bone-in pork loin roast	½ cup diced onion
	½ cup diced celery
2 tablespoons oil	½ cup diced green bell pepper
¼ cup Cajun seasoning	1 tablespoon minced garlic

1. Cut 5 slits across the pork roast. Spritz it with oil, coating it completely. Evenly sprinkle the Cajun seasoning over the pork roast. 2. In a medium bowl, stir together the onion, celery, green bell pepper, and garlic until combined. Set aside. 3. Preheat the air fryer to 360ºF (182ºC). Line the air fryer basket with parchment paper. 4. Place the pork roast on the parchment and spritz with oil. 5. Cook for 5 minutes. Flip the roast and cook for 5 minutes more. Continue to flip and cook in 5-minute increments for a total cook time of 20 minutes. 6. Increase the air fryer temperature to 390ºF (199ºC). 7. Cook the roast for 8 minutes more and flip. Add the vegetable mixture to the basket and cook for a final 5 minutes. Let the roast sit for 5 minutes before serving.

Red Curry Flank Steak

Prep time: 30 minutes | Cook time: 12 to 18 minutes | Serves 4

²3 tablespoons red curry paste	3 scallions, minced
¼ cup olive oil	1½ pounds (680 g) flank steak
2 teaspoons grated fresh ginger	Fresh cilantro (or parsley)
2 tablespoons soy sauce	leaves
2 tablespoons rice wine vinegar	

1. Mix the red curry paste, olive oil, ginger, soy sauce, rice vinegar and scallions together in a bowl. Place the flank steak in a shallow glass dish and pour half the marinade over the steak. Pierce the steak several times with a fork or meat tenderizer to let the marinade penetrate the meat. Turn the steak over, pour the remaining marinade over the top and pierce the steak several times again. Cover and marinate the steak in the refrigerator for 6 to 8 hours. 2. When you are ready to cook, remove the steak from the refrigerator and let it sit at room temperature for 30 minutes. 3. Preheat the air fryer to 400ºF (204ºC). 4. Cut the flank steak in half so that it fits more easily into the air fryer and transfer both pieces to the air fryer basket. Pour the marinade over the steak. Air fry for 12 to 18 minutes, depending on your preferred degree of doneness of the steak (12 minutes = medium rare). Flip the steak over halfway through the cooking time. 5. When your desired degree of doneness has been reached, remove the steak to a cutting board and let it rest for 5 minutes before slicing. Thinly slice the flank steak against the grain of the meat. Transfer the slices to a serving platter, pour any juice from the bottom of the air fryer over the sliced flank steak and sprinkle the fresh cilantro on top.

Sumptuous Pizza Tortilla Rolls

Prep time: 10 minutes | Cook time: 6 minutes | Serves 4

1 teaspoon butter
½ medium onion, slivered
½ red or green bell pepper, julienned
4 ounces (113 g) fresh white mushrooms, chopped
½ cup pizza sauce
8 flour tortillas
8 thin slices deli ham
24 pepperoni slices
1 cup shredded Mozzarella cheese
Cooking spray

1. Preheat the air fryer to 390°F (199°C). 2. Put butter, onions, bell pepper, and mushrooms in a baking pan. Bake in the preheated air fryer for 3 minutes. Stir and cook 3 to 4 minutes longer until just crisp and tender. Remove pan and set aside. 3. To assemble rolls, spread about 2 teaspoons of pizza sauce on one half of each tortilla. Top with a slice of ham and 3 slices of pepperoni. Divide sautéed vegetables among tortillas and top with cheese. 4. Roll up tortillas, secure with toothpicks if needed, and spray with oil. 5. Put 4 rolls in air fryer basket and air fry for 4 minutes. Turn and air fry 4 minutes, until heated through and lightly browned. 6. Repeat step 4 to air fry remaining pizza rolls. 7. Serve immediately.

Pigs in a Blanket

Prep time: 10 minutes | Cook time: 7 minutes | Serves 2

½ cup shredded Mozzarella cheese
2 tablespoons blanched finely ground almond flour
1 ounce (28 g) full-fat cream
cheese
2 (2-ounce / 57-g) beef smoked sausages
½ teaspoon sesame seeds

1. Place Mozzarella, almond flour, and cream cheese in a large microwave-safe bowl. Microwave for 45 seconds and stir until smooth. Roll dough into a ball and cut in half. 2. Press each half out into a 4 × 5-inch rectangle. Roll one sausage up in each dough half and press seams closed. Sprinkle the top with sesame seeds. 3. Place each wrapped sausage into the air fryer basket. 4. Adjust the temperature to 400°F (204°C) and air fry for 7 minutes. 5. The outside will be golden when completely cooked. Serve immediately.

Easy Beef Satay

Prep time: 30 minutes | Cook time: 8 minutes | Serves 4

1 pound (454 g) beef flank steak, thinly sliced into long strips
2 tablespoons vegetable oil
1 tablespoon fish sauce
1 tablespoon soy sauce
1 tablespoon minced fresh ginger
1 tablespoon minced garlic
1 tablespoon sugar
1 teaspoon Sriracha or other hot sauce
1 teaspoon ground coriander
½ cup chopped fresh cilantro
¼ cup chopped roasted peanuts

1. Place the beef strips in a large bowl or resealable plastic bag. Add the vegetable oil, fish sauce, soy sauce, ginger, garlic, sugar, Sriracha, coriander, and ¼ cup of the cilantro to the bag. Seal and massage the bag to thoroughly coat and combine. Marinate at room temperature for 30 minutes, or cover and refrigerate for up to 24

hours. 2. Using tongs, remove the beef strips from the bag and lay them flat in the air fryer basket, minimizing overlap as much as possible; discard the marinade. Set the air fryer to 400°F (204°C) for 8 minutes, turning the beef strips halfway through the cooking time. 3. Transfer the meat to a serving platter. Sprinkle with the remaining ¼ cup cilantro and the peanuts. Serve.

Pork and Beef Egg Rolls

Prep time: 30 minutes | Cook time: 7 to 8 minutes per batch | Makes 8 egg rolls

¼ pound (113 g) very lean ground beef
¼ pound (113 g) lean ground pork
1 tablespoon soy sauce
1 teaspoon olive oil
½ cup grated carrots
2 green onions, chopped
2 cups grated Napa cabbage
¼ cup chopped water chestnuts
¼ teaspoon salt
¼ teaspoon garlic powder
¼ teaspoon black pepper
1 egg
1 tablespoon water
8 egg roll wraps
Oil for misting or cooking spray

1. In a large skillet, brown beef and pork with soy sauce. Remove cooked meat from skillet, drain, and set aside. 2. Pour off any excess grease from skillet. Add olive oil, carrots, and onions. Sauté until barely tender, about 1 minute. 3. Stir in cabbage, cover, and cook for 1 minute or just until cabbage slightly wilts. Remove from heat. 4. In a large bowl, combine the cooked meats and vegetables, water chestnuts, salt, garlic powder, and pepper. Stir well. If needed, add more salt to taste. 5. Beat together egg and water in a small bowl. 6. Fill egg roll wrappers, using about ¼ cup of filling for each wrap. Roll up and brush all over with egg wash to seal. Spray very lightly with olive oil or cooking spray. 7. Place 4 egg rolls in air fryer basket and air fry at 390°F (199°C) for 4 minutes. Turn over and cook 3 to 4 more minutes, until golden brown and crispy. 8. Repeat to cook remaining egg rolls.

Rosemary Roast Beef

Prep time: 30 minutes | Cook time: 30 to 35 minutes | Serves 8

1 (2-pound / 907-g) top round beef roast, tied with kitchen string
Sea salt and freshly ground black pepper, to taste
2 teaspoons minced garlic
2 tablespoons finely chopped fresh rosemary
¼ cup avocado oil

1. Season the roast generously with salt and pepper. 2. In a small bowl, whisk together the garlic, rosemary, and avocado oil. Rub this all over the roast. Cover loosely with aluminum foil or plastic wrap and refrigerate for at least 12 hours or up to 2 days. 3. Remove the roast from the refrigerator and allow to sit at room temperature for about 1 hour. 4. Set the air fryer to 325°F (163°C). Place the roast in the air fryer basket and roast for 15 minutes. Flip the roast and cook for 15 to 20 minutes more, until the meat is browned and an instant-read thermometer reads 120°F (49°C) at the thickest part (for medium-rare). 5. Transfer the meat to a cutting board, and let it rest for 15 minutes before thinly slicing and serving.

Sausage and Pork Meatballs

Prep time: 15 minutes | Cook time: 8 to 12 minutes | Serves 8

1 large egg
1 teaspoon gelatin
1 pound (454 g) ground pork
½ pound (227 g) Italian sausage, casings removed, crumbled
⅓ cup Parmesan cheese
¼ cup finely diced onion

1 tablespoon tomato paste
1 teaspoon minced garlic
1 teaspoon dried oregano
¼ teaspoon red pepper flakes
Sea salt and freshly ground black pepper, to taste
Keto-friendly marinara sauce, for serving

1. Beat the egg in a small bowl and sprinkle with the gelatin. Allow to sit for 5 minutes. 2. In a large bowl, combine the ground pork, sausage, Parmesan, onion, tomato paste, garlic, oregano, and red pepper flakes. Season with salt and black pepper. 3. Stir the gelatin mixture, then add it to the other ingredients and, using clean hands, mix to ensure that everything is well combined. Form into 1½-inch round meatballs. 4. Set the air fryer to 400°F (204°C). Place the meatballs in the air fryer basket in a single layer, cooking in batches as needed. Air fry for 5 minutes. Flip and cook for 3 to 7 minutes more, or until an instant-read thermometer reads 160°F (71°C).

Fruited Ham

Prep time: 15 minutes | Cook time: 8 to 10 minutes | Serves 4

1 cup orange marmalade
¼ cup packed light brown sugar
¼ teaspoon ground cloves
½ teaspoon dry mustard
1 to 2 tablespoons oil

1 pound (454 g) cooked ham, cut into 1-inch cubes
½ cup canned mandarin oranges, drained and chopped

1. In a small bowl, stir together the orange marmalade, brown sugar, cloves, and dry mustard until blended. Set aside. 2. Preheat the air fryer to 320°F (160°C). Spritz a baking pan with oil. 3. Place the ham cubes in the prepared pan. Pour the marmalade sauce over the ham to glaze it. 4. Cook for 4 minutes. Stir and cook for 2 minutes more. 5. Add the mandarin oranges and cook for 2 to 4 minutes more until the sauce begins to thicken and the ham is tender.

Herbed Beef

Prep time: 5 minutes | Cook time: 22 minutes | Serves 6

1 teaspoon dried dill
1 teaspoon dried thyme
1 teaspoon garlic powder

2 pounds (907 g) beef steak
3 tablespoons butter

1. Preheat the air fryer to 360°F (182°C). 2. Combine the dill, thyme, and garlic powder in a small bowl, and massage into the steak. 3. Air fry the steak in the air fryer for 20 minutes, then remove, shred, and return to the air fryer. 4. Add the butter and air fry the shredded steak for a further 2 minutes at 365°F (185°C). Make sure the beef is coated in the butter before serving.

Carne Asada

Prep time: 5 minutes | Cook time: 15 minutes | Serves 4

3 chipotle peppers in adobo, chopped
⅓ cup chopped fresh oregano
⅓ cup chopped fresh parsley
4 cloves garlic, minced
Juice of 2 limes

1 teaspoon ground cumin seeds
⅓ cup olive oil
1 to 1½ pounds (454 g to 680 g) flank steak
Salt, to taste

1. Combine the chipotle, oregano, parsley, garlic, lime juice, cumin, and olive oil in a large bowl. Stir to mix well. 2. Dunk the flank steak in the mixture and press to coat well. Wrap the bowl in plastic and marinate under room temperature for at least 30 minutes. 3. Preheat the air fryer to 390°F (199°C). 4. Discard the marinade and place the steak in the preheated air fryer. Sprinkle with salt. 5. Air fry for 15 minutes or until the steak is medium-rare or it reaches your desired doneness. Flip the steak halfway through the cooking time. 6. Remove the steak from the air fryer and slice to serve.

Panko Crusted Calf's Liver Strips

Prep time: 15 minutes | Cook time: 23 to 25 minutes | Serves 4

1 pound (454 g) sliced calf's liver, cut into ½-inch wide strips
2 eggs
2 tablespoons milk

½ cup whole wheat flour
2 cups panko breadcrumbs
Salt and ground black pepper, to taste
Cooking spray

1. Preheat the air fryer to 390°F (199°C) and spritz with cooking spray. 2. Rub the calf's liver strips with salt and ground black pepper on a clean work surface. 3. Whisk the eggs with milk in a large bowl. Pour the flour in a shallow dish. Pour the panko on a separate shallow dish. 4. Dunk the liver strips in the flour, then in the egg mixture. Shake the excess off and roll the strips over the panko to coat well. 5. Arrange half of the liver strips in a single layer in the preheated air fryer and spritz with cooking spray. 6. Air fry for 5 minutes or until browned. Flip the strips halfway through. Repeat with the remaining strips. 7. Serve immediately.

Dijon Porterhouse Steak

Prep time: 20 minutes | Cook time: 14 minutes | Serves 2

1 pound (454 g) porterhouse steak, cut meat from bones in 2 pieces
½ teaspoon ground black pepper
1 teaspoon cayenne pepper

½ teaspoon salt
1 teaspoon garlic powder
½ teaspoon dried thyme
½ teaspoon dried marjoram
1 teaspoon Dijon mustard
1 tablespoon butter, melted

1. Sprinkle the porterhouse steak with all the seasonings. 2. Spread the mustard and butter evenly over the meat. 3. Cook in the preheated air fryer at 390°F (199°C) for 12 to 14 minutes. 4. Taste for doneness with a meat thermometer and serve immediately.

Bean and Beef Meatball Taco Pizza

Prep time: 10 minutes | Cook time: 7 to 9 minutes per batch | Serves 4

¾ cup refried beans (from a 16-ounce / 454-g can)
½ cup salsa
10 frozen precooked beef meatballs, thawed and sliced
1 jalapeño pepper, sliced
4 whole-wheat pita breads

1 cup shredded pepper Jack cheese
½ cup shredded Colby cheese
Cooking oil spray
⅓ cup sour cream

1. In a medium bowl, stir together the refried beans, salsa, meatballs, and jalapeño. 2. Insert the crisper plate into the basket and the basket into the unit. Preheat the unit by selecting BAKE, setting the temperature to 375ºF (191ºC), and setting the time to 3 minutes. Select START/STOP to begin. 3. Top the pitas with the refried bean mixture and sprinkle with the cheeses. 4. Once the unit is preheated, spray the crisper plate with cooking oil. Working in batches, place the pizzas into the basket. Select BAKE, set the temperature to 375ºF (191ºC), and set the time to 9 minutes. Select START/STOP to begin. 5. After about 7 minutes, check the pizzas. They are done when the cheese is melted and starts to brown. If not ready, resume cooking. 6. When the cooking is complete, top each pizza with a dollop of sour cream and serve warm.

Cantonese BBQ Pork

Prep time: 30 minutes | Cook time: 15 minutes | Serves 4

¼ cup honey
2 tablespoons dark soy sauce
1 tablespoon sugar
1 tablespoon Shaoxing wine (rice cooking wine)
1 tablespoon hoisin sauce

2 teaspoons minced garlic
2 teaspoons minced fresh ginger
1 teaspoon Chinese five-spice powder
1 pound (454 g) fatty pork shoulder, cut into long, 1-inch-thick pieces

1. In a small microwave-safe bowl, combine the honey, soy sauce, sugar, wine, hoisin, garlic, ginger, and five-spice powder. Microwave in 10-second intervals, stirring in between, until the honey has dissolved. 2. Use a fork to pierce the pork slices to allow the marinade to penetrate better. Place the pork in a large bowl or resealable plastic bag and pour in half the marinade; set aside the remaining marinade to use for the sauce. Toss to coat. Marinate the pork at room temperature for 30 minutes, or cover and refrigerate for up 24 hours. 3. Place the pork in a single layer in the air fryer basket. Set the air fryer to 400ºF (204ºC) for 15 minutes, turning and basting the pork halfway through the cooking time. 4. While the pork is cooking, microwave the reserved marinade on high for 45 to 60 seconds, stirring every 15 seconds, to thicken it slightly to the consistency of a sauce. 5. Transfer the pork to a cutting board and let rest for 10 minutes. Brush with the sauce and serve.

Chapter 6 Fish and Seafood

Snapper Scampi

Prep time: 5 minutes | Cook time: 8 to 10 minutes | Serves 4

4 (6-ounce / 170-g) skinless snapper or arctic char fillets
1 tablespoon olive oil
3 tablespoons lemon juice, divided
½ teaspoon dried basil
Pinch salt
Freshly ground black pepper, to taste
2 tablespoons butter
2 cloves garlic, minced

1. Rub the fish fillets with olive oil and 1 tablespoon of the lemon juice. Sprinkle with the basil, salt, and pepper, and place in the air fryer basket. 2. Air fry the fish at 380ºF (193ºC) for 7 to 8 minutes or until the fish just flakes when tested with a fork. Remove the fish from the basket and put on a serving plate. Cover to keep warm. 3. In a baking pan, combine the butter, remaining 2 tablespoons lemon juice, and garlic. Bake in the air fryer for 1 to 2 minutes or until the garlic is sizzling. Pour this mixture over the fish and serve

Garlic Shrimp

Prep time: 15 minutes | Cook time: 10 minutes | Serves 3

Shrimp:
Oil, for spraying
1 pound (454 g) medium raw shrimp, peeled and deveined
6 tablespoons unsalted butter, melted
1 cup panko bread crumbs
2 tablespoons granulated garlic
1 teaspoon salt
½ teaspoon freshly ground black pepper
Garlic Butter Sauce:
½ cup unsalted butter
2 teaspoons granulated garlic
¾ teaspoon salt (omit if using salted butter)

Make the Shrimp 1. Preheat the air fryer to 400ºF (204ºC). Line the air fryer basket with parchment and spray lightly with oil. 2. Place the shrimp and melted butter in a zip-top plastic bag, seal, and shake well, until evenly coated. 3. In a medium bowl, mix together the bread crumbs, garlic, salt, and black pepper. 4. Add the shrimp to the panko mixture and toss until evenly coated. Shake off any excess coating. 5. Place the shrimp in the prepared basket and spray lightly with oil. 6. Cook for 8 to 10 minutes, flipping and spraying with oil after 4 to 5 minutes, until golden brown and crispy. Make the Garlic Butter Sauce 7. In a microwave-safe bowl, combine the butter, garlic, and salt and microwave on 50% power for 30 to 60 seconds, stirring every 15 seconds, until completely melted. 8. Serve the shrimp immediately with the garlic butter sauce on the side for dipping.

Cod with Creamy Mustard Sauce

Prep time: 10 minutes | Cook time: 10 minutes | Serves 4

Fish:
Oil, for spraying
1 pound (454 g) cod fillets
2 tablespoons olive oil
1 tablespoon lemon juice
1 teaspoon salt
½ teaspoon freshly ground
black pepper
Mustard Sauce:
½ cup heavy cream
3 tablespoons Dijon mustard
1 tablespoon unsalted butter
1 teaspoon salt

Make the Fish 1. Line the air fryer basket with parchment and spray lightly with oil. 2. Rub the cod with the olive oil and lemon juice. Season with the salt and black pepper. 3. Place the cod in the prepared basket. You may need to work in batches, depending on the size of your air fryer. 4. Roast at 350ºF (177ºC) for 5 minutes. Increase the temperature to 400ºF (204ºC) and cook for another 5 minutes, until flaky and the internal temperature reaches 145ºF (63ºC). Make the Mustard Sauce 5. In a small saucepan, mix together the heavy cream, mustard, butter, and salt and bring to a simmer over low heat. Cook for 3 to 4 minutes, or until the sauce starts to thicken. 6. Transfer the cod to a serving plate and drizzle with the mustard sauce. Serve immediately.

Tuna Patties with Spicy Sriracha Sauce

Prep time: 10 minutes | Cook time: 10 minutes | Serves 4

2 (6-ounce / 170-g) cans tuna packed in oil, drained
3 tablespoons almond flour
2 tablespoons mayonnaise
1 teaspoon dried dill
½ teaspoon onion powder
Pinch of salt and pepper
Spicy Sriracha Sauce:
¼ cup mayonnaise
1 tablespoon Sriracha sauce
1 teaspoon garlic powder

1. Preheat the air fryer to 380ºF (193ºC). Line the basket with parchment paper. 2. In a large bowl, combine the tuna, almond flour, mayonnaise, dill, and onion powder. Season to taste with salt and freshly ground black pepper. Use a fork to stir, mashing with the back of the fork as necessary, until thoroughly combined. 3. Use an ice cream scoop to form the tuna mixture patties. Place the patties in a single layer on the parchment paper in the air fryer basket. Press lightly with the bottom of the scoop to flatten into a circle about ½ inch thick. Pausing halfway through the cooking time to turn the patties, air fry for 10 minutes until lightly browned. 4. To make the Sriracha sauce: In a small bowl, combine the mayonnaise, Sriracha, and garlic powder. Serve the tuna patties topped with the Sriracha sauce.

Paprika Shrimp

Prep time: 5 minutes | Cook time: 6 minutes | Serves 2

8 ounces (227 g) medium shelled and deveined shrimp
2 tablespoons salted butter, melted

1 teaspoon paprika
½ teaspoon garlic powder
¼ teaspoon onion powder
½ teaspoon Old Bay seasoning

1. Toss all ingredients together in a large bowl. Place shrimp into the air fryer basket. 2. Adjust the temperature to 400ºF (204ºC) and set the timer for 6 minutes. 3. Turn the shrimp halfway through the cooking time to ensure even cooking. Serve immediately.

Creamy Haddock

Prep time: 10 minutes | Cook time: 8 minutes | Serves 4

1 pound (454 g) haddock fillet
1 teaspoon cayenne pepper
1 teaspoon salt

1 teaspoon coconut oil
½ cup heavy cream

1. Grease a baking pan with coconut oil. 2. Then put haddock fillet inside and sprinkle it with cayenne pepper, salt, and heavy cream. Put the baking pan in the air fryer basket and cook at 375ºF (191ºC) for 8 minutes.

Coconut Cream Mackerel

Prep time: 10 minutes | Cook time: 6 minutes | Serves 4

2 pounds (907 g) mackerel fillet
1 cup coconut cream
1 teaspoon ground coriander

1 teaspoon cumin seeds
1 garlic clove, peeled, chopped

1. Chop the mackerel roughly and sprinkle it with coconut cream, ground coriander, cumin seeds, and garlic. 2. Then put the fish in the air fryer and cook at 400ºF (204ºC) for 6 minutes.

Butter-Wine Baked Salmon

Prep time: 5 minutes | Cook time: 10 minutes | Serves 4

4 tablespoons butter, melted
2 cloves garlic, minced
Sea salt and ground black pepper, to taste
¼ cup dry white wine

1 tablespoon lime juice
1 teaspoon smoked paprika
½ teaspoon onion powder
4 salmon steaks
Cooking spray

1. Place all the ingredients except the salmon and oil in a shallow dish and stir to mix well. 2. Add the salmon steaks, turning to coat well on both sides. Transfer the salmon to the refrigerator to marinate for 30 minutes. 3. Preheat the air fryer to 360ºF (182ºC). 4. Place the salmon steaks in the air fryer basket, discarding any excess marinade. Spray the salmon steaks with cooking spray. 5. Air fry for about 10 minutes, flipping the salmon steaks halfway through, or until cooked to your preferred doneness. 6. Divide the salmon steaks among four plates and serve.

Parmesan-Crusted Hake with Garlic Sauce

Prep time: 5 minutes | Cook time: 10 minutes | Serves 3

Fish:
6 tablespoons mayonnaise
1 tablespoon fresh lime juice
1 teaspoon Dijon mustard
1 cup grated Parmesan cheese
Salt, to taste
¼ teaspoon ground black pepper, or more to taste

3 hake fillets, patted dry
Nonstick cooking spray
Garlic Sauce:
¼ cup plain Greek yogurt
2 tablespoons olive oil
2 cloves garlic, minced
½ teaspoon minced tarragon leaves

1. Preheat the air fryer to 395ºF (202ºC). 2. Mix the mayo, lime juice, and mustard in a shallow bowl and whisk to combine. In another shallow bowl, stir together the grated Parmesan cheese, salt, and pepper. 3. Dredge each fillet in the mayo mixture, then roll them in the cheese mixture until they are evenly coated on both sides. 4. Spray the air fryer basket with nonstick cooking spray. Arrange the fillets in the basket and air fry for 10 minutes, or until the fish flakes easily with a fork. Flip the fillets halfway through the cooking time. 5. Meanwhile, in a small bowl, whisk all the ingredients for the sauce until well incorporated. 6. Serve the fish warm alongside the sauce.

Tuna-Stuffed Quinoa Patties

Prep time: 10 minutes | Cook time: 15 minutes | Serves 4

12 ounces (340 g) quinoa
4 slices white bread with crusts removed
½ cup milk
3 eggs
10 ounces (283 g) tuna packed

in olive oil, drained
2 to 3 lemons
Kosher salt and pepper, to taste
1¼ cups panko bread crumbs
Vegetable oil, for spraying
Lemon wedges, for serving

1. Rinse the quinoa in a fine-mesh sieve until the water runs clear. Bring 4 cups of salted water to a boil. Add the quinoa, cover, and reduce heat to low. Simmer the quinoa covered until most of the water is absorbed and the quinoa is tender, 15 to 20 minutes. Drain and allow to cool to room temperature. Meanwhile, soak the bread in the milk. 2. Mix the drained quinoa with the soaked bread and 2 of the eggs in a large bowl and mix thoroughly. In a medium bowl, combine the tuna, the remaining egg, and the juice and zest of 1 of the lemons. Season well with salt and pepper. Spread the panko on a plate. 3. Scoop up approximately ½ cup of the quinoa mixture and flatten into a patty. Place a heaping tablespoon of the tuna mixture in the center of the patty and close the quinoa around the tuna. Flatten the patty slightly to create an oval-shaped croquette. Dredge both sides of the croquette in the panko. Repeat with the remaining quinoa and tuna. 4. Spray the air fryer basket with oil to prevent sticking, and preheat the air fryer to 400ºF (204ºC). Arrange 4 or 5 of the croquettes in the basket, taking care to avoid overcrowding. Spray the tops of the croquettes with oil. Air fry for 8 minutes until the top side is browned and crispy. Carefully turn the croquettes over and spray the second side with oil. Air fry until the second side is browned and crispy, another 7 minutes. Repeat with the remaining croquettes. 5. Serve the croquetas warm with plenty of lemon wedges for spritzing.

Tuna-Stuffed Tomatoes

Prep time: 5 minutes | Cook time: 5 minutes | Serves 2

2 medium beefsteak tomatoes, tops removed, seeded, membranes removed
2 (2.6-ounce / 74-g) pouches tuna packed in water, drained
1 medium stalk celery, trimmed and chopped
2 tablespoons mayonnaise
¼ teaspoon salt
¼ teaspoon ground black pepper
2 teaspoons coconut oil
¼ cup shredded mild Cheddar cheese

1. Scoop pulp out of each tomato, leaving ½-inch shell. 2. In a medium bowl, mix tuna, celery, mayonnaise, salt, and pepper. Drizzle with coconut oil. Spoon ½ mixture into each tomato and top each with 2 tablespoons Cheddar. 3. Place tomatoes into ungreased air fryer basket. Adjust the temperature to 320ºF (160ºC) and air fry for 5 minutes. Cheese will be melted when done. Serve warm.

Tuna Steak

Prep time: 10 minutes | Cook time: 12 minutes | Serves 4

1 pound (454 g) tuna steaks, boneless and cubed
1 tablespoon mustard
1 tablespoon avocado oil
1 tablespoon apple cider vinegar

1. Mix avocado oil with mustard and apple cider vinegar. 2. Then brush tuna steaks with mustard mixture and put in the air fryer basket. 3. Cook the fish at 360ºF (182ºC) for 6 minutes per side.

Popcorn Crawfish

Prep time: 15 minutes | Cook time: 18 to 20 minutes | Serves 4

½ cup flour, plus 2 tablespoons
½ teaspoon garlic powder
1½ teaspoons Old Bay Seasoning
½ teaspoon onion powder
½ cup beer, plus 2 tablespoons
1 (12-ounce / 340-g) package frozen crawfish tail meat,
thawed and drained
Oil for misting or cooking spray
Coating:
1½ cups panko crumbs
1 teaspoon Old Bay Seasoning
½ teaspoon ground black pepper

1. In a large bowl, mix together the flour, garlic powder, Old Bay Seasoning, and onion powder. Stir in beer to blend. 2. Add crawfish meat to batter and stir to coat. 3. Combine the coating ingredients in food processor and pulse to finely crush the crumbs. Transfer crumbs to shallow dish. 4. Preheat the air fryer to 390ºF (199ºC). 5. Pour the crawfish and batter into a colander to drain. Stir with a spoon to drain excess batter. 6. Working with a handful of crawfish at a time, roll in crumbs and place on a cookie sheet. It's okay if some of the smaller pieces of crawfish meat stick together. 7. Spray breaded crawfish with oil or cooking spray and place all at once into air fryer basket. 8. Air fry at 390ºF (199ºC) for 5 minutes. Shake basket or stir and mist again with olive oil or spray. Cook 5 more minutes, shake basket again, and mist lightly again. Continue cooking 3 to 5 more minutes, until browned and crispy.

Chili Prawns

Prep time: 10 minutes | Cook time: 8 minutes | Serves 2

8 prawns, cleaned
Salt and black pepper, to taste
½ teaspoon ground cayenne pepper
½ teaspoon garlic powder
½ teaspoon ground cumin
½ teaspoon red chili flakes
Cooking spray

1. Preheat the air fryer to 340ºF (171ºC). Spritz the air fryer basket with cooking spray. 2. Toss the remaining ingredients in a large bowl until the prawns are well coated. 3. Spread the coated prawns evenly in the basket and spray them with cooking spray. 4. Air fry for 8 minutes, flipping the prawns halfway through, or until the prawns are pink. 5. Remove the prawns from the basket to a plate.

Parmesan Lobster Tails

Prep time: 5 minutes | Cook time: 7 minutes | Serves 4

4 (4-ounce / 113-g) lobster tails
2 tablespoons salted butter, melted
1½ teaspoons Cajun seasoning, divided
¼ teaspoon salt
¼ teaspoon ground black pepper
¼ cup grated Parmesan cheese
½ ounce (14 g) plain pork rinds, finely crushed

1. Cut lobster tails open carefully with a pair of scissors and gently pull meat away from shells, resting meat on top of shells. 2. Brush lobster meat with butter and sprinkle with 1 teaspoon Cajun seasoning, ¼ teaspoon per tail. 3. In a small bowl, mix remaining Cajun seasoning, salt, pepper, Parmesan, and pork rinds. Gently press ¼ mixture onto meat on each lobster tail. 4. Carefully place tails into ungreased air fryer basket. Adjust the temperature to 400ºF (204ºC) and air fry for 7 minutes. Lobster tails will be crispy and golden on top and have an internal temperature of at least 145ºF (63ºC) when done. Serve warm.

Lemon Mahi-Mahi

Prep time: 5 minutes | Cook time: 14 minutes | Serves 2

Oil, for spraying
2 (6-ounce / 170-g) mahi-mahi fillets
1 tablespoon lemon juice
1 tablespoon olive oil
¼ teaspoon salt
¼ teaspoon freshly ground black pepper
1 tablespoon chopped fresh dill
2 lemon slices

1. Line the air fryer basket with parchment and spray lightly with oil. 2. Place the mahi-mahi in the prepared basket. 3. In a small bowl, whisk together the lemon juice and olive oil. Brush the mixture evenly over the mahi-mahi. 4. Sprinkle the mahi-mahi with the salt and black pepper and top with the dill. 5. Air fry at 400ºF (204ºC) for 12 to 14 minutes, depending on the thickness of the fillets, until they flake easily. 6. Transfer to plates, top each with a lemon slice, and serve.

Stuffed Shrimp

Prep time: 20 minutes | Cook time: 12 minutes per batch | Serves 4

16 tail-on shrimp, peeled and deveined (last tail section intact)
¾ cup crushed panko bread crumbs
Oil for misting or cooking spray
Stuffing:
2 (6-ounce / 170-g) cans lump crab meat
2 tablespoons chopped shallots
2 tablespoons chopped green onions
2 tablespoons chopped celery
2 tablespoons chopped green bell pepper
½ cup crushed saltine crackers
1 teaspoon Old Bay Seasoning
1 teaspoon garlic powder
¼ teaspoon ground thyme
2 teaspoons dried parsley flakes
2 teaspoons fresh lemon juice
2 teaspoons Worcestershire sauce
1 egg, beaten

1. Rinse shrimp. Remove tail section (shell) from 4 shrimp, discard, and chop the meat finely. 2. To prepare the remaining 12 shrimp, cut a deep slit down the back side so that the meat lies open flat. Do not cut all the way through. 3. Preheat the air fryer to 360°F (182°C). 4. Place chopped shrimp in a large bowl with all of the stuffing ingredients and stir to combine. 5. Divide stuffing into 12 portions, about 2 tablespoons each. 6. Place one stuffing portion onto the back of each shrimp and form into a ball or oblong shape. Press firmly so that stuffing sticks together and adheres to shrimp. 7. Gently roll each stuffed shrimp in panko crumbs and mist with oil or cooking spray. 8. Place 6 shrimp in air fryer basket and air fry at 360°F (182°C) for 10 minutes. Mist with oil or spray and cook 2 minutes longer or until stuffing cooks through inside and is crispy outside. 9. Repeat step 8 to cook remaining shrimp.

Fish Tacos with Jalapeño-Lime Sauce

Prep time: 25 minutes | Cook time: 7 to 10 minutes | Serves 4

Fish Tacos:
1 pound (454 g) fish fillets
¼ teaspoon cumin
¼ teaspoon coriander
⅛ teaspoon ground red pepper
1 tablespoon lime zest
¼ teaspoon smoked paprika
1 teaspoon oil
Cooking spray
6 to 8 corn or flour tortillas (6-inch size)
Jalapeño-Lime Sauce:
½ cup sour cream
1 tablespoon lime juice
¼ teaspoon grated lime zest
½ teaspoon minced jalapeño (flesh only)
¼ teaspoon cumin
Napa Cabbage Garnish:
1 cup shredded Napa cabbage
¼ cup slivered red or green bell pepper
¼ cup slivered onion

1. Slice the fish fillets into strips approximately ½-inch thick. 2. Put the strips into a sealable plastic bag along with the cumin, coriander, red pepper, lime zest, smoked paprika, and oil. Massage seasonings into the fish until evenly distributed. 3. Spray the air fryer basket with nonstick cooking spray and place seasoned fish inside. 4. Air fry at 390°F (199°C) for approximately 5 minutes. Shake basket to distribute fish. Cook an additional 2 to 5 minutes, until fish flakes easily. 5. While the fish is cooking, prepare the Jalapeño-Lime Sauce by mixing the sour cream, lime juice, lime zest, jalapeño, and cumin together to make a smooth sauce. Set

aside. 6. Mix the cabbage, bell pepper, and onion together and set aside. 7. To warm refrigerated tortillas, wrap in damp paper towels and microwave for 30 to 60 seconds. 8. To serve, spoon some of fish into a warm tortilla. Add one or two tablespoons Napa Cabbage Garnish and drizzle with Jalapeño-Lime Sauce.

Tuna with Herbs

Prep time: 20 minutes | Cook time: 17 minutes | Serves 4

1 tablespoon butter, melted
1 medium-sized leek, thinly sliced
1 tablespoon chicken stock
1 tablespoon dry white wine
1 pound (454 g) tuna
½ teaspoon red pepper flakes, crushed
Sea salt and ground black pepper, to taste
½ teaspoon dried rosemary
½ teaspoon dried basil
½ teaspoon dried thyme
2 small ripe tomatoes, puréed
1 cup Parmesan cheese, grated

1. Melt ½ tablespoon of butter in a sauté pan over medium-high heat. Now, cook the leek and garlic until tender and aromatic. Add the stock and wine to deglaze the pan. 2. Preheat the air fryer to 370°F (188°C). 3. Grease a casserole dish with the remaining ½ tablespoon of melted butter. Place the fish in the casserole dish. Add the seasonings. Top with the sautéed leek mixture. Add the tomato purée. Cook for 10 minutes in the preheated air fryer. Top with grated Parmesan cheese; cook an additional 7 minutes until the crumbs are golden. Bon appétit!

Tuna Cakes

Prep time: 10 minutes | Cook time: 10 minutes | Serves 4

4 (3-ounce / 85-g) pouches tuna, drained
1 large egg, whisked
2 tablespoons peeled and chopped white onion
½ teaspoon Old Bay seasoning

1. In a large bowl, mix all ingredients together and form into four patties. 2. Place patties into ungreased air fryer basket. Adjust the temperature to 400°F (204°C) and air fry for 10 minutes. Patties will be browned and crispy when done. Let cool 5 minutes before serving.

Simple Buttery Cod

Prep time: 5 minutes | Cook time: 8 minutes | Serves 2

2 (4-ounce / 113-g) cod fillets
2 tablespoons salted butter, melted
1 teaspoon Old Bay seasoning
½ medium lemon, sliced

1. Place cod fillets into a round baking dish. Brush each fillet with butter and sprinkle with Old Bay seasoning. Lay two lemon slices on each fillet. Cover the dish with foil and place into the air fryer basket. 2. Adjust the temperature to 350°F (177°C) and bake for 8 minutes. Flip halfway through the cooking time. When cooked, internal temperature should be at least 145°F (63°C). Serve warm.

Teriyaki Salmon

Prep time: 30 minutes | Cook time: 12 minutes | Serves 4

4 (6-ounce / 170-g) salmon fillets	¼ teaspoon ground ginger
½ cup soy sauce	2 teaspoons olive oil
¼ cup packed light brown sugar	½ teaspoon salt
2 teaspoons rice vinegar	¼ teaspoon freshly ground black pepper
1 teaspoon minced garlic	Oil, for spraying

1. Place the salmon in a small pan, skin-side up. 2. In a small bowl, whisk together the soy sauce, brown sugar, rice vinegar, garlic, ginger, olive oil, salt, and black pepper. 3. Pour the mixture over the salmon and marinate for about 30 minutes. 4. Line the air fryer basket with parchment and spray lightly with oil. Place the salmon in the prepared basket, skin-side down. You may need to work in batches, depending on the size of your air fryer. 5. Air fry at 400°F (204°C) for 6 minutes, brush the salmon with more marinade, and cook for another 6 minutes, or until the internal temperature reaches 145°F (63°C). Serve immediately.

Flounder Fillets

Prep time: 10 minutes | Cook time: 5 to 8 minutes | Serves 4

1 egg white	4 (4-ounce / 113-g) flounder fillets
1 tablespoon water	
1 cup panko bread crumbs	Salt and pepper, to taste
2 tablespoons extra-light virgin olive oil	Oil for misting or cooking spray

1. Preheat the air fryer to 390°F (199°C). 2. Beat together egg white and water in shallow dish. 3. In another shallow dish, mix panko crumbs and oil until well combined and crumbly (best done by hand). 4. Season flounder fillets with salt and pepper to taste. Dip each fillet into egg mixture and then roll in panko crumbs, pressing in crumbs so that fish is nicely coated. 5. Spray the air fryer basket with nonstick cooking spray and add fillets. Air fry at 390°F (199°C) for 3 minutes. 6. Spray fish fillets but do not turn. Cook 2 to 5 minutes longer or until golden brown and crispy. Using a spatula, carefully remove fish from basket and serve.

Cayenne Flounder Cutlets

Prep time: 15 minutes | Cook time: 10 minutes | Serves 2

1 egg	taste
1 cup Pecorino Romano cheese, grated	½ teaspoon cayenne pepper
	1 teaspoon dried parsley flakes
Sea salt and white pepper, to	2 flounder fillets

1. To make a breading station, whisk the egg until frothy. 2. In another bowl, mix Pecorino Romano cheese, and spices. 3. Dip the fish in the egg mixture and turn to coat evenly; then, dredge in the cracker crumb mixture, turning a couple of times to coat evenly. 4. Cook in the preheated air fryer at 390°F (199°C) for 5 minutes; turn them over and cook another 5 minutes. Enjoy!

Crab-Stuffed Avocado Boats

Prep time: 5 minutes | Cook time: 7 minutes | Serves 4

2 medium avocados, halved and pitted	¼ teaspoon Old Bay seasoning
	2 tablespoons peeled and diced yellow onion
8 ounces (227 g) cooked crab meat	2 tablespoons mayonnaise

1. Scoop out avocado flesh in each avocado half, leaving ½ inch around edges to form a shell. Chop scooped-out avocado. 2. In a medium bowl, combine crab meat, Old Bay seasoning, onion, mayonnaise, and chopped avocado. Place ¼ mixture into each avocado shell. 3. Place avocado boats into ungreased air fryer basket. Adjust the temperature to 350°F (177°C) and air fry for 7 minutes. Avocado will be browned on the top and mixture will be bubbling when done. Serve warm.

Jalea

Prep time: 20 minutes | Cook time: 10 minutes | Serves 4

Salsa Criolla:	20 large or jumbo shrimp, shelled and deveined
½ red onion, thinly sliced	
2 tomatoes, diced	¼ cup all-purpose flour
1 serrano or jalapeño pepper, deseeded and diced	¼ cup cornstarch
	1 teaspoon garlic powder
1 clove garlic, minced	1 teaspoon kosher salt
¼ cup chopped fresh cilantro	¼ teaspoon cayenne pepper
Pinch of kosher salt	2 cups panko bread crumbs
3 limes	2 eggs, beaten with 2 tablespoons water
Fried Seafood:	
1 pound (454 g) firm, white-fleshed fish such as cod (add an extra ½-pound /227-g fish if not using shrimp)	Vegetable oil, for spraying
	Mayonnaise or tartar sauce, for serving (optional)

1. To make the Salsa Criolla, combine the red onion, tomatoes, pepper, garlic, cilantro, and salt in a medium bowl. Add the juice and zest of 2 of the limes. Refrigerate the salad while you make the fish. 2. To make the seafood, cut the fish fillets into strips approximately 2 inches long and 1 inch wide. Place the flour, cornstarch, garlic powder, salt, and cayenne pepper on a plate and whisk to combine. Place the panko on a separate plate. Dredge the fish strips in the seasoned flour mixture, shaking off any excess. Dip the strips in the egg mixture, coating them completely, then dredge in the panko, shaking off any excess. Place the fish strips on a plate or rack. Repeat with the shrimp, if using. 3. Spray the air fryer basket with oil, and preheat the air fryer to 400°F (204°C). Working in 2 or 3 batches, arrange the fish and shrimp in a single layer in the basket, taking care not to crowd the basket. Spray with oil. Air fry for 5 minutes, then flip and air fry for another 4 to 5 minutes until the outside is brown and crisp and the inside of the fish is opaque and flakes easily with a fork. Repeat with the remaining seafood. 4. Place the fried seafood on a platter. Use a slotted spoon to remove the salsa criolla from the bowl, leaving behind any liquid that has accumulated. Place the salsa criolla on top of the fried seafood. Serve immediately with the remaining lime, cut into wedges, and mayonnaise or tartar sauce as desired.

Tilapia with Pecans

Prep time: 20 minutes | Cook time: 16 minutes | Serves 5

2 tablespoons ground flaxseeds
1 teaspoon paprika
Sea salt and white pepper, to taste
1 teaspoon garlic paste

2 tablespoons extra-virgin olive oil
½ cup pecans, ground
5 tilapia fillets, sliced into halves

1. Combine the ground flaxseeds, paprika, salt, white pepper, garlic paste, olive oil, and ground pecans in a Ziploc bag. Add the fish fillets and shake to coat well. 2. Spritz the air fryer basket with cooking spray. Cook in the preheated air fryer at 400°F (204°C) for 10 minutes; turn them over and cook for 6 minutes more. Work in batches. 3. Serve with lemon wedges, if desired. Enjoy!

Miso Salmon

Prep time: 10 minutes | Cook time: 12 minutes | Serves 2

2 tablespoons brown sugar
2 tablespoons soy sauce
2 tablespoons white miso paste
1 teaspoon minced garlic
1 teaspoon minced fresh ginger
½ teaspoon freshly cracked black pepper

2 (5-ounce / 142-g) salmon fillets
Vegetable oil spray
1 teaspoon sesame seeds
2 scallions, thinly sliced, for garnish

1. In a small bowl, whisk together the brown sugar, soy sauce, miso, garlic, ginger, and pepper to combine. 2. Place the salmon fillets on a plate. Pour half the sauce over the fillets; turn the fillets to coat the other sides with sauce. 3. Spray the air fryer basket with vegetable oil spray. Place the sauce-covered salmon in the basket. Set the air fryer to 400°F (204°C) for 12 minutes. Halfway through the cooking time, brush additional miso sauce on the salmon. 4. Sprinkle the salmon with the sesame seeds and scallions and serve.

Parmesan-Crusted Halibut Fillets

Prep time: 5 minutes | Cook time: 10 minutes | Serves 4

2 medium-sized halibut fillets
Dash of tabasco sauce
1 teaspoon curry powder
½ teaspoon ground coriander
½ teaspoon hot paprika

Kosher salt and freshly cracked mixed peppercorns, to taste
2 eggs
1½ tablespoons olive oil
½ cup grated Parmesan cheese

1. Preheat the air fryer to 365°F (185°C). 2. On a clean work surface, drizzle the halibut fillets with the tabasco sauce. Sprinkle with the curry powder, coriander, hot paprika, salt, and cracked mixed peppercorns. Set aside. 3. In a shallow bowl, beat the eggs until frothy. In another shallow bowl, combine the olive oil and Parmesan cheese. 4. One at a time, dredge the halibut fillets in the beaten eggs, shaking off any excess, then roll them over the Parmesan cheese until evenly coated. 5. Arrange the halibut fillets in the air fryer basket in a single layer and air fry for 10 minutes, or until the fish is golden brown and crisp. 6. Cool for 5 minutes before serving.

Crustless Shrimp Quiche

Prep time: 15 minutes | Cook time: 20 minutes | Serves 2

Vegetable oil
4 large eggs
½ cup half-and-half
4 ounces (113 g) raw shrimp, chopped (about 1 cup)
1 cup shredded Parmesan or Swiss cheese

¼ cup chopped scallions
1 teaspoon sweet smoked paprika
1 teaspoon herbes de Provence
1 teaspoon black pepper
½ to 1 teaspoon kosher salt

1. Generously grease a baking pan with vegetable oil. (Be sure to grease the pan well, the proteins in eggs stick something fierce. Alternatively, line the bottom of the pan with parchment paper cut to fit and spray the parchment and sides of the pan generously with vegetable oil spray.) 2. In a large bowl, beat together the eggs and half-and-half. Add the shrimp, ¾ cup of the cheese, the scallions, paprika, herbes de Provence, pepper, and salt. Stir with a fork to thoroughly combine. Pour the egg mixture into the prepared pan. 3. Place the pan in the air fryer basket. Set the air fryer to 300°F (149°C) for 20 minutes. After 17 minutes, sprinkle the remaining ¼ cup cheese on top and cook for the remaining 3 minutes, or until the cheese has melted, the eggs are set, and a toothpick inserted into the center comes out clean. 4. Serve the quiche warm or at room temperature.

Almond Pesto Salmon

Prep time: 5 minutes | Cook time: 12 minutes | Serves 2

¼ cup pesto
¼ cup sliced almonds, roughly chopped
2 (1½-inch-thick) salmon fillets

(about 4 ounces / 113 g each)
2 tablespoons unsalted butter, melted

1. In a small bowl, mix pesto and almonds. Set aside. 2. Place fillets into a round baking dish. 3. Brush each fillet with butter and place half of the pesto mixture on the top of each fillet. Place dish into the air fryer basket. 4. Adjust the temperature to 390°F (199°C) and set the timer for 12 minutes. 5. Salmon will easily flake when fully cooked and reach an internal temperature of at least 145°F (63°C). Serve warm.

Shrimp with Swiss Chard

Prep time: 10 minutes | Cook time: 10 minutes | Serves 4

1 pound (454 g) shrimp, peeled and deveined
½ teaspoon smoked paprika
½ cup Swiss chard, chopped

2 tablespoons apple cider vinegar
1 tablespoon coconut oil
¼ cup heavy cream

1. Mix shrimps with smoked paprika and apple cider vinegar. 2. Put the shrimps in the air fryer and add coconut oil. 3. Cook the shrimps at 350°F (177°C) for 10 minutes. 4. Then mix cooked shrimps with remaining ingredients and carefully mix.

Tuna Patty Sliders

Prep time: 15 minutes | Cook time: 10 to 15 minutes | Serves 4

3 (5-ounce / 142-g) cans tuna, packed in water
⅔ cup whole-wheat panko bread crumbs
⅓ cup shredded Parmesan
cheese
1 tablespoon sriracha
¾ teaspoon black pepper
10 whole-wheat slider buns
Cooking spray

1. Preheat the air fryer to 350ºF (177ºC). 2. Spray the air fryer basket lightly with cooking spray. 3. In a medium bowl combine the tuna, bread crumbs, Parmesan cheese, sriracha, and black pepper and stir to combine. 4. Form the mixture into 10 patties. 5. Place the patties in the air fryer basket in a single layer. Spray the patties lightly with cooking spray. You may need to cook them in batches. 6. Air fry for 6 to 8 minutes. Turn the patties over and lightly spray with cooking spray. Air fry until golden brown and crisp, another 4 to 7 more minutes. Serve warm.

Coconut Shrimp

Prep time: 5 minutes | Cook time: 6 minutes | Serves 2

8 ounces (227 g) medium shelled and deveined shrimp
2 tablespoons salted butter, melted
½ teaspoon Old Bay seasoning
¼ cup unsweetened shredded coconut

1. In a large bowl, toss the shrimp in butter and Old Bay seasoning. 2. Place shredded coconut in bowl. Coat each piece of shrimp in the coconut and place into the air fryer basket. 3. Adjust the temperature to 400ºF (204ºC) and air fry for 6 minutes. 4. Gently turn the shrimp halfway through the cooking time. Serve immediately.

Pecan-Crusted Tilapia

Prep time: 10minutes | Cook time: 10 minutes | Serves 4

1¼ cups pecans
¾ cup panko bread crumbs
½ cup all-purpose flour
2 tablespoons Cajun seasoning
2 eggs, beaten with 2
tablespoons water
4 (6-ounce/ 170-g) tilapia fillets
Vegetable oil, for spraying
Lemon wedges, for serving

1. Grind the pecans in the food processor until they resemble coarse meal. Combine the ground pecans with the panko on a plate. On a second plate, combine the flour and Cajun seasoning. Dry the tilapia fillets using paper towels and dredge them in the flour mixture, shaking off any excess. Dip the fillets in the egg mixture and then dredge them in the pecan and panko mixture, pressing the coating onto the fillets. Place the breaded fillets on a plate or rack. 2. Preheat the air fryer to 375ºF (191ºC). Spray both sides of the breaded fillets with oil. Carefully transfer 2 of the fillets to the air fryer basket and air fry for 9 to 10 minutes, flipping once halfway through, until the flesh is opaque and flaky. Repeat with the remaining fillets. 3. Serve immediately with lemon wedges.

Cilantro Lime Baked Salmon

Prep time: 10 minutes | Cook time: 12 minutes | Serves 2

2 (3-ounce / 85-g) salmon fillets, skin removed
1 tablespoon salted butter, melted
1 teaspoon chili powder
½ teaspoon finely minced garlic
¼ cup sliced pickled jalapeños
½ medium lime, juiced
2 tablespoons chopped cilantro

1. Place salmon fillets into a round baking pan. Brush each with butter and sprinkle with chili powder and garlic. 2. Place jalapeño slices on top and around salmon. Pour half of the lime juice over the salmon and cover with foil. Place pan into the air fryer basket. 3. Adjust the temperature to 370ºF (188ºC) and bake for 12 minutes. 4. When fully cooked, salmon should flake easily with a fork and reach an internal temperature of at least 145ºF (63ºC). 5. To serve, spritz with remaining lime juice and garnish with cilantro.

Foil-Packet Lobster Tail

Prep time: 15 minutes | Cook time: 12 minutes | Serves 2

2 (6-ounce / 170-g) lobster tails, halved
2 tablespoons salted butter, melted
½ teaspoon Old Bay seasoning
Juice of ½ medium lemon
1 teaspoon dried parsley

1. Place the two halved tails on a sheet of aluminum foil. Drizzle with butter, Old Bay seasoning, and lemon juice. 2. Seal the foil packets, completely covering tails. Place into the air fryer basket. 3. Adjust the temperature to 375ºF (191ºC) and air fry for 12 minutes. 4. Once done, sprinkle with dried parsley and serve immediately.

Pecan-Crusted Catfish

Prep time: 5 minutes | Cook time: 12 minutes | Serves 4

½ cup pecan meal
1 teaspoon fine sea salt
¼ teaspoon ground black pepper
4 (4-ounce / 113-g) catfish
fillets
For Garnish (Optional):
Fresh oregano
Pecan halves

1. Spray the air fryer basket with avocado oil. Preheat the air fryer to 375ºF (191ºC). 2. In a large bowl, mix the pecan meal, salt, and pepper. One at a time, dredge the catfish fillets in the mixture, coating them well. Use your hands to press the pecan meal into the fillets. Spray the fish with avocado oil and place them in the air fryer basket. 3. Air fry the coated catfish for 12 minutes, or until it flakes easily and is no longer translucent in the center, flipping halfway through. 4. Garnish with oregano sprigs and pecan halves, if desired. 5. Store leftovers in an airtight container in the fridge for up to 3 days. Reheat in a preheated 350ºF (177ºC) air fryer for 4 minutes, or until heated through.

Black Cod with Grapes and Kale

Prep time: 10 minutes | Cook time: 15 minutes | Serves 2

2 (6- to 8-ounce / 170- to 227- g) fillets of black cod	¼-inch thick
Salt and freshly ground black pepper, to taste	½ cup pecans
	3 cups shredded kale
Olive oil	2 teaspoons white balsamic vinegar or white wine vinegar
1 cup grapes, halved	2 tablespoons extra-virgin olive oil
1 small bulb fennel, sliced	

1. Preheat the air fryer to 400ºF (204ºC). 2. Season the cod fillets with salt and pepper and drizzle, brush or spray a little olive oil on top. Place the fish, presentation side up (skin side down), into the air fryer basket. Air fry for 10 minutes. 3. When the fish has finished cooking, remove the fillets to a side plate and loosely tent with foil to rest. 4. Toss the grapes, fennel and pecans in a bowl with a drizzle of olive oil and season with salt and pepper. Add the grapes, fennel and pecans to the air fryer basket and air fry for 5 minutes at 400ºF (204ºC), shaking the basket once during the cooking time. 5. Transfer the grapes, fennel and pecans to a bowl with the kale. Dress the kale with the balsamic vinegar and olive oil, season to taste with salt and pepper and serve along side the cooked fish.

Parmesan Mackerel with Coriander

Prep time: 10 minutes | Cook time: 7 minutes | Serves 2

12 ounces (340 g) mackerel fillet	grated
	1 teaspoon ground coriander
2 ounces (57 g) Parmesan,	1 tablespoon olive oil

1. Sprinkle the mackerel fillet with olive oil and put it in the air fryer basket. 2. Top the fish with ground coriander and Parmesan. 3. Cook the fish at 390ºF (199ºC) for 7 minutes.

Coconut Shrimp with Spicy Dipping Sauce

Prep time: 15 minutes | Cook time: 8 minutes | Serves 4

1 (2½-ounce / 71-g) bag pork rinds	shrimp, peeled and deveined
	½ teaspoon salt
¾ cup unsweetened shredded coconut flakes	¼ teaspoon freshly ground black pepper
¾ cup coconut flour	Spicy Dipping Sauce:
1 teaspoon onion powder	½ cup mayonnaise
1 teaspoon garlic powder	2 tablespoons Sriracha
2 eggs	Zest and juice of ½ lime
1½ pounds (680 g) large	1 clove garlic, minced

1. Preheat the air fryer to 390ºF (199ºC). 2. In a food processor fitted with a metal blade, combine the pork rinds and coconut flakes. Pulse until the mixture resembles coarse crumbs. Transfer to a shallow bowl. 3. In another shallow bowl, combine the coconut flour, onion powder, and garlic powder; mix until thoroughly combined. 4. In a third shallow bowl, whisk the eggs until slightly frothy. 5. In a large bowl, season the shrimp with the salt and pepper, tossing gently to coat. 6. Working a few pieces at a time, dredge the shrimp in the flour mixture, followed by the eggs, and finishing with the pork rind crumb mixture. Arrange the shrimp on a baking sheet until ready to air fry. 7. Working in batches if necessary, arrange the shrimp in a single layer in the air fryer basket. Pausing halfway through the cooking time to turn the shrimp, air fry for 8 minutes until cooked through. 8. To make the sauce: In a small bowl, combine the mayonnaise, Sriracha, lime zest and juice, and garlic. Whisk until thoroughly combined. Serve alongside the shrimp.

Lemon-Dill Salmon Burgers

Prep time: 10 minutes | Cook time: 8 minutes | Serves 4

2 (6-ounce / 170-g) fillets of salmon, finely chopped by hand or in a food processor	1 teaspoon salt
	Freshly ground black pepper, to taste
1 cup fine bread crumbs	2 eggs, lightly beaten
1 teaspoon freshly grated lemon zest	4 brioche or hamburger buns
	Lettuce, tomato, red onion, avocado, mayonnaise or mustard, for serving
2 tablespoons chopped fresh dill weed	

1. Preheat the air fryer to 400ºF (204ºC). 2. Combine all the ingredients in a bowl. Mix together well and divide into four balls. Flatten the balls into patties, making an indentation in the center of each patty with your thumb (this will help the burger stay flat as it cooks) and flattening the sides of the burgers so that they fit nicely into the air fryer basket. 3. Transfer the burgers to the air fryer basket and air fry for 4 minutes. Flip the burgers over and air fry for another 3 to 4 minutes, until nicely browned and firm to the touch. 4. Serve on soft brioche buns with your choice of topping: lettuce, tomato, red onion, avocado, mayonnaise or mustard

Crawfish Creole Casserole

Prep time: 20 minutes | Cook time: 25 minutes | Serves 4

1½ cups crawfish meat	1 tablespoon cornstarch
½ cup chopped celery	1 teaspoon Creole seasoning
½ cup chopped onion	¾ teaspoon salt
½ cup chopped green bell pepper	½ teaspoon freshly ground black pepper
2 large eggs, beaten	1 cup shredded Cheddar cheese
1 cup half-and-half	Cooking spray
1 tablespoon butter, melted	

1. In a medium bowl, stir together the crawfish, celery, onion, and green pepper. 2. In another medium bowl, whisk the eggs, half-and-half, butter, cornstarch, Creole seasoning, salt, and pepper until blended. Stir the egg mixture into the crawfish mixture. Add the cheese and stir to combine. 3. Preheat the air fryer to 300ºF (149ºC). Spritz a baking pan with oil. 4. Transfer the crawfish mixture to the prepared pan and place it in the air fryer basket. 5. Bake for 25 minutes, stirring every 10 minutes, until a knife inserted into the center comes out clean. 6. Serve immediately.

Greek Fish Pitas

Prep time: 10 minutes | Cook time: 15 minutes | Serves 4

1 pound (454 g) pollock, cut
into 1-inch pieces
¼ cup olive oil
1 teaspoon salt
½ teaspoon dried oregano
½ teaspoon dried thyme
½ teaspoon garlic powder

¼ teaspoon cayenne
4 whole wheat pitas
1 cup shredded lettuce
2 Roma tomatoes, diced
Nonfat plain Greek yogurt
Lemon, quartered

1. Preheat the air fryer to 380°F(193°C). 2. In a medium bowl, combine the pollock with olive oil, salt, oregano, thyme, garlic powder, and cayenne. 3. Put the pollock into the air fryer basket and roast for 15 minutes. 4. Serve inside pitas with lettuce, tomato, and Greek yogurt with a lemon wedge on the side.

Salmon Burgers with Creamy Broccoli Slaw

Prep time: 15 minutes | Cook time: 10 minutes | Serves 4

For the salmon burgers
1 pound (454 g) salmon fillets,
bones and skin removed
1 egg
¼ cup fresh dill, chopped
1 cup whole wheat bread
crumbs
½ teaspoon salt
½ teaspoon cayenne pepper
2 garlic cloves, minced
4 whole wheat buns

For the broccoli slaw
3 cups chopped or shredded
broccoli
½ cup shredded carrots
¼ cup sunflower seeds
2 garlic cloves, minced
½ teaspoon salt
2 tablespoons apple cider
vinegar
1 cup nonfat plain Greek yogurt

Make the salmon burgers 1. Preheat the air fryer to 360°F(182°C). 2. In a food processor, pulse the salmon fillets until they are finely chopped. 3. In a large bowl, combine the chopped salmon, egg, dill, bread crumbs, salt, cayenne, and garlic until it comes together. 4. Form the salmon into 4 patties. Place them into the air fryer basket, making sure that they don't touch each other. 5. Bake for 5 minutes. Flip the salmon patties and bake for 5 minutes more. Make the broccoli slaw 6. In a large bowl, combine all of the ingredients for the broccoli slaw. Mix well. 7. Serve the salmon burgers on toasted whole wheat buns, and top with a generous portion of broccoli slaw.

Southern-Style Catfish

**Prep time: 10 minutes | Cook time: 12 minutes |
Serves 4**

4 (7-ounce / 198-g) catfish
fillets
⅓ cup heavy whipping cream
1 tablespoon lemon juice
1 cup blanched finely ground

almond flour
2 teaspoons Old Bay seasoning
½ teaspoon salt
¼ teaspoon ground black
pepper

1. Place catfish fillets into a large bowl with cream and pour in lemon juice. Stir to coat. 2. In a separate large bowl, mix flour and Old Bay seasoning. 3. Remove each fillet and gently shake off excess cream. Sprinkle with salt and pepper. Press each fillet gently into flour mixture on both sides to coat. 4. Place fillets into ungreased air fryer basket. Adjust the temperature to 400°F (204°C) and air fry for 12 minutes, turning fillets halfway through cooking. Catfish will be golden brown and have an internal temperature of at least 145°F (63°C) when done. Serve warm.

Tortilla Shrimp Tacos

Prep time: 10 minutes | Cook time: 6 minutes | Serves 4

Spicy Mayo:
3 tablespoons mayonnaise
1 tablespoon Louisiana-style
Cilantro-Lime Slaw:
2 cups shredded green cabbage
½ small red onion, thinly sliced
1 small jalapeño, thinly sliced
2 tablespoons chopped fresh
Shrimp:
1 large egg, beaten
1 cup crushed tortilla chips
24 jumbo shrimp (about 1
pound / 454 g), peeled and

hot pepper sauce

cilantro
Juice of 1 lime
¼ teaspoon kosher salt

deveined
⅛ teaspoon kosher salt
Cooking spray
8 corn tortillas, for serving

1. For the spicy mayo: In a small bowl, mix the mayonnaise and hot pepper sauce. 2. For the cilantro-lime slaw: In a large bowl, toss together the cabbage, onion, jalapeño, cilantro, lime juice, and salt to combine. Cover and refrigerate to chill. 3. For the shrimp: Place the egg in a shallow bowl and the crushed tortilla chips in another. Season the shrimp with the salt. Dip the shrimp in the egg, then in the crumbs, pressing gently to adhere. Place on a work surface and spray both sides with oil. 4. Preheat the air fryer to 360°F (182°C). 5. Working in batches, arrange a single layer of the shrimp in the air fryer basket. Air fry for 6 minutes, flipping halfway, until golden and cooked through in the center. 6. To serve, place 2 tortillas on each plate and top each with 3 shrimp. Top each taco with ¼ cup slaw, then drizzle with spicy mayo.

Firecracker Shrimp

Prep time: 10 minutes | Cook time: 7 minutes | Serves 4

1 pound (454 g) medium
shelled and deveined shrimp
2 tablespoons salted butter,
melted
½ teaspoon Old Bay seasoning
¼ teaspoon garlic powder

2 tablespoons sriracha
¼ teaspoon powdered erythritol
¼ cup full-fat mayonnaise
⅛ teaspoon ground black
pepper

1. In a large bowl, toss shrimp in butter, Old Bay seasoning, and garlic powder. Place shrimp into the air fryer basket. 2. Adjust the temperature to 400°F (204°C) and set the timer for 7 minutes. 3. Flip the shrimp halfway through the cooking time. Shrimp will be bright pink when fully cooked. 4. In another large bowl, mix sriracha, powdered erythritol, mayonnaise, and pepper. Toss shrimp in the spicy mixture and serve immediately.

Shrimp Curry

Prep time: 30 minutes | Cook time: 10 minutes | Serves 4

¾ cup unsweetened full-fat coconut milk	1 teaspoon salt
¼ cup finely chopped yellow onion	¼ to ½ teaspoon cayenne pepper
2 teaspoons garam masala	1 pound (454 g) raw shrimp (21 to 25 count), peeled and deveined
1 tablespoon minced fresh ginger	
1 tablespoon minced garlic	2 teaspoons chopped fresh cilantro
1 teaspoon ground turmeric	

1. In a large bowl, stir together the coconut milk, onion, garam masala, ginger, garlic, turmeric, salt and cayenne, until well blended. 2. Add the shrimp and toss until coated with sauce on all sides. Marinate at room temperature for 30 minutes. 3. Transfer the shrimp and marinade to a baking pan. Place the pan in the air fryer basket. Set the air fryer to 375°F (191°C) for 10 minutes, stirring halfway through the cooking time. 4. Transfer the shrimp to a serving bowl or platter. Sprinkle with the cilantro and serve.

Balsamic Tilapia

Prep time: 5 minutes | Cook time: 15 minutes | Serves 4

4 tilapia fillets, boneless	1 teaspoon avocado oil
2 tablespoons balsamic vinegar	1 teaspoon dried basil

1. Sprinkle the tilapia fillets with balsamic vinegar, avocado oil, and dried basil. 2. Then put the fillets in the air fryer basket and cook at 365°F (185°C) for 15 minutes.

Shrimp Scampi

Prep time: 8 minutes | Cook time: 8 minutes | Serves 4

4 tablespoons (½ stick) salted butter or ghee	2 tablespoons chicken broth or dry white wine
1 tablespoon fresh lemon juice	2 tablespoons chopped fresh basil, plus more for sprinkling, or 1 teaspoon dried
1 tablespoon minced garlic	
2 teaspoons red pepper flakes	
1 pound (454 g) shrimp (21 to 25 count), peeled and deveined	1 tablespoon chopped fresh chives, or 1 teaspoon dried

1. Place a baking pan in the air fryer basket. Set the air fryer to 325°F (163°C) for 8 minutes (this will preheat the pan so the butter will melt faster). 2. Carefully remove the pan from the fryer and add the butter, lemon juice, garlic, and red pepper flakes. Place the pan back in the fryer. 3. Cook for 2 minutes, stirring once, until the butter has melted. (Do not skip this step; this is what infuses the butter with garlic flavor, which is what makes it all taste so good.) 4. Carefully remove the pan from the fryer and add the shrimp, broth, basil, and chives. Stir gently until the ingredients are well combined. 5. Return the pan to the air fryer and cook for 5 minutes, stirring once. 6. Thoroughly stir the shrimp mixture and let it rest for 1 minute on a wire rack. (This is so the shrimp cooks in the residual heat rather than getting overcooked and rubbery.) 7. Stir once more, sprinkle with additional chopped fresh basil, and serve.

Crunchy Air Fried Cod Fillets

Prep time: 10 minutes | Cook time: 12 minutes | Serves 2

⅓ cup panko bread crumbs	1 tablespoon mayonnaise
1 teaspoon vegetable oil	1 large egg yolk
1 small shallot, minced	¼ teaspoon grated lemon zest, plus lemon wedges for serving
1 small garlic clove, minced	
½ teaspoon minced fresh thyme	2 (8-ounce / 227-g) skinless cod fillets, 1¼ inches thick
Salt and pepper, to taste	
1 tablespoon minced fresh parsley	Vegetable oil spray

1. Preheat the air fryer to 300°F (149°C). 2. Make foil sling for air fryer basket by folding 1 long sheet of aluminum foil so it is 4 inches wide. Lay sheet of foil widthwise across basket, pressing foil into and up sides of basket. Fold excess foil as needed so that edges of foil are flush with top of basket. Lightly spray the foil and basket with vegetable oil spray. 3. Toss the panko with the oil in a bowl until evenly coated. Stir in the shallot, garlic, thyme, ¼ teaspoon salt, and ⅛ teaspoon pepper. Microwave, stirring frequently, until the panko is light golden brown, about 2 minutes. Transfer to a shallow dish and let cool slightly; stir in the parsley. Whisk the mayonnaise, egg yolk, lemon zest, and ⅛ teaspoon pepper together in another bowl. 4. Pat the cod dry with paper towels and season with salt and pepper. Arrange the fillets, skinned-side down, on plate and brush tops evenly with mayonnaise mixture. (Tuck thinner tail ends of fillets under themselves as needed to create uniform pieces.) Working with 1 fillet at a time, dredge the coated side in panko mixture, pressing gently to adhere. Arrange the fillets, crumb-side up, on sling in the prepared basket, spaced evenly apart. 5. Bake for 12 to 16 minutes, using a sling to rotate fillets halfway through cooking. Using a sling, carefully remove cod from air fryer. Serve with the lemon wedges.

Italian Tuna Roast

Prep time: 15 minutes | Cook time: 21 to 24 minutes | Serves 8

Cooking spray	oil
1 tablespoon Italian seasoning	1 teaspoon lemon juice
⅛ teaspoon ground black pepper	1 tuna loin (approximately 2 pounds / 907 g, 3 to 4 inches thick)
1 tablespoon extra-light olive	

1. Spray baking dish with cooking spray and place in air fryer basket. Preheat the air fryer to 390°F (199°C). 2. Mix together the Italian seasoning, pepper, oil, and lemon juice. 3. Using a dull table knife or butter knife, pierce top of tuna about every half inch: Insert knife into top of tuna roast and pierce almost all the way to the bottom. 4. Spoon oil mixture into each of the holes and use the knife to push seasonings into the tuna as deeply as possible. 5. Spread any remaining oil mixture on all outer surfaces of tuna. 6. Place tuna roast in baking dish and roast at 390°F (199°C) for 20 minutes. Check temperature with a meat thermometer. Cook for an additional 1 to 4 minutes or until temperature reaches 145°F (63°C). 7. Remove basket from the air fryer and let tuna sit in the basket for 10 minutes.

Catfish Bites

Prep time: 15 minutes | Cook time: 20 minutes | Serves 4

Oil, for spraying
1 pound (454 g) catfish fillets, cut into 2-inch pieces
1 cup buttermilk
½ cup cornmeal
¼ cup all-purpose flour
2 teaspoons Creole seasoning
½ cup yellow mustard

1. Line the air fryer basket with parchment and spray lightly with oil. 2. Place the catfish pieces and buttermilk in a zip-top plastic bag, seal, and refrigerate for about 10 minutes. 3. In a shallow bowl, mix together the cornmeal, flour, and Creole seasoning. 4. Remove the catfish from the bag and pat dry with a paper towel. 5. Spread the mustard on all sides of the catfish, then dip them in the cornmeal mixture until evenly coated. 6. Place the catfish in the prepared basket. You may need to work in batches, depending on the size of your air fryer. Spray lightly with oil. 7. Air fry at 400°F (204°C) for 10 minutes, flip carefully, spray with oil, and cook for another 10 minutes. Serve immediately.

Asian Swordfish

Prep time: 10 minutes | Cook time: 6 to 11 minutes | Serves 4

4 (4-ounce / 113-g) swordfish steaks
½ teaspoon toasted sesame oil
1 jalapeño pepper, finely minced
2 garlic cloves, grated
1 tablespoon grated fresh ginger
½ teaspoon Chinese five-spice powder
⅛ teaspoon freshly ground black pepper
2 tablespoons freshly squeezed lemon juice

1. Place the swordfish steaks on a work surface and drizzle with the sesame oil. 2. In a small bowl, mix the jalapeño, garlic, ginger, five-spice powder, pepper, and lemon juice. Rub this mixture into the fish and let it stand for 10 minutes. 3. Roast the swordfish in the air fryer at 380°F (193°C) for 6 to 11 minutes, or until the swordfish reaches an internal temperature of at least 140°F (60°C) on a meat thermometer. Serve immediately.

Chinese Ginger-Scallion Fish

Prep time: 15 minutes | Cook time: 15 minutes | Serves 2

Bean Sauce:
2 tablespoons soy sauce
1 tablespoon rice wine
1 tablespoon doubanjiang
Vegetables and Fish:
1 tablespoon peanut oil
¼ cup julienned green onions (white and green parts)
¼ cup chopped fresh cilantro
2 tablespoons julienned fresh
(Chinese black bean paste)
1 teaspoon minced fresh ginger
1 clove garlic, minced

ginger
2 (6-ounce / 170-g) white fish fillets, such as tilapia

1. For the sauce: In a small bowl, combine all the ingredients and stir until well combined; set aside. 2. For the vegetables and fish: In a medium bowl, combine the peanut oil, green onions, cilantro, and ginger. Toss to combine. 3. Cut two squares of parchment large

enough to hold one fillet and half of the vegetables. Place one fillet on each parchment square, top with the vegetables, and pour over the sauce. Fold over the parchment paper and crimp the sides in small, tight folds to hold the fish, vegetables, and sauce securely inside the packet. 4. Place the packets in a single layer in the air fryer basket. Set fryer to 350°F (177°C) for 15 minutes. 5. Transfer each packet to a dinner plate. Cut open with scissors just before serving.

Seasoned Tuna Steaks

Prep time: 5 minutes | Cook time: 9 minutes | Serves 4

1 teaspoon garlic powder
½ teaspoon salt
¼ teaspoon dried thyme
¼ teaspoon dried oregano
4 tuna steaks
2 tablespoons olive oil
1 lemon, quartered

1. Preheat the air fryer to 380°F(193°C). 2. In a small bowl, whisk together the garlic powder, salt, thyme, and oregano. 3. Coat the tuna steaks with olive oil. Season both sides of each steak with the seasoning blend. Place the steaks in a single layer in the air fryer basket. 4. Roast for 5 minutes, then flip and roast for an additional 3 to 4 minutes.

Sweet Tilapia Fillets

Prep time: 5 minutes | Cook time: 14 minutes | Serves 4

2 tablespoons erythritol
1 tablespoon apple cider vinegar
4 tilapia fillets, boneless
1 teaspoon olive oil

1. Mix apple cider vinegar with olive oil and erythritol. 2. Then rub the tilapia fillets with the sweet mixture and put in the air fryer basket in one layer. Cook the fish at 360°F (182°C) for 7 minutes per side.

Panko Crab Sticks with Mayo Sauce

Prep time: 5 minutes | Cook time: 12 minutes | Serves 4

Crab Sticks:
2 eggs
1 cup flour
⅓ cup panko bread crumbs
Mayo Sauce:
½ cup mayonnaise
1 lime, juiced
1 tablespoon old bay seasoning
1 pound (454 g) crab sticks
Cooking spray

2 garlic cloves, minced

1. Preheat air fryer to 390°F (199°C). 2. In a bowl, beat the eggs. In a shallow bowl, place the flour. In another shallow bowl, thoroughly combine the panko bread crumbs and old bay seasoning. 3. Dredge the crab sticks in the flour, shaking off any excess, then in the beaten eggs, finally press them in the bread crumb mixture to coat well. 4. Arrange the crab sticks in the air fryer basket and spray with cooking spray. 5. Air fry for 12 minutes until golden brown. Flip the crab sticks halfway through the cooking time. 6. Meanwhile, make the sauce by whisking together the mayo, lime juice, and garlic in a small bowl. 7. Serve the crab sticks with the mayo sauce on the side.

Salmon with Fennel and Carrot

Prep time: 15 minutes | Cook time: 15 minutes | Serves 4

1 fennel bulb, thinly sliced
2 large carrots, sliced
1 large onion, thinly sliced
2 teaspoons extra-virgin olive oil
½ cup sour cream

1 teaspoon dried tarragon leaves
4 (5-ounce / 142-g) salmon fillets
⅛ teaspoon salt
¼ teaspoon coarsely ground black pepper

1. Insert the crisper plate into the basket and the basket into the unit. Preheat the unit by selecting AIR ROAST, setting the temperature to 400ºF (204ºC), and setting the time to 3 minutes. Select START/STOP to begin. 2. In a medium bowl, toss together the fennel, carrots, and onion. Add the olive oil and toss again to coat the vegetables. Put the vegetables into a 6-inch round metal pan. 3. Once the unit is preheated, place the pan into the basket. 4. Select AIR ROAST, set the temperature to 400ºF (204ºC), and set the time to 15 minutes. Select START/STOP to begin. 5. After 5 minutes, the vegetables should be crisp-tender. Remove the pan and stir in the sour cream and tarragon. Top with the salmon fillets and sprinkle the fish with the salt and pepper. Reinsert the pan into the basket and resume cooking. 6. When the cooking is complete, the salmon should flake easily with a fork and a food thermometer should register at least 145ºF (63ºC). Serve the salmon on top of the vegetables.

Chapter 7 Snacks and Appetizers

Crispy Phyllo Artichoke Triangles

Prep time: 15 minutes | Cook time: 9 to 12 minutes | Makes 18 triangles

¼ cup Ricotta cheese	cheese
1 egg white	½ teaspoon dried thyme
⅓ cup minced and drained artichoke hearts	6 sheets frozen phyllo dough, thawed
3 tablespoons grated Mozzarella	2 tablespoons melted butter

1. Preheat the air fryer to 400°F (204°C). 2. In a small bowl, combine the Ricotta cheese, egg white, artichoke hearts, Mozzarella cheese, and thyme, and mix well. 3. Cover the phyllo dough with a damp kitchen towel while you work so it doesn't dry out. Using one sheet at a time, place on the work surface and cut into thirds lengthwise. 4. Put about 1½ teaspoons of the filling on each strip at the base. Fold the bottom right-hand tip of phyllo over the filling to meet the other side in a triangle, then continue folding in a triangle. Brush each triangle with butter to seal the edges. Repeat with the remaining phyllo dough and filling. 5. Place the triangles in the air fryer basket. Bake, 6 at a time, for about 3 to 4 minutes, or until the phyllo is golden brown and crisp. 6. Serve hot.

Garlicky and Cheesy French Fries

Prep time: 5 minutes | Cook time: 20 to 25 minutes | Serves 4

3 medium russet potatoes, rinsed, dried, and cut into thin wedges or classic fry shapes	½ teaspoon salt
2 tablespoons extra-virgin olive oil	¼ teaspoon freshly ground black pepper
1 tablespoon granulated garlic	Cooking oil spray
⅓ cup grated Parmesan cheese	2 tablespoons finely chopped fresh parsley (optional)

1. In a large bowl combine the potato wedges or fries and the olive oil. Toss to coat. 2. Sprinkle the potatoes with the granulated garlic, Parmesan cheese, salt, and pepper, and toss again. 3. Insert the crisper plate into the basket and the basket into the unit. Preheat the unit by selecting AIR FRY, setting the temperature to 400°F (204°C), and setting the time to 3 minutes. Select START/STOP to begin. 4. Once the unit is preheated, spray the crisper plate with cooking oil. Place the potatoes into the basket. 5. Select AIR FRY, set the temperature to 400°F (204°C), and set the time to 20 to 25 minutes. Select START/STOP to begin. 6. After about 10 minutes, remove the basket and shake it so the fries at the bottom come up to the top. Reinsert the basket to resume cooking. 7. When the cooking is complete, top the fries with the parsley (if using) and serve hot.

Corn Dog Muffins

Prep time: 10 minutes | Cook time: 8 to 10 minutes per batch | Makes 8 muffins

1¼ cups sliced kosher hotdogs (3 or 4, depending on size)	2 tablespoons canola oil
½ cup flour	8 foil muffin cups, paper liners removed
½ cup yellow cornmeal	Cooking spray
2 teaspoons baking powder	Mustard or your favorite dipping sauce
½ cup skim milk	
1 egg	

1. Slice each hotdog in half lengthwise, then cut in ¼-inch half-moon slices. Set aside. 2. Preheat the air fryer to 390°F (199°C). 3. In a large bowl, stir together flour, cornmeal, and baking powder. 4. In a small bowl, beat together the milk, egg, and oil until just blended. 5. Pour egg mixture into dry ingredients and stir with a spoon to mix well. 6. Stir in sliced hot dogs. 7. Spray the foil cups lightly with cooking spray. 8. Divide mixture evenly into muffin cups. 9. Place 4 muffin cups in the air fryer basket and cook for 5 minutes. 10. Reduce temperature to 360°F (182°C) and cook 3 to 5 minutes or until toothpick inserted in center of muffin comes out clean. 11. Repeat steps 9 and 10 to bake remaining corn dog muffins. 12. Serve with mustard or other sauces for dipping.

String Bean Fries

Prep time: 15 minutes | Cook time: 5 to 6 minutes | Serves 4

½ pound (227 g) fresh string beans	¼ teaspoon salt
2 eggs	¼ teaspoon ground black pepper
4 teaspoons water	¼ teaspoon dry mustard (optional)
½ cup white flour	Oil for misting or cooking spray
½ cup bread crumbs	

1. Preheat the air fryer to 360°F (182°C). 2. Trim stem ends from string beans, wash, and pat dry. 3. In a shallow dish, beat eggs and water together until well blended. 4. Place flour in a second shallow dish. 5. In a third shallow dish, stir together the bread crumbs, salt, pepper, and dry mustard if using. 6. Dip each string bean in egg mixture, flour, egg mixture again, then bread crumbs. 7. When you finish coating all the string beans, open air fryer and place them in basket. 8. Cook for 3 minutes. 9. Stop and mist string beans with oil or cooking spray. 10. Cook for 2 to 3 more minutes or until string beans are crispy and nicely browned.

Spinach and Crab Meat Cups

Prep time: 10 minutes | Cook time: 10 minutes |
Makes 30 cups

1 (6-ounce / 170-g) can crab
meat, drained to yield ⅓ cup
meat
¼ cup frozen spinach, thawed,
drained, and chopped
1 clove garlic, minced
½ cup grated Parmesan cheese

3 tablespoons plain yogurt
¼ teaspoon lemon juice
½ teaspoon Worcestershire
sauce
30 mini frozen phyllo shells,
thawed
Cooking spray

1. Preheat the air fryer to 390°F (199°C). 2. Remove any bits of shell that might remain in the crab meat. 3. Mix the crab meat, spinach, garlic, and cheese together. 4. Stir in the yogurt, lemon juice, and Worcestershire sauce and mix well. 5. Spoon a teaspoon of filling into each phyllo shell. 6. Spray the air fryer basket with cooking spray and arrange half the shells in the basket. Air fry for 5 minutes. Repeat with the remaining shells. 7. Serve immediately.

Homemade Sweet Potato Chips

Prep time: 5 minutes | Cook time: 15 minutes | Serves 2

1 large sweet potato, sliced thin
⅛ teaspoon salt

2 tablespoons olive oil

1. Preheat the air fryer to 380°F (193°C). 2. In a small bowl, toss the sweet potatoes, salt, and olive oil together until the potatoes are well coated. 3. Put the sweet potato slices into the air fryer and spread them out in a single layer. 4. Fry for 10 minutes. Stir, then air fry for 3 to 5 minutes more, or until the chips reach the preferred level of crispiness.

Pork and Cabbage Egg Rolls

Prep time: 15 minutes | Cook time: 12 minutes |
Makes 12 egg rolls

Cooking oil spray
2 garlic cloves, minced
12 ounces (340 g) ground pork
1 teaspoon sesame oil
¼ cup soy sauce
2 teaspoons grated peeled fresh

ginger
2 cups shredded green cabbage
4 scallions, green parts (white
parts optional), chopped
24 egg roll wrappers

1. Spray a skillet with the cooking oil and place it over medium-high heat. Add the garlic and cook for 1 minute until fragrant. 2. Add the ground pork to the skillet. Using a spoon, break the pork into smaller chunks. 3. In a small bowl, whisk the sesame oil, soy sauce, and ginger until combined. Add the sauce to the skillet. Stir to combine and continue cooking for about 5 minutes until the pork is browned and thoroughly cooked. 4. Stir in the cabbage and scallions. Transfer the pork mixture to a large bowl. 5. Lay the egg roll wrappers on a flat surface. Dip a basting brush in water and glaze each egg roll wrapper along the edges with the wet brush. This will soften the dough and make it easier to roll. 6. Stack 2 egg roll wrappers (it works best if you double-wrap the egg rolls). Scoop 1 to 2 tablespoons of the pork mixture into the center of each wrapper stack. 7. Roll one long side of the wrappers up over the filling. Press firmly on the area with the filling, tucking it in lightly to secure it in place. Fold in the left and right sides. Continue rolling to close. Use the basting brush to wet the seam and seal the egg roll. Repeat with the remaining ingredients. 8. Insert the crisper plate into the basket and the basket into the unit. Preheat the unit by selecting AIR FRY, setting the temperature to 400°F (204°C), and setting the time to 3 minutes. Select START/STOP to begin. 9. Once the unit is preheated, spray the crisper plate with cooking oil. Place the egg rolls into the basket. It is okay to stack them. Spray them with cooking oil. 10. Select AIR FRY, set the temperature to 400°F (204°C), and set the time to 12 minutes. Insert the basket into the unit. Select START/STOP to begin. 11. After 8 minutes, use tongs to flip the egg rolls. Reinsert the basket to resume cooking. 12. When the cooking is complete, serve the egg rolls hot.

Cinnamon-Apple Chips

Prep time: 10 minutes | Cook time: 32 minutes | Serves 4

Oil, for spraying
2 Red Delicious or Honeycrisp
apples

¼ teaspoon ground cinnamon,
divided

1. Line the air fryer basket with parchment and spray lightly with oil. 2. Trim the uneven ends off the apples. Using a mandoline on the thinnest setting or a sharp knife, cut the apples into very thin slices. Discard the cores. 3. Place half of the apple slices in a single layer in the prepared basket and sprinkle with half of the cinnamon. 4. Place a metal air fryer trivet on top of the apples to keep them from flying around while they are cooking. 5. Air fry at 300°F (149°C) for 16 minutes, flipping every 5 minutes to ensure even cooking. Repeat with the remaining apple slices and cinnamon. 6. Let cool to room temperature before serving. The chips will firm up as they cool.

Pickle Chips

Prep time: 30 minutes | Cook time: 12 minutes | Serves 4

Oil, for spraying
2 cups sliced dill or sweet
pickles, drained
1 cup buttermilk

2 cups all-purpose flour
2 large eggs, beaten
2 cups panko bread crumbs
¼ teaspoon salt

1. Line the air fryer basket with parchment and spray lightly with oil. 2. In a shallow bowl, combine the pickles and buttermilk and let soak for at least 1 hour, then drain. 3. Place the flour, beaten eggs, and bread crumbs in separate bowls. 4. Coat each pickle chip lightly in the flour, dip in the eggs, and dredge in the bread crumbs. Be sure each one is evenly coated. 5. Place the pickle chips in the prepared basket, sprinkle with the salt, and spray lightly with oil. You may need to work in batches, depending on the size of your air fryer. 6. Air fry at 390°F (199°C) for 5 minutes, flip, and cook for another 5 to 7 minutes, or until crispy. Serve hot.

Veggie Salmon Nachos

Prep time: 10 minutes | Cook time: 9 to 12 minutes | Serves 6

2 ounces (57 g) baked no-salt corn tortilla chips
1 (5-ounce / 142-g) baked salmon fillet, flaked
½ cup canned low-sodium black beans, rinsed and drained

1 red bell pepper, chopped
½ cup grated carrot
1 jalapeño pepper, minced
⅓ cup shredded low-sodium low-fat Swiss cheese
1 tomato, chopped

1. Preheat the air fryer to 360ºF (182ºC). 2. In a baking pan, layer the tortilla chips. Top with the salmon, black beans, red bell pepper, carrot, jalapeño, and Swiss cheese. 3. Bake in the air fryer for 9 to 12 minutes, or until the cheese is melted and starts to brown. 4. Top with the tomato and serve.

Rumaki

Prep time: 30 minutes | Cook time: 10 to 12 minutes per batch | Makes about 24 rumaki

10 ounces (283 g) raw chicken livers
1 can sliced water chestnuts, drained

¼ cup low-sodium teriyaki sauce
12 slices turkey bacon

1. Cut livers into 1½-inch pieces, trimming out tough veins as you slice. 2. Place livers, water chestnuts, and teriyaki sauce in small container with lid. If needed, add another tablespoon of teriyaki sauce to make sure livers are covered. Refrigerate for 1 hour. 3. When ready to cook, cut bacon slices in half crosswise. 4. Wrap 1 piece of liver and 1 slice of water chestnut in each bacon strip. Secure with toothpick. 5. When you have wrapped half of the livers, place them in the air fryer basket in a single layer. 6. Air fry at 390ºF (199ºC) for 10 to 12 minutes, until liver is done and bacon is crispy. 7. While first batch cooks, wrap the remaining livers. Repeat step 6 to cook your second batch.

Fried Artichoke Hearts

Prep time: 10 minutes | Cook time: 12 minutes | Serves 10

Oil, for spraying
3 (14-ounce / 397-g) cans quartered artichokes, drained and patted dry
½ cup mayonnaise

1 cup panko bread crumbs
⅓ cup grated Parmesan cheese
Salt and freshly ground black pepper, to taste

1. Line the air fryer basket with parchment and spray lightly with oil. 2. Place the artichokes on a plate. Put the mayonnaise and bread crumbs in separate bowls. 3. Working one at a time, dredge each artichoke piece in the mayonnaise, then in the bread crumbs to cover. 4. Place the artichokes in the prepared basket. You may need to work in batches, depending on the size of your air fryer. 5. Air fry at 370ºF (188ºC) for 10 to 12 minutes, or until crispy and golden brown. 6. Sprinkle with the Parmesan cheese and season with salt and black pepper. Serve immediately.

Taco-Spiced Chickpeas

Prep time: 5 minutes | Cook time: 17 minutes | Serves 3

Oil, for spraying
1 (15½-ounce / 439-g) can chickpeas, drained
1 teaspoon chili powder

½ teaspoon ground cumin
½ teaspoon salt
½ teaspoon granulated garlic
2 teaspoons lime juice

1. Line the air fryer basket with parchment and spray lightly with oil. Place the chickpeas in the prepared basket. 2. Air fry at 390ºF (199ºC) for 17 minutes, shaking or stirring the chickpeas and spraying lightly with oil every 5 to 7 minutes. 3. In a small bowl, mix together the chili powder, cumin, salt, and garlic. 4. When 2 to 3 minutes of cooking time remain, sprinkle half of the seasoning mix over the chickpeas. Finish cooking. 5. Transfer the chickpeas to a medium bowl and toss with the remaining seasoning mix and the lime juice. Serve immediately.

Mozzarella Arancini

Prep time: 5 minutes | Cook time: 8 to 11 minutes | Makes 16 arancini

2 cups cooked rice, cooled
2 eggs, beaten
1½ cups panko bread crumbs, divided
½ cup grated Parmesan cheese

2 tablespoons minced fresh basil
16 ¾-inch cubes Mozzarella cheese
2 tablespoons olive oil

1. Preheat the air fryer to 400ºF (204ºC). 2. In a medium bowl, combine the rice, eggs, ½ cup of the bread crumbs, Parmesan cheese, and basil. Form this mixture into 16 1½-inch balls. 3. Poke a hole in each of the balls with your finger and insert a Mozzarella cube. Form the rice mixture firmly around the cheese. 4. On a shallow plate, combine the remaining 1 cup of the bread crumbs with the olive oil and mix well. Roll the rice balls in the bread crumbs to coat. 5. Air fry the arancini in batches for 8 to 11 minutes or until golden brown. 6. Serve hot.

Spicy Chicken Bites

Prep time: 10 minutes | Cook time: 10 to 12 minutes | Makes 30 bites

8 ounces boneless and skinless chicken thighs, cut into 30 pieces

¼ teaspoon kosher salt
2 tablespoons hot sauce
Cooking spray

1. Preheat the air fryer to 390ºF (199ºC). 2. Spray the air fryer basket with cooking spray and season the chicken bites with the kosher salt, then place in the basket and air fry for 10 to 12 minutes or until crispy. 3. While the chicken bites cook, pour the hot sauce into a large bowl. 4. Remove the bites and add to the sauce bowl, tossing to coat. Serve warm.

Crunchy Basil White Beans

Prep time: 2 minutes | Cook time: 19 minutes | Serves 2

1 (15-ounce / 425-g) can cooked white beans	¼ teaspoon garlic powder
2 tablespoons olive oil	¼ teaspoon salt, divided
1 teaspoon fresh sage, chopped	1 teaspoon chopped fresh basil

1. Preheat the air fryer to 380°F(193°C). 2. In a medium bowl, mix together the beans, olive oil, sage, garlic, ⅛ teaspoon salt, and basil. 3. Pour the white beans into the air fryer and spread them out in a single layer. 4. Bake for 10 minutes. Stir and continue cooking for an additional 5 to 9 minutes, or until they reach your preferred level of crispiness. 5. Toss with the remaining ⅛ teaspoon salt before serving.

Apple Wedges

Prep time: 10 minutes | Cook time: 8 to 9 minutes | Serves 4

¼ cup panko bread crumbs	1 egg white
¼ cup pecans	2 teaspoons water
1½ teaspoons cinnamon	1 medium apple
1½ teaspoons brown sugar	Oil for misting or cooking spray
¼ cup cornstarch	

1. In a food processor, combine panko, pecans, cinnamon, and brown sugar. Process to make small crumbs. 2. Place cornstarch in a plastic bag or bowl with lid. In a shallow dish, beat together the egg white and water until slightly foamy. 3. Preheat the air fryer to 390°F (199°C). 4. Cut apple into small wedges. The thickest edge should be no more than ⅜- to ½-inch thick. Cut away the core, but do not peel. 5. Place apple wedges in cornstarch, reseal bag or bowl, and shake to coat. 6. Dip wedges in egg wash, shake off excess, and roll in crumb mixture. Spray with oil. 7. Place apples in air fryer basket in single layer and cook for 5 minutes. Shake basket and break apart any apples that have stuck together. Mist lightly with oil and cook 3 to 4 minutes longer, until crispy.

Eggplant Fries

Prep time: 10 minutes | Cook time: 7 to 8 minutes per batch | Serves 4

1 medium eggplant	1 cup crushed panko bread crumbs
1 teaspoon ground coriander	
1 teaspoon cumin	1 large egg
1 teaspoon garlic powder	2 tablespoons water
½ teaspoon salt	Oil for misting or cooking spray

1. Peel and cut the eggplant into fat fries, ⅜- to ½-inch thick. 2. Preheat the air fryer to 390°F (199°C). 3. In a small cup, mix together the coriander, cumin, garlic, and salt. 4. Combine 1 teaspoon of the seasoning mix and panko crumbs in a shallow dish. 5. Place eggplant fries in a large bowl, sprinkle with remaining seasoning, and stir well to combine. 6. Beat eggs and water together and pour over eggplant fries. Stir to coat. 7. Remove eggplant from egg wash, shaking off excess, and roll in panko crumbs. 8. Spray with oil. 9. Place half of the fries in air fryer basket. You should have only a single layer, but it's fine if they overlap a little. 10. Cook for 5 minutes. Shake basket, mist lightly with oil, and cook 2 to 3 minutes longer, until browned and crispy. 11. Repeat step 10 to cook remaining eggplant.

Poutine with Waffle Fries

Prep time: 10 minutes | Cook time: 15 to 17 minutes | Serves 4

2 cups frozen waffle cut fries	2 green onions, sliced
2 teaspoons olive oil	1 cup shredded Swiss cheese
1 red bell pepper, chopped	½ cup bottled chicken gravy

1. Preheat the air fryer to 380°F (193°C). 2. Toss the waffle fries with the olive oil and place in the air fryer basket. Air fry for 10 to 12 minutes, or until the fries are crisp and light golden brown, shaking the basket halfway through the cooking time. 3. Transfer the fries to a baking pan and top with the pepper, green onions, and cheese. Air fry for 3 minutes, or until the vegetables are crisp and tender. 4. Remove the pan from the air fryer and drizzle the gravy over the fries. Air fry for 2 minutes, or until the gravy is hot. 5. Serve immediately.

Pepperoni Pizza Dip

Prep time: 10 minutes | Cook time: 10 minutes | Serves 6

6 ounces (170 g) cream cheese, softened	¾ cup pizza sauce
¾ cup shredded Italian cheese blend	½ cup sliced miniature pepperoni
¼ cup sour cream	¼ cup sliced black olives
1½ teaspoons dried Italian seasoning	1 tablespoon thinly sliced green onion
¼ teaspoon garlic salt	Cut-up raw vegetables, toasted baguette slices, pita chips, or tortilla chips, for serving
¼ teaspoon onion powder	

1. In a small bowl, combine the cream cheese, ¼ cup of the shredded cheese, the sour cream, Italian seasoning, garlic salt, and onion powder. Stir until smooth and the ingredients are well blended. 2. Spread the mixture in a baking pan. Top with the pizza sauce, spreading to the edges. Sprinkle with the remaining ½ cup shredded cheese. Arrange the pepperoni slices on top of the cheese. Top with the black olives and green onion. 3. Place the pan in the air fryer basket. Set the air fryer to 350°F (177°C) for 10 minutes, or until the pepperoni is beginning to brown on the edges and the cheese is bubbly and lightly browned. 4. Let stand for 5 minutes before serving with vegetables, toasted baguette slices, pita chips, or tortilla chips.

Cheesy Hash Brown Bruschetta

Prep time: 5 minutes | Cook time: 6 to 8 minutes |
Serves 4

4 frozen hash brown patties
1 tablespoon olive oil
⅓ cup chopped cherry tomatoes
3 tablespoons diced fresh
Mozzarella

2 tablespoons grated Parmesan
cheese
1 tablespoon balsamic vinegar
1 tablespoon minced fresh basil

1. Preheat the air fryer to 400°F (204°C). 2. Place the hash brown patties in the air fryer in a single layer. Air fry for 6 to 8 minutes, or until the potatoes are crisp, hot, and golden brown. 3. Meanwhile, combine the olive oil, tomatoes, Mozzarella, Parmesan, vinegar, and basil in a small bowl. 4. When the potatoes are done, carefully remove from the basket and arrange on a serving plate. Top with the tomato mixture and serve.

Veggie Shrimp Toast

Prep time: 15 minutes | Cook time: 3 to 6 minutes |
Serves 4

8 large raw shrimp, peeled and
finely chopped
1 egg white
2 garlic cloves, minced
3 tablespoons minced red bell
pepper

1 medium celery stalk, minced
2 tablespoons cornstarch
¼ teaspoon Chinese five-spice
powder
3 slices firm thin-sliced no-
sodium whole-wheat bread

1. Preheat the air fryer to 350°F (177°C). 2. In a small bowl, stir together the shrimp, egg white, garlic, red bell pepper, celery, cornstarch, and five-spice powder. Top each slice of bread with one-third of the shrimp mixture, spreading it evenly to the edges. With a sharp knife, cut each slice of bread into 4 strips. 3. Place the shrimp toasts in the air fryer basket in a single layer. You may need to cook them in batches. Air fry for 3 to 6 minutes, until crisp and golden brown. 4. Serve hot.

Crunchy Chickpeas

Prep time: 5 minutes | Cook time: 15 to 20 minutes |
Serves 4

½ teaspoon chili powder
½ teaspoon ground cumin
¼ teaspoon cayenne pepper
¼ teaspoon salt

1 (19-ounce / 539-g) can
chickpeas, drained and rinsed
Cooking spray

1. Preheat the air fryer to 390°F (199°C). Lightly spritz the air fryer basket with cooking spray. 2. Mix the chili powder, cumin, cayenne pepper, and salt in a small bowl. 3. Place the chickpeas in a medium bowl and lightly mist with cooking spray. 4. Add the spice mixture to the chickpeas and toss until evenly coated. 5. Place the chickpeas in the air fryer basket and air fry for 15 to 20 minutes, or until the chickpeas are cooked to your preferred crunchiness. Shake the basket three or four times during cooking. 6. Let the chickpeas cool for 5 minutes before serving.

Crispy Breaded Beef Cubes

Prep time: 10 minutes | Cook time: 12 to 16 minutes
| Serves 4

1 pound (454 g) sirloin tip, cut
into 1-inch cubes
1 cup cheese pasta sauce

1½ cups soft bread crumbs
2 tablespoons olive oil
½ teaspoon dried marjoram

1. Preheat the air fryer to 360°F (182°C). 2. In a medium bowl, toss the beef with the pasta sauce to coat. 3. In a shallow bowl, combine the bread crumbs, oil, and marjoram, and mix well. Drop the beef cubes, one at a time, into the bread crumb mixture to coat thoroughly. 4. Air fry the beef in two batches for 6 to 8 minutes, shaking the basket once during cooking time, until the beef is at least 145°F (63°C) and the outside is crisp and brown. 5. Serve hot.

Spicy Tortilla Chips

Prep time: 5 minutes | Cook time: 8 to 12 minutes |
Serves 4

½ teaspoon ground cumin
½ teaspoon paprika
½ teaspoon chili powder
½ teaspoon salt

Pinch cayenne pepper
8 (6-inch) corn tortillas, each
cut into 6 wedges
Cooking spray

1. Preheat the air fryer to 375°F (191°C). Lightly spritz the air fryer basket with cooking spray. 2. Stir together the cumin, paprika, chili powder, salt, and pepper in a small bowl. 3. Working in batches, arrange the tortilla wedges in the air fryer basket in a single layer. Lightly mist them with cooking spray. Sprinkle some seasoning mixture on top of the tortilla wedges. 4. Air fry for 4 to 6 minutes, shaking the basket halfway through, or until the chips are lightly browned and crunchy. 5. Repeat with the remaining tortilla wedges and seasoning mixture. 6. Let the tortilla chips cool for 5 minutes and serve.

Peppery Chicken Meatballs

Prep time: 5 minutes | Cook time: 13 to 20 minutes |
Makes 16 meatballs

2 teaspoons olive oil
¼ cup minced onion
¼ cup minced red bell pepper
2 vanilla wafers, crushed

1 egg white
½ teaspoon dried thyme
½ pound (227 g) ground
chicken breast

1. Preheat the air fryer to 370°F (188°C). 2. In a baking pan, mix the olive oil, onion, and red bell pepper. Put the pan in the air fryer. Air fry for 3 to 5 minutes, or until the vegetables are tender. 3. In a medium bowl, mix the cooked vegetables, crushed wafers, egg white, and thyme until well combined 4. Mix in the chicken, gently but thoroughly, until everything is combined. 5. Form the mixture into 16 meatballs and place them in the air fryer basket. Air fry for 10 to 15 minutes, or until the meatballs reach an internal temperature of 165°F (74°C) on a meat thermometer. 6. Serve immediately.

Browned Ricotta with Capers and Lemon

Prep time: 10 minutes | Cook time: 8 to 10 minutes |
Serves 4 to 6

1½ cups whole milk ricotta cheese	1 teaspoon finely chopped fresh rosemary
2 tablespoons extra-virgin olive oil	Pinch crushed red pepper flakes
2 tablespoons capers, rinsed	Salt and freshly ground black pepper, to taste
Zest of 1 lemon, plus more for garnish	1 tablespoon grated Parmesan cheese

1. Preheat the air fryer to 380°F (193°C). 2. In a mixing bowl, stir together the ricotta cheese, olive oil, capers, lemon zest, rosemary, red pepper flakes, salt, and pepper until well combined. 3. Spread the mixture evenly in a baking dish and place it in the air fryer basket. 4. Air fry for 8 to 10 minutes until the top is nicely browned. 5. Remove from the basket and top with a sprinkle of grated Parmesan cheese. 6. Garnish with the lemon zest and serve warm.

Garlic-Roasted Tomatoes and Olives

Prep time: 5 minutes | Cook time: 20 minutes | Serves 6

2 cups cherry tomatoes	1 tablespoon fresh basil, minced
4 garlic cloves, roughly chopped	1 tablespoon fresh oregano, minced
½ red onion, roughly chopped	2 tablespoons olive oil
1 cup black olives	¼ to ½ teaspoon salt
1 cup green olives	

1. Preheat the air fryer to 380°F(193°C). 2. In a large bowl, combine all of the ingredients and toss together so that the tomatoes and olives are coated well with the olive oil and herbs. 3. Pour the mixture into the air fryer basket, and roast for 10 minutes. Stir the mixture well, then continue roasting for an additional 10 minutes. 4. Remove from the air fryer, transfer to a serving bowl, and enjoy.

Mexican Potato Skins

Prep time: 10 minutes | Cook time: 55 minutes | Serves 6

Olive oil	beans
6 medium russet potatoes, scrubbed	1 tablespoon taco seasoning
	½ cup salsa
Salt and freshly ground black pepper, to taste	¾ cup reduced-fat shredded Cheddar cheese
1 cup fat-free refried black	

1. Spray the air fryer basket lightly with olive oil. 2. Spray the potatoes lightly with oil and season with salt and pepper. Pierce each potato a few times with a fork. 3. Place the potatoes in the air fryer basket. Air fry at 400°F (204°C) until fork-tender, 30 to 40 minutes. The cooking time will depend on the size of the potatoes. You can cook the potatoes in the microwave or a standard oven, but they won't get the same lovely crispy skin they will get in the air fryer. 4. While the potatoes are cooking, in a small bowl, mix together the beans and taco seasoning. Set aside until the potatoes are cool enough to handle. 5. Cut each potato in half lengthwise. Scoop out most of the insides, leaving about ¼ inch in the skins so the potato skins hold their shape. 6. Season the insides of the potato skins with salt and black pepper. Lightly spray the insides of the potato skins with oil. You may need to cook them in batches. 7. Place them into the air fryer basket, skin-side down, and air fry until crisp and golden, 8 to 10 minutes. 8. Transfer the skins to a work surface and spoon ½ tablespoon of seasoned refried black beans into each one. Top each with 2 teaspoons salsa and 1 tablespoon shredded Cheddar cheese. 9. Place filled potato skins in the air fryer basket in a single layer. Lightly spray with oil. 10. Air fry until the cheese is melted and bubbly, 2 to 3 minutes.

Grilled Ham and Cheese on Raisin Bread

Prep time: 5 minutes | Cook time: 10 minutes | Serves 1

2 slices raisin bread	(about 3 ounces / 85 g)
2 tablespoons butter, softened	4 slices Muenster cheese (about
2 teaspoons honey mustard	3 ounces / 85 g)
3 slices thinly sliced honey ham	2 toothpicks

1. Preheat the air fryer to 370°F (188°C). 2. Spread the softened butter on one side of both slices of raisin bread and place the bread, buttered side down on the counter. Spread the honey mustard on the other side of each slice of bread. Layer 2 slices of cheese, the ham and the remaining 2 slices of cheese on one slice of bread and top with the other slice of bread. Remember to leave the buttered side of the bread on the outside. 3. Transfer the sandwich to the air fryer basket and secure the sandwich with toothpicks. 4. Air fry for 5 minutes. Flip the sandwich over, remove the toothpicks and air fry for another 5 minutes. Cut the sandwich in half and enjoy!

Stuffed Fried Mushrooms

Prep time: 20 minutes | Cook time: 10 to 11 minutes
| Serves 10

½ cup panko bread crumbs	cream cheese, at room temperature
½ teaspoon freshly ground black pepper	20 cremini or button mushrooms, stemmed
½ teaspoon onion powder	1 to 2 tablespoons oil
½ teaspoon cayenne pepper	
1 (8-ounce / 227-g) package	

1. In a medium bowl, whisk the bread crumbs, black pepper, onion powder, and cayenne until blended. 2. Add the cream cheese and mix until well blended. Fill each mushroom top with 1 teaspoon of the cream cheese mixture 3. Preheat the air fryer to 360°F (182°C). Line the air fryer basket with a piece of parchment paper. 4. Place the mushrooms on the parchment and spritz with oil. 5. Cook for 5 minutes. Shake the basket and cook for 5 to 6 minutes more until the filling is firm and the mushrooms are soft.

Dark Chocolate and Cranberry Granola Bars

Prep time: 5 minutes | Cook time: 15 minutes | Serves 6

2 cups certified gluten-free quick oats	3 tablespoons unsweetened shredded coconut
2 tablespoons sugar-free dark chocolate chunks	½ cup raw honey
2 tablespoons unsweetened dried cranberries	1 teaspoon ground cinnamon
	⅛ teaspoon salt
	2 tablespoons olive oil

1. Preheat the air fryer to 360°F(182°C). Line an 8-by-8-inch baking dish with parchment paper that comes up the side so you can lift it out after cooking. 2. In a large bowl, mix together all of the ingredients until well combined. 3. Press the oat mixture into the pan in an even layer. 4. Place the pan into the air fryer basket and bake for 15 minutes. 5. Remove the pan from the air fryer, and lift the granola cake out of the pan using the edges of the parchment paper. 6. Allow to cool for 5 minutes before slicing into 6 equal bars. 7. Serve immediately, or wrap in plastic wrap and store at room temperature for up to 1 week.

Mushroom Tarts

Prep time: 15 minutes | Cook time: 38 minutes |

Makes 15 tarts

2 tablespoons extra-virgin olive oil, divided	¼ cup dry white wine
1 small white onion, sliced	1 sheet frozen puff pastry, thawed
8 ounces (227 g) shiitake mushrooms, sliced	1 cup shredded Gruyère cheese
¼ teaspoon sea salt	Cooking oil spray
¼ teaspoon freshly ground black pepper	1 tablespoon thinly sliced fresh chives

1. Insert the crisper plate into the basket and the basket into the unit. Preheat the unit by selecting BAKE, setting the temperature to 300°F (149°C), and setting the time to 3 minutes. Select START/STOP to begin. 2. In a heatproof bowl that fits into the basket, stir together 1 tablespoon of olive oil, the onion, and the mushrooms. 3. Once the unit is preheated, place the bowl into the basket. 4. Select BAKE, set the temperature to 300°F (149°C), and set the time to 7 minutes. Select START/STOP to begin. 5. After about 2½ minutes, stir the vegetables. Resume cooking. After another 2½ minutes, the vegetables should be browned and tender. Season with the salt and pepper and add the wine. Resume cooking until the liquid evaporates, about 2 minutes. 6. When the cooking is complete, place the bowl on a heatproof surface. 7. Increase the air fryer temperature to 390°F (199°C) and set the time to 3 minutes. Select START/STOP to begin. 8. Unfold the puff pastry and cut it into 15 (3-by-3-inch) squares. Using a fork, pierce the dough and brush both sides with the remaining 1 tablespoon of olive oil. 9. Evenly distribute half the cheese among the puff pastry squares, leaving a ½-inch border around the edges. Divide the mushroom-onion mixture among the pastry squares and top with the remaining cheese. 10. Once the unit is preheated, spray the crisper plate with cooking oil. Working in batches, place 5 tarts into the basket; do not stack or overlap. 11. Select BAKE, set the temperature to 390°F (199°C), and set the time to 8 minutes. Select START/STOP to begin. 12. After 6 minutes, check the tarts; if not yet golden brown, resume cooking for about 2 minutes more. 13. When the cooking is complete, remove the tarts and transfer to a wire rack to cool. Repeat steps 10, 11, and 12 with the remaining tarts. 14. Serve garnished with the chives.

Root Veggie Chips with Herb Salt

Prep time: 10 minutes | Cook time: 8 minutes | Serves 2

1 parsnip, washed	Cooking spray
1 small beet, washed	Herb Salt:
1 small turnip, washed	¼ teaspoon kosher salt
½ small sweet potato, washed	2 teaspoons finely chopped fresh parsley
1 teaspoon olive oil	

1. Preheat the air fryer to 360°F (182°C). 2. Peel and thinly slice the parsnip, beet, turnip, and sweet potato, then place the vegetables in a large bowl, add the olive oil, and toss. 3. Spray the air fryer basket with cooking spray, then place the vegetables in the basket and air fry for 8 minutes, gently shaking the basket halfway through. 4. While the chips cook, make the herb salt in a small bowl by combining the kosher salt and parsley. 5. Remove the chips and place on a serving plate, then sprinkle the herb salt on top and allow to cool for 2 to 3 minutes before serving.

Shrimp Pirogues

Prep time: 15 minutes | Cook time: 4 to 5 minutes |

Serves 8

12 ounces (340 g) small, peeled, and deveined raw shrimp	1 teaspoon dried dill weed, crushed
3 ounces (85 g) cream cheese, room temperature	Salt, to taste
2 tablespoons plain yogurt	4 small hothouse cucumbers, each approximately 6 inches long
1 teaspoon lemon juice	

1. Pour 4 tablespoons water in bottom of air fryer drawer. 2. Place shrimp in air fryer basket in single layer and air fry at 390°F (199°C) for 4 to 5 minutes, just until done. Watch carefully because shrimp cooks quickly, and overcooking makes it tough. 3. Chop shrimp into small pieces, no larger than ½ inch. Refrigerate while mixing the remaining ingredients. 4. With a fork, mash and whip the cream cheese until smooth. 5. Stir in the yogurt and beat until smooth. Stir in lemon juice, dill weed, and chopped shrimp. 6. Taste for seasoning. If needed, add ¼ to ½ teaspoon salt to suit your taste. 7. Store in refrigerator until serving time. 8. When ready to serve, wash and dry cucumbers and split them lengthwise. Scoop out the seeds and turn cucumbers upside down on paper towels to drain for 10 minutes. 9. Just before filling, wipe centers of cucumbers dry. Spoon the shrimp mixture into the pirogues and cut in half crosswise. Serve immediately.

Skinny Fries

Prep time: 10 minutes | Cook time: 15 minutes per batch | Serves 2

2 to 3 russet potatoes, peeled and cut into ¼-inch sticks
2 to 3 teaspoons olive or

vegetable oil
Salt, to taste

1. Cut the potatoes into ¼-inch strips. (A mandolin with a julienne blade is really helpful here.) Rinse the potatoes with cold water several times and let them soak in cold water for at least 10 minutes or as long as overnight. 2. Preheat the air fryer to 380°F (193°C). 3. Drain and dry the potato sticks really well, using a clean kitchen towel. Toss the fries with the oil in a bowl and then air fry the fries in two batches at 380°F (193°C) for 15 minutes, shaking the basket a couple of times while they cook. 4. Add the first batch of French fries back into the air fryer basket with the finishing batch and let everything warm through for a few minutes. As soon as the fries are done, season them with salt and transfer to a plate or basket. Serve them warm with ketchup or your favorite dip.

Cheesy Steak Fries

Prep time: 5 minutes | Cook time: 20 minutes | Serves 5

1 (28-ounce / 794-g) bag frozen steak fries
Cooking spray
Salt and pepper, to taste
½ cup beef gravy

1 cup shredded Mozzarella cheese
2 scallions, green parts only, chopped

1. Preheat the air fryer to 400°F (204°C). 2. Place the frozen steak fries in the air fryer. Air fry for 10 minutes. Shake the basket and spritz the fries with cooking spray. Sprinkle with salt and pepper. Air fry for an additional 8 minutes. 3. Pour the beef gravy into a medium, microwave-safe bowl. Microwave for 30 seconds, or until the gravy is warm. 4. Sprinkle the fries with the cheese. Air fry for an additional 2 minutes, until the cheese is melted. 5. Transfer the fries to a serving dish. Drizzle the fries with gravy and sprinkle the scallions on top for a green garnish. Serve.

Chile-Brined Fried Calamari

Prep time: 20 minutes | Cook time: 8 minutes | Serves 2

1 (8-ounce / 227-g) jar sweet or hot pickled cherry peppers
½ pound (227 g) calamari bodies and tentacles, bodies cut into ½-inch-wide rings
1 lemon
2 cups all-purpose flour
Kosher salt and freshly ground

black pepper, to taste
3 large eggs, lightly beaten
Cooking spray
½ cup mayonnaise
1 teaspoon finely chopped rosemary
1 garlic clove, minced

1. Drain the pickled pepper brine into a large bowl and tear the peppers into bite-size strips. Add the pepper strips and calamari to the brine and let stand in the refrigerator for 20 minutes or up to 2 hours. 2. Grate the lemon zest into a large bowl then whisk in the flour and season with salt and pepper. Dip the calamari and pepper strips in the egg, then toss them in the flour mixture until fully coated. Spray the calamari and peppers liberally with cooking spray, then transfer half to the air fryer. Air fry at 400°F (204°C), shaking the basket halfway into cooking, until the calamari is cooked through and golden brown, about 8 minutes. Transfer to a plate and repeat with the remaining pieces. 3. In a small bowl, whisk together the mayonnaise, rosemary, and garlic. Squeeze half the zested lemon to get 1 tablespoon of juice and stir it into the sauce. Season with salt and pepper. Cut the remaining zested lemon half into 4 small wedges and serve alongside the calamari, peppers, and sauce.

Shishito Peppers with Herb Dressing

Prep time: 10 minutes | Cook time: 6 minutes | Serves 2 to 4

6 ounces (170 g) shishito peppers
1 tablespoon vegetable oil
Kosher salt and freshly ground black pepper, to taste
½ cup mayonnaise
2 tablespoons finely chopped fresh basil leaves
2 tablespoons finely chopped

fresh flat-leaf parsley
1 tablespoon finely chopped fresh tarragon
1 tablespoon finely chopped fresh chives
Finely grated zest of ½ lemon
1 tablespoon fresh lemon juice
Flaky sea salt, for serving

1. Preheat the air fryer to 400°F (204°C). 2. In a bowl, toss together the shishitos and oil to evenly coat and season with kosher salt and black pepper. Transfer to the air fryer and air fry for 6 minutes, shaking the basket halfway through, or until the shishitos are blistered and lightly charred. 3. Meanwhile, in a small bowl, whisk together the mayonnaise, basil, parsley, tarragon, chives, lemon zest, and lemon juice. 4. Pile the peppers on a plate, sprinkle with flaky sea salt, and serve hot with the dressing.

Cheese Wafers

Prep time: 30 minutes | Cook time: 5 to 6 minutes per batch | Makes 4 dozen

4 ounces (113 g) sharp Cheddar cheese, grated
¼ cup butter
½ cup flour

¼ teaspoon salt
½ cup crisp rice cereal
Oil for misting or cooking spray

1. Cream the butter and grated cheese together. You can do it by hand, but using a stand mixer is faster and easier. 2. Sift flour and salt together. Add it to the cheese mixture and mix until well blended. 3. Stir in cereal. 4. Place dough on wax paper and shape into a long roll about 1 inch in diameter. Wrap well with the wax paper and chill for at least 4 hours. 5. When ready to cook, preheat the air fryer to 360°F (182°C). 6. Cut cheese roll into ¼-inch slices. 7. Spray the air fryer basket with oil or cooking spray and place slices in a single layer, close but not touching. 8. Cook for 5 to 6 minutes or until golden brown. When done, place them on paper towels to cool. 9. Repeat previous step to cook remaining cheese bites.

Parmesan Cauliflower

Prep time: 15 minutes | Cook time: 15 minutes |
Makes 5 cups

8 cups small cauliflower florets (about 1¼ pounds / 567 g)
3 tablespoons olive oil
1 teaspoon garlic powder
½ teaspoon salt
½ teaspoon turmeric
¼ cup shredded Parmesan cheese

1. Preheat the air fryer to 390ºF (199ºC). 2. In a bowl, combine the cauliflower florets, olive oil, garlic powder, salt, and turmeric and toss to coat. 3. Transfer to the air fryer basket and air fry for 15 minutes, or until the florets are crisp-tender. Shake the basket twice during cooking. 4. Remove from the basket to a plate. Sprinkle with the shredded Parmesan cheese and toss well. Serve warm.

Lemon-Pepper Chicken Drumsticks

Prep time: 30 minutes | Cook time: 30 minutes | Serves 2

2 teaspoons freshly ground coarse black pepper
1 teaspoon baking powder
½ teaspoon garlic powder
4 chicken drumsticks (4 ounces / 113 g each)
Kosher salt, to taste
1 lemon

1. In a small bowl, stir together the pepper, baking powder, and garlic powder. Place the drumsticks on a plate and sprinkle evenly with the baking powder mixture, turning the drumsticks so they're well coated. Let the drumsticks stand in the refrigerator for at least 1 hour or up to overnight. 2. Sprinkle the drumsticks with salt, then transfer them to the air fryer, standing them bone-end up and leaning against the wall of the air fryer basket. Air fry at 375ºF (191ºC) until cooked through and crisp on the outside, about 30 minutes. 3. Transfer the drumsticks to a serving platter and finely grate the zest of the lemon over them while they're hot. Cut the lemon into wedges and serve with the warm drumsticks.

Crispy Green Bean Fries with Lemon-Yogurt Sauce

Prep time: 5 minutes | Cook time: 5 minutes | Serves 4

Green Beans:
1 egg
2 tablespoons water
1 tablespoon whole wheat flour
¼ teaspoon paprika
½ teaspoon garlic powder
½ teaspoon salt
¼ cup whole wheat bread crumbs
½ pound (227 g) whole green beans
Lemon-Yogurt Sauce:
½ cup nonfat plain Greek yogurt
1 tablespoon lemon juice
¼ teaspoon salt
⅛ teaspoon cayenne pepper

Make the Green Beans: 1. Preheat the air fryer to 380°F(193ºC). 2. In a medium shallow bowl, beat together the egg and water until frothy. 3. In a separate medium shallow bowl, whisk together the flour, paprika, garlic powder, and salt, then mix in the bread crumbs. 4. Spray the bottom of the air fryer with cooking spray. 5. Dip each green bean into the egg mixture, then into the bread crumb mixture, coating the outside with the crumbs. Place the green beans in a single layer in the bottom of the air fryer basket. 6. Fry in the air fryer for 5 minutes, or until the breading is golden brown. Make the Lemon-Yogurt Sauce: 7. In a small bowl, combine the yogurt, lemon juice, salt, and cayenne. 8. Serve the green bean fries alongside the lemon-yogurt sauce as a snack or appetizer.

Cheesy Zucchini Tots

Prep time: 15 minutes | Cook time: 6 minutes | Serves 8

2 medium zucchini (about 12 ounces / 340 g), shredded
1 large egg, whisked
½ cup grated pecorino romano cheese
½ cup panko bread crumbs
¼ teaspoon black pepper
1 clove garlic, minced
Cooking spray

1. Using your hands, squeeze out as much liquid from the zucchini as possible. In a large bowl, mix the zucchini with the remaining ingredients except the oil until well incorporated. 2. Make the zucchini tots: Use a spoon or cookie scoop to place tablespoonfuls of the zucchini mixture onto a lightly floured cutting board and form into 1-inch logs. 3. Preheat air fryer to 375ºF (191ºC). Spritz the air fryer basket with cooking spray. 4. Place the tots in the basket. You may need to cook in batches to avoid overcrowding. 5. Air fry for 6 minutes until golden brown. 6. Remove from the basket to a serving plate and repeat with the remaining zucchini tots. 7. Serve immediately.

Hush Puppies

Prep time: 45 minutes | Cook time: 10 minutes |
Serves 12

1 cup self-rising yellow cornmeal
½ cup all-purpose flour
1 teaspoon sugar
1 teaspoon salt
1 teaspoon freshly ground black pepper
1 large egg
⅓ cup canned creamed corn
1 cup minced onion
2 teaspoons minced jalapeño pepper
2 tablespoons olive oil, divided

1. Thoroughly combine the cornmeal, flour, sugar, salt, and pepper in a large bowl. 2. Whisk together the egg and corn in a small bowl. Pour the egg mixture into the bowl of cornmeal mixture and stir to combine. Stir in the minced onion and jalapeño. Cover the bowl with plastic wrap and place in the refrigerator for 30 minutes. 3. Preheat the air fryer to 375ºF (191ºC). Line the air fryer basket with parchment paper and lightly brush it with 1 tablespoon of olive oil. 4. Scoop out the cornmeal mixture and form into 24 balls, about 1 inch. 5. Arrange the balls in the parchment paper-lined basket, leaving space between each ball. 6. Air fry in batches for 5 minutes. Shake the basket and brush the balls with the remaining 1 tablespoon of olive oil. Continue cooking for 5 minutes until golden brown. 7. Remove the balls (hush puppies) from the basket and serve on a plate.

Garlic Edamame

Prep time: 5 minutes | Cook time: 10 minutes | Serves 4

Olive oil	¼ teaspoon freshly ground
1 (16-ounce / 454-g) bag frozen	black pepper
edamame in pods	½ teaspoon red pepper flakes
½ teaspoon salt	(optional)
½ teaspoon garlic salt	

1. Spray the air fryer basket lightly with olive oil. 2. In a medium bowl, add the frozen edamame and lightly spray with olive oil. Toss to coat. 3. In a small bowl, mix together the salt, garlic salt, black pepper, and red pepper flakes (if using). Add the mixture to the edamame and toss until evenly coated. 4. Place half the edamame in the air fryer basket. Do not overfill the basket. 5. Air fry at 375°F (191°C) for 5 minutes. Shake the basket and cook until the edamame is starting to brown and get crispy, 3 to 5 more minutes. 6. Repeat with the remaining edamame and serve immediately.

Polenta Fries with Chili-Lime Mayo

Prep time: 10 minutes | Cook time: 28 minutes | Serves 4

Polenta Fries:	½ cup mayonnaise
2 teaspoons vegetable or olive	1 teaspoon chili powder
oil	1 teaspoon chopped fresh
¼ teaspoon paprika	cilantro
1 pound (454 g) prepared	¼ teaspoon ground cumin
polenta, cut into 3-inch ×	Juice of ½ lime
½-inch strips	Salt and freshly ground black
Chili-Lime Mayo:	pepper, to taste

1. Preheat the air fryer to 400°F (204°C). 2. Mix the oil and paprika in a bowl. Add the polenta strips and toss until evenly coated. 3. Transfer the polenta strips to the air fry basket and air fry for 28 minutes until the fries are golden brown, shaking the basket once during cooking. Season as desired with salt and pepper. 4. Meanwhile, whisk together all the ingredients for the chili-lime mayo in a small bowl. 5. Remove the polenta fries from the air fryer to a plate and serve alongside the chili-lime mayo as a dipping sauce.

Greek Potato Skins with Olives and Feta

Prep time: 5 minutes | Cook time: 45 minutes | Serves 4

2 russet potatoes	2 tablespoons fresh cilantro,
3 tablespoons olive oil,	chopped, plus more for serving
divided, plus more for drizzling	¼ cup Kalamata olives, diced
(optional)	¼ cup crumbled feta
1 teaspoon kosher salt, divided	Chopped fresh parsley, for
¼ teaspoon black pepper	garnish (optional)

1. Preheat the air fryer to 380°F(193°C). 2. Using a fork, poke 2 to 3 holes in the potatoes, then coat each with about ½ tablespoon olive oil and ½ teaspoon salt. 3. Place the potatoes into the air fryer basket and bake for 30 minutes. 4. Remove the potatoes from the air fryer, and slice in half. Using a spoon, scoop out the flesh of the potatoes, leaving a ½-inch layer of potato inside the skins, and set the skins aside. 5. In a medium bowl, combine the scooped potato middles with the remaining 2 tablespoons of olive oil, ½ teaspoon of salt, black pepper, and cilantro. Mix until well combined. 6. Divide the potato filling into the now-empty potato skins, spreading it evenly over them. Top each potato with a tablespoon each of the olives and feta. 7. Place the loaded potato skins back into the air fryer and bake for 15 minutes. 8. Serve with additional chopped cilantro or parsley and a drizzle of olive oil, if desired.

Lemon Shrimp with Garlic Olive Oil

Prep time: 5 minutes | Cook time: 6 minutes | Serves 4

1 pound (454 g) medium	½ teaspoon salt
shrimp, cleaned and deveined	¼ teaspoon red pepper flakes
¼ cup plus 2 tablespoons olive	Lemon wedges, for serving
oil, divided	(optional)
Juice of ½ lemon	Marinara sauce, for dipping
3 garlic cloves, minced and	(optional)
divided	

1. Preheat the air fryer to 380°F(193°C). 2. In a large bowl, combine the shrimp with 2 tablespoons of the olive oil, as well as the lemon juice, ⅓ of the minced garlic, salt, and red pepper flakes. Toss to coat the shrimp well. 3. In a small ramekin, combine the remaining ¼ cup of olive oil and the remaining minced garlic. 4. Tear off a 12-by-12-inch sheet of aluminum foil. Pour the shrimp into the center of the foil, then fold the sides up and crimp the edges so that it forms an aluminum foil bowl that is open on top. Place this packet into the air fryer basket. 5. Roast the shrimp for 4 minutes, then open the air fryer and place the ramekin with oil and garlic in the basket beside the shrimp packet. Cook for 2 more minutes. 6. Transfer the shrimp on a serving plate or platter with the ramekin of garlic olive oil on the side for dipping. You may also serve with lemon wedges and marinara sauce, if desired.

Roasted Grape Dip

Prep time: 10 minutes | Cook time: 8 to 12 minutes | Serves 6

2 cups seedless red grapes,	1 cup low-fat Greek yogurt
rinsed and patted dry	2 tablespoons 2% milk
1 tablespoon apple cider	2 tablespoons minced fresh
vinegar	basil
1 tablespoon honey	

1. In the air fryer basket, sprinkle the grapes with the cider vinegar and drizzle with the honey. Toss to coat. Roast the grapes at 380°F (193°C) for 8 to 12 minutes, or until shriveled but still soft. Remove from the air fryer. 2. In a medium bowl, stir together the yogurt and milk. 3. Gently blend in the grapes and basil. Serve immediately, or cover and chill for 1 to 2 hours.

Baked Ricotta

Prep time: 10 minutes | Cook time: 15 minutes | Makes 2 cups

1 (15-ounce / 425-g) container whole milk Ricotta cheese
3 tablespoons grated Parmesan cheese, divided
2 tablespoons extra-virgin olive oil
1 teaspoon chopped fresh thyme leaves

1 teaspoon grated lemon zest
1 clove garlic, crushed with press
¼ teaspoon salt
¼ teaspoon pepper
Toasted baguette slices or crackers, for serving

1. Preheat the air fryer to 380°F (193°C). 2. To get the baking dish in and out of the air fryer, create a sling using a 24-inch length of foil, folded lengthwise into thirds. 3. Whisk together the Ricotta, 2 tablespoons of the Parmesan, oil, thyme, lemon zest, garlic, salt, and pepper. Pour into a baking dish. Cover the dish tightly with foil. 4. Place the sling under dish and lift by the ends into the air fryer, tucking the ends of the sling around the dish. Bake for 10 minutes. Remove the foil cover and sprinkle with the remaining 1 tablespoon of the Parmesan. Air fry for 5 more minutes, or until bubbly at edges and the top is browned. 5. Serve warm with toasted baguette slices or crackers.

Artichoke and Olive Pita Flatbread

Prep time: 5 minutes | Cook time: 10 minutes | Serves 4

2 whole wheat pitas
2 tablespoons olive oil, divided
2 garlic cloves, minced
¼ teaspoon salt
½ cup canned artichoke hearts, sliced

¼ cup Kalamata olives
¼ cup shredded Parmesan
¼ cup crumbled feta
Chopped fresh parsley, for garnish (optional)

1. Preheat the air fryer to 380°F(193°C). 2. Brush each pita with 1 tablespoon olive oil, then sprinkle the minced garlic and salt over the top. 3. Distribute the artichoke hearts, olives, and cheeses evenly between the two pitas, and place both into the air fryer to bake for 10 minutes. 4. Remove the pitas and cut them into 4 pieces each before serving. Sprinkle parsley over the top, if desired.

Sweet Potato Fries with Mayonnaise

Prep time: 5 minutes | Cook time: 20 minutes | Serves 2 to 3

1 large sweet potato (about 1 pound / 454 g), scrubbed
1 teaspoon vegetable or canola oil
Salt, to taste
Dipping Sauce:

¼ cup light mayonnaise
½ teaspoon sriracha sauce
1 tablespoon spicy brown mustard
1 tablespoon sweet Thai chili sauce

1. Preheat the air fryer to 200°F (93°C). 2. On a flat work surface, cut the sweet potato into fry-shaped strips about ¼ inch wide and ¼ inch thick. You can use a mandoline to slice the sweet potato quickly and uniformly. 3. In a medium bowl, drizzle the sweet potato strips with the oil and toss well. 4. Transfer to the air fryer basket and air fry for 10 minutes, shaking the basket twice during cooking. 5. Remove the air fryer basket and sprinkle with the salt and toss to coat. 6. Increase the air fryer temperature to 400°F (204°C) and air fry for an additional 10 minutes, or until the fries are crispy and tender. Shake the basket a few times during cooking. 7. Meanwhile, whisk together all the ingredients for the sauce in a small bowl. 8. Remove the sweet potato fries from the basket to a plate and serve warm alongside the dipping sauce.

Asian Rice Logs

Prep time: 30 minutes | Cook time: 5 minutes | Makes 8 rice logs

1½ cups cooked jasmine or sushi rice
¼ teaspoon salt
2 teaspoons five-spice powder
2 teaspoons diced shallots
1 tablespoon tamari sauce
1 egg, beaten
1 teaspoon sesame oil
2 teaspoons water

⅓ cup plain bread crumbs
¾ cup panko bread crumbs
2 tablespoons sesame seeds
Orange Marmalade Dipping Sauce:
½ cup all-natural orange marmalade
1 tablespoon soy sauce

1. Make the rice according to package instructions. While the rice is cooking, make the dipping sauce by combining the marmalade and soy sauce and set aside. 2. Stir together the cooked rice, salt, five-spice powder, shallots, and tamari sauce. 3. Divide rice into 8 equal pieces. With slightly damp hands, mold each piece into a log shape. Chill in freezer for 10 to 15 minutes. 4. Mix the egg, sesame oil, and water together in a shallow bowl. 5. Place the plain bread crumbs on a sheet of wax paper. 6. Mix the panko bread crumbs with the sesame seeds and place on another sheet of wax paper. 7. Roll the rice logs in plain bread crumbs, then dip in egg wash, and then dip in the panko and sesame seeds. 8. Cook the logs at 390°F (199°C) for approximately 5 minutes, until golden brown. 9. Cool slightly before serving with Orange Marmalade Dipping Sauce.

Garlic-Parmesan Croutons

Prep time: 3 minutes | Cook time: 12 minutes | Serves 4

Oil, for spraying
4 cups cubed French bread
1 tablespoon grated Parmesan cheese

3 tablespoons olive oil
1 tablespoon granulated garlic
½ teaspoon unsalted salt

1. Line the air fryer basket with parchment and spray lightly with oil. 2. In a large bowl, mix together the bread, Parmesan cheese, olive oil, garlic, and salt, tossing with your hands to evenly distribute the seasonings. Transfer the coated bread cubes to the prepared basket. 3. Air fry at 350°F (177°C) for 10 to 12 minutes, stirring once after 5 minutes, or until crisp and golden brown.

Classic Spring Rolls

Prep time: 10 minutes | Cook time: 9 minutes |
Makes 16 spring rolls

4 teaspoons toasted sesame oil
6 medium garlic cloves, minced
or pressed
1 tablespoon grated peeled
fresh ginger
2 cups thinly sliced shiitake
mushrooms
4 cups chopped green cabbage

1 cup grated carrot
½ teaspoon sea salt
16 rice paper wrappers
Cooking oil spray (sunflower,
safflower, or refined coconut)
Gluten-free sweet and sour
sauce or Thai sweet chili sauce,
for serving (optional)

1. Place a wok or sauté pan over medium heat until hot. 2. Add the sesame oil, garlic, ginger, mushrooms, cabbage, carrot, and salt. Cook for 3 to 4 minutes, stirring often, until the cabbage is lightly wilted. Remove the pan from the heat. 3. Gently run a rice paper under water. Lay it on a flat nonabsorbent surface. Place about ¼ cup of the cabbage filling in the middle. Once the wrapper is soft enough to roll, fold the bottom up over the filling, fold in the sides, and roll the wrapper all the way up. (Basically, make a tiny burrito.) 4. Repeat step 3 to make the remaining spring rolls until you have the number of spring rolls you want to cook right now (and the amount that will fit in the air fryer basket in a single layer without them touching each other). Refrigerate any leftover filling in an airtight container for about 1 week. 5. Insert the crisper plate into the basket and the basket into the unit. Preheat the unit by selecting AIR FRY, setting the temperature to 390ºF (199ºC), and setting the time to 3 minutes. Select START/STOP to begin. 6. Once the unit is preheated, spray the crisper plate and the basket with cooking oil. Place the spring rolls into the basket, leaving a little room between them so they don't stick to each other. Spray the top of each spring roll with cooking oil. 7. Select AIR FRY, set the temperature to 390ºF (199ºC), and set the time to 9 minutes. Select START/STOP to begin. 8. When the cooking is complete, the egg rolls should be crisp-ish and lightly browned. Serve immediately, plain or with a sauce of choice.

Old Bay Chicken Wings

Prep time: 10 minutes | Cook time: 12 to 15 minutes
| Serves 4

2 tablespoons Old Bay
seasoning
2 teaspoons baking powder
2 teaspoons salt

2 pounds (907 g) chicken
wings, patted dry
Cooking spray

1. Preheat the air fryer to 400ºF (204ºC). Lightly spray the air fryer basket with cooking spray. 2. Combine the Old Bay seasoning, baking powder, and salt in a large zip-top plastic bag. Add the chicken wings, seal, and shake until the wings are thoroughly coated in the seasoning mixture. 3. Lay the chicken wings in the air fryer basket in a single layer and lightly mist with cooking spray. You may need to work in batches to avoid overcrowding. 4. Air fry

for 12 to 15 minutes, flipping the wings halfway through, or until the wings are lightly browned and the internal temperature reaches at least 165ºF (74ºC) on a meat thermometer. 5. Remove from the basket to a plate and repeat with the remaining chicken wings. 6. Serve hot.

Greens Chips with Curried Yogurt Sauce

Prep time: 10 minutes | Cook time: 5 to 6 minutes |
Serves 4

1 cup low-fat Greek yogurt
1 tablespoon freshly squeezed
lemon juice
1 tablespoon curry powder
½ bunch curly kale, stemmed,
ribs removed and discarded,

leaves cut into 2- to 3-inch
pieces
½ bunch chard, stemmed, ribs
removed and discarded, leaves
cut into 2- to 3-inch pieces
1½ teaspoons olive oil

1. In a small bowl, stir together the yogurt, lemon juice, and curry powder. Set aside. 2. In a large bowl, toss the kale and chard with the olive oil, working the oil into the leaves with your hands. This helps break up the fibers in the leaves so the chips are tender. 3. Air fry the greens in batches at 390ºF (199ºC) for 5 to 6 minutes, until crisp, shaking the basket once during cooking. Serve with the yogurt sauce.

Vegetable Pot Stickers

Prep time: 12 minutes | Cook time: 11 to 18 minutes
| Makes 12 pot stickers

1 cup shredded red cabbage
¼ cup chopped button
mushrooms
¼ cup grated carrot
2 tablespoons minced onion

2 garlic cloves, minced
2 teaspoons grated fresh ginger
12 gyoza/pot sticker wrappers
2½ teaspoons olive oil, divided

1. In a baking pan, combine the red cabbage, mushrooms, carrot, onion, garlic, and ginger. Add 1 tablespoon of water. Place in the air fryer and air fry at 370ºF (188ºC) for 3 to 6 minutes, until the vegetables are crisp-tender. Drain and set aside. 2. Working one at a time, place the pot sticker wrappers on a work surface. Top each wrapper with a scant 1 tablespoon of the filling. Fold half of the wrapper over the other half to form a half circle. Dab one edge with water and press both edges together. 3. To another pan, add 1¼ teaspoons of olive oil. Put half of the pot stickers, seam-side up, in the pan. Air fry for 5 minutes, or until the bottoms are light golden brown. Add 1 tablespoon of water and return the pan to the air fryer. 4. Air fry for 4 to 6 minutes more, or until hot. Repeat with the remaining pot stickers, remaining 1¼ teaspoons of oil, and another tablespoon of water. Serve immediately.

Sweet Bacon Tater Tots

Prep time: 5 minutes | Cook time: 7 minutes | Serves 4

24 frozen tater tots
6 slices cooked bacon

2 tablespoons maple syrup
1 cup shredded Cheddar cheese

1. Preheat the air fryer to 400°F (204°C). 2. Put the tater tots in the air fryer basket. Air fry for 10 minutes, shaking the basket halfway through the cooking time. 3. Meanwhile, cut the bacon into 1-inch pieces. 4. Remove the tater tots from the air fryer basket and put into a baking pan. Top with the bacon and drizzle with the maple syrup. Air fry for 5 minutes, or until the tots and bacon are crisp. 5. Top with the cheese and air fry for 2 minutes, or until the cheese is melted. 6. Serve hot.

Chapter 8 Vegetables and Sides

Dinner Rolls

Prep time: 10 minutes | Cook time: 12 minutes | Serves 6

1 cup shredded Mozzarella cheese
1 ounce (28 g) full-fat cream cheese
1 cup blanched finely ground

almond flour
¼ cup ground flaxseed
½ teaspoon baking powder
1 large egg

1. Place Mozzarella, cream cheese, and almond flour in a large microwave-safe bowl. Microwave for 1 minute. Mix until smooth. 2. Add flaxseed, baking powder, and egg until fully combined and smooth. Microwave an additional 15 seconds if it becomes too firm. 3. Separate the dough into six pieces and roll into balls. Place the balls into the air fryer basket. 4. Adjust the temperature to 320ºF (160ºC) and air fry for 12 minutes. 5. Allow rolls to cool completely before serving.

Glazed Sweet Potato Bites

Prep time: 10 minutes | Cook time: 25 minutes | Serves 4

Oil, for spraying
3 medium sweet potatoes, peeled and cut into 1-inch pieces

2 tablespoons honey
1 tablespoon olive oil
2 teaspoons ground cinnamon

1. Line the air fryer basket with parchment and spray lightly with oil. 2. In a large bowl, toss together the sweet potatoes, honey, olive oil, and cinnamon until evenly coated. 3. Place the potatoes in the prepared basket. 4. Air fry at 400ºF (204ºC) for 20 to 25 minutes, or until crispy and easily pierced with a fork.

Sausage-Stuffed Mushroom Caps

Prep time: 10 minutes | Cook time: 8 minutes | Serves 2

6 large portobello mushroom caps
½ pound (227 g) Italian sausage
¼ cup chopped onion

2 tablespoons blanched finely ground almond flour
¼ cup grated Parmesan cheese
1 teaspoon minced fresh garlic

1. Use a spoon to hollow out each mushroom cap, reserving scrapings. 2. In a medium skillet over medium heat, brown the sausage about 10 minutes or until fully cooked and no pink remains. Drain and then add reserved mushroom scrapings, onion, almond flour, Parmesan, and garlic. Gently fold ingredients together and continue cooking an additional minute, then remove from heat.

3. Evenly spoon the mixture into mushroom caps and place the caps into a 6-inch round pan. Place pan into the air fryer basket. 4. Adjust the temperature to 375ºF (191ºC) and set the timer for 8 minutes. 5. When finished cooking, the tops will be browned and bubbling. Serve warm.

Chiles Rellenos with Red Chile Sauce

Prep time: 20 minutes | Cook time: 20 minutes | Serves 2

Peppers:
2 poblano peppers, rinsed and dried
⅔ cup thawed frozen or drained canned corn kernels
1 scallion, sliced
2 tablespoons chopped fresh cilantro
½ teaspoon kosher salt
¼ teaspoon black pepper
⅔ cup grated Monterey Jack cheese
Sauce:
3 tablespoons extra-virgin olive oil

½ cup finely chopped yellow onion
2 teaspoons minced garlic
1 (6-ounce / 170-g) can tomato paste
2 tablespoons ancho chile powder
1 teaspoon dried oregano
1 teaspoon ground cumin
½ teaspoon kosher salt
2 cups chicken broth
2 tablespoons fresh lemon juice
Mexican crema or sour cream, for serving

1. For the peppers: Place the peppers in the air fryer basket. Set the air fryer to 400ºF (204ºC) for 10 minutes, turning the peppers halfway through the cooking time, until their skins are charred. Transfer the peppers to a resealable plastic bag, seal, and set aside to steam for 5 minutes. Peel the peppers and discard the skins. Cut a slit down the center of each pepper, starting at the stem and continuing to the tip. Remove the seeds, being careful not to tear the chile. 2. In a medium bowl, combine the corn, scallion, cilantro, salt, black pepper, and cheese; set aside. 3. Meanwhile, for the sauce: In a large skillet, heat the olive oil over medium-high heat. Add the onion and cook, stirring, until tender, about 5 minutes. Add the garlic and cook, stirring, for 30 seconds. Stir in the tomato paste, chile powder, oregano, and cumin, and salt. Cook, stirring, for 1 minute. Whisk in the broth and lemon juice. Bring to a simmer and cook, stirring occasionally, while the stuffed peppers finish cooking. 4. Cut a slit down the center of each poblano pepper, starting at the stem and continuing to the tip. Remove the seeds, being careful not to tear the chile. 5. Carefully stuff each pepper with half the corn mixture. Place the stuffed peppers in a baking pan. Place the pan in the air fryer basket. Set the air fryer to 400ºF (204ºC) for 10 minutes, or until the cheese has melted. 6. Transfer the stuffed peppers to a serving platter and drizzle with the sauce and some crema.

Golden Pickles

Prep time: 10 minutes | Cook time: 15 minutes | Serves 4

14 dill pickles, sliced
¼ cup flour
⅛ teaspoon baking powder
Pinch of salt
2 tablespoons cornstarch plus 3

tablespoons water
6 tablespoons panko bread crumbs
½ teaspoon paprika
Cooking spray

1. Preheat the air fryer to 400ºF (204ºC). 2. Drain any excess moisture out of the dill pickles on a paper towel. 3. In a bowl, combine the flour, baking powder and salt. 4. Throw in the cornstarch and water mixture and combine well with a whisk. 5. Put the panko bread crumbs in a shallow dish along with the paprika. Mix thoroughly. 6. Dip the pickles in the flour batter, before coating in the bread crumbs. Spritz all the pickles with the cooking spray. 7. Transfer to the air fryer basket and air fry for 15 minutes, or until golden brown. 8. Serve immediately.

Zucchini Fritters

Prep time: 10 minutes | Cook time: 10 minutes | Serves 4

2 zucchini, grated (about 1 pound / 454 g)
1 teaspoon salt
¼ cup almond flour
¼ cup grated Parmesan cheese
1 large egg

¼ teaspoon dried thyme
¼ teaspoon ground turmeric
¼ teaspoon freshly ground black pepper
1 tablespoon olive oil
½ lemon, sliced into wedges

1. Preheat the air fryer to 400ºF (204ºC). Cut a piece of parchment paper to fit slightly smaller than the bottom of the air fryer. 2. Place the zucchini in a large colander and sprinkle with the salt. Let sit for 5 to 10 minutes. Squeeze as much liquid as you can from the zucchini and place in a large mixing bowl. Add the almond flour, Parmesan, egg, thyme, turmeric, and black pepper. Stir gently until thoroughly combined. 3. Shape the mixture into 8 patties and arrange on the parchment paper. Brush lightly with the olive oil. Pausing halfway through the cooking time to turn the patties, air fry for 10 minutes until golden brown. Serve warm with the lemon wedges.

Broccoli Salad

Prep time: 5 minutes | Cook time: 7 minutes | Serves 4

2 cups fresh broccoli florets, chopped
1 tablespoon olive oil
¼ teaspoon salt
⅛ teaspoon ground black

pepper
¼ cup lemon juice, divided
¼ cup shredded Parmesan cheese
¼ cup sliced roasted almonds

1. In a large bowl, toss broccoli and olive oil together. Sprinkle with salt and pepper, then drizzle with 2 tablespoons lemon juice. 2. Place broccoli into ungreased air fryer basket. Adjust the temperature to 350ºF (177ºC) and set the timer for 7 minutes, shaking the basket halfway through cooking. Broccoli will be golden on the edges when done. 3. Place broccoli into a large serving bowl and drizzle with remaining lemon juice. Sprinkle with Parmesan and almonds. Serve warm.

Creamed Spinach

Prep time: 10 minutes | Cook time: 15 minutes | Serves 4

Vegetable oil spray
1 (10-ounce / 283-g) package frozen spinach, thawed and squeezed dry
½ cup chopped onion
2 cloves garlic, minced

4 ounces (113 g) cream cheese, diced
½ teaspoon ground nutmeg
1 teaspoon kosher salt
1 teaspoon black pepper
½ cup grated Parmesan cheese

1. Spray a baking pan with vegetable oil spray. 2. In a medium bowl, combine the spinach, onion, garlic, cream cheese, nutmeg, salt, and pepper. Transfer to the prepared pan. 3. Place the pan in the air fryer basket. Set the air fryer to 350ºF (177ºC) for 10 minutes. Open and stir to thoroughly combine the cream cheese and spinach. 4. Sprinkle the Parmesan cheese on top. Set the air fryer to 400ºF (204ºC) for 5 minutes, or until the cheese has melted and browned.

Herbed Shiitake Mushrooms

Prep time: 10 minutes | Cook time: 5 minutes | Serves 4

8 ounces (227 g) shiitake mushrooms, stems removed and caps roughly chopped
1 tablespoon olive oil
½ teaspoon salt
Freshly ground black pepper, to taste

1 teaspoon chopped fresh thyme leaves
1 teaspoon chopped fresh oregano
1 tablespoon chopped fresh parsley

1. Preheat the air fryer to 400ºF (204ºC). 2. Toss the mushrooms with the olive oil, salt, pepper, thyme and oregano. Air fry for 5 minutes, shaking the basket once or twice during the cooking process. The mushrooms will still be somewhat chewy with a meaty texture. If you'd like them a little more tender, add a couple of minutes to this cooking time. 3. Once cooked, add the parsley to the mushrooms and toss. Season again to taste and serve.

Garlic Roasted Broccoli

Prep time: 8 minutes | Cook time: 10 to 14 minutes | Serves 6

1 head broccoli, cut into bite-size florets
1 tablespoon avocado oil
2 teaspoons minced garlic
⅛ teaspoon red pepper flakes

Sea salt and freshly ground black pepper, to taste
1 tablespoon freshly squeezed lemon juice
½ teaspoon lemon zest

1. In a large bowl, toss together the broccoli, avocado oil, garlic, red pepper flakes, salt, and pepper. 2. Set the air fryer to 375ºF (191ºC). Arrange the broccoli in a single layer in the air fryer basket, working in batches if necessary. Roast for 10 to 14 minutes, until the broccoli is lightly charred. 3. Place the florets in a medium bowl and toss with the lemon juice and lemon zest. Serve.

Sesame Taj Tofu

Prep time: 5 minutes | Cook time: 25 minutes | Serves 4

1 block firm tofu, pressed and cut into 1-inch thick cubes	seeds
2 tablespoons soy sauce	1 teaspoon rice vinegar
2 teaspoons toasted sesame	1 tablespoon cornstarch

1. Preheat the air fryer to 400°F (204°C). 2. Add the tofu, soy sauce, sesame seeds, and rice vinegar in a bowl together and mix well to coat the tofu cubes. Then cover the tofu in cornstarch and put it in the air fryer basket. 3. Air fry for 25 minutes, giving the basket a shake at five-minute intervals to ensure the tofu cooks evenly. 4. Serve immediately.

Easy Potato Croquettes

Prep time: 15 minutes | Cook time: 15 minutes | Serves 10

¼ cup nutritional yeast	Salt and ground black pepper, to taste
2 cups boiled potatoes, mashed	2 tablespoons vegetable oil
1 flax egg	¼ cup bread crumbs
1 tablespoon flour	
2 tablespoons chopped chives	

1. Preheat the air fryer to 400°F (204°C). 2. In a bowl, combine the nutritional yeast, potatoes, flax egg, flour, and chives. Sprinkle with salt and pepper as desired. 3. In a separate bowl, mix the vegetable oil and bread crumbs to achieve a crumbly consistency. 4. Shape the potato mixture into small balls and dip each one into the bread crumb mixture. 5. Put the croquettes inside the air fryer and air fry for 15 minutes, ensuring the croquettes turn golden brown. 6. Serve immediately.

Fried Brussels Sprouts

Prep time: 10 minutes | Cook time: 18 minutes | Serves 4

1 teaspoon plus 1 tablespoon extra-virgin olive oil, divided	2 tablespoons sriracha
2 teaspoons minced garlic	1 pound (454 g) Brussels sprouts, stems trimmed and any tough leaves removed, rinsed, halved lengthwise, and dried
2 tablespoons honey	
1 tablespoon sugar	
2 tablespoons freshly squeezed lemon juice	½ teaspoon salt
2 tablespoons rice vinegar	Cooking oil spray

1. In a small saucepan over low heat, combine 1 teaspoon of olive oil, the garlic, honey, sugar, lemon juice, vinegar, and sriracha. Cook for 2 to 3 minutes, or until slightly thickened. Remove the pan from the heat, cover, and set aside. 2. Place the Brussels sprouts in a resealable bag or small bowl. Add the remaining olive oil and the salt, and toss to coat. 3. Insert the crisper plate into the basket and the basket into the unit. Preheat the unit by selecting AIR FRY, setting the temperature to 390°F (199°C), and setting the time to 3 minutes. Select START/STOP to begin. 4. Once the unit is preheated, spray the crisper plate with cooking oil. Add the Brussels sprouts to the basket. 5. Select AIR FRY, set the temperature to 390°F (199°C), and set the time to 15 minutes. Select START/STOP to begin. 6. After 7 or 8 minutes, remove the basket and shake it to toss the sprouts. Reinsert the basket to resume cooking. 7. When the cooking is complete, the leaves should be crispy and light brown and the sprout centers tender. 8. Place the sprouts in a medium serving bowl and drizzle the sauce over the top. Toss to coat, and serve immediately.

Spicy Roasted Bok Choy

Prep time: 10 minutes | Cook time: 7 to 10 minutes | Serves 4

2 tablespoons olive oil	2 cloves garlic, minced
2 tablespoons reduced-sodium coconut aminos	1 head (about 1 pound / 454 g) bok choy, sliced lengthwise into quarters
2 teaspoons sesame oil	
2 teaspoons chili-garlic sauce	2 teaspoons black sesame seeds

1. Preheat the air fryer to 400°F (204°C). 2. In a large bowl, combine the olive oil, coconut aminos, sesame oil, chili-garlic sauce, and garlic. Add the bok choy and toss, massaging the leaves with your hands if necessary, until thoroughly coated. 3. Arrange the bok choy in the basket of the air fryer. Pausing about halfway through the cooking time to shake the basket, air fry for 7 to 10 minutes until the bok choy is tender and the tips of the leaves begin to crisp. 4.Remove from the basket and let cool for a few minutes before coarsely chopping. Serve sprinkled with the sesame seeds.

Citrus-Roasted Broccoli Florets

Prep time: 5 minutes | Cook time: 12 minutes | Serves 6

4 cups broccoli florets (approximately 1 large head)	½ cup orange juice
2 tablespoons olive oil	1 tablespoon raw honey
½ teaspoon salt	Orange wedges, for serving (optional)

1. Preheat the air fryer to 360°F(182°C). 2. In a large bowl, combine the broccoli, olive oil, salt, orange juice, and honey. Toss the broccoli in the liquid until well coated. 3. Pour the broccoli mixture into the air fryer basket and roast for 6 minutes. Stir and roast for 6 minutes more. 4. Serve alone or with orange wedges for additional citrus flavor, if desired.

Parmesan and Herb Sweet Potatoes

Prep time: 10 minutes | Cook time: 18 minutes | Serves 4

2 large sweet potatoes, peeled and cubed	½ teaspoon salt
¼ cup olive oil	2 tablespoons shredded Parmesan
1 teaspoon dried rosemary	

1. Preheat the air fryer to 360°F(182°C). 2. In a large bowl, toss the sweet potatoes with the olive oil, rosemary, and salt. 3. Pour the potatoes into the air fryer basket and roast for 10 minutes, then stir the potatoes and sprinkle the Parmesan over the top. Continue roasting for 8 minutes more. 4. Serve hot and enjoy.

Butternut Squash Croquettes

Prep time: 5 minutes | Cook time: 17 minutes | Serves 4

⅓ butternut squash, peeled and grated
⅓ cup all-purpose flour
2 eggs, whisked
4 cloves garlic, minced
1½ tablespoons olive oil

1 teaspoon fine sea salt
⅓ teaspoon freshly ground black pepper, or more to taste
⅓ teaspoon dried sage
A pinch of ground allspice

1. Preheat the air fryer to 345°F (174°C). Line the air fryer basket with parchment paper. 2. In a mixing bowl, stir together all the ingredients until well combined. 3. Make the squash croquettes: Use a small cookie scoop to drop tablespoonfuls of the squash mixture onto a lightly floured surface and shape into balls with your hands. Transfer them to the air fryer basket. 4. Air fry for 17 minutes until the squash croquettes are golden brown. 5. Remove from the basket to a plate and serve warm.

Lemon-Garlic Mushrooms

Prep time: 10 minutes | Cook time: 10 to 15 minutes | Serves 6

12 ounces (340 g) sliced mushrooms
1 tablespoon avocado oil
Sea salt and freshly ground black pepper, to taste
3 tablespoons unsalted butter

1 teaspoon minced garlic
1 teaspoon freshly squeezed lemon juice
½ teaspoon red pepper flakes
2 tablespoons chopped fresh parsley

1. Place the mushrooms in a medium bowl and toss with the oil. Season to taste with salt and pepper. 2. Place the mushrooms in a single layer in the air fryer basket. Set your air fryer to 375°F (191°C) and roast for 10 to 15 minutes, until the mushrooms are tender. 3. While the mushrooms cook, melt the butter in a small pot or skillet over medium-low heat. Stir in the garlic and cook for 30 seconds. Remove the pot from the heat and stir in the lemon juice and red pepper flakes. 4. Toss the mushrooms with the lemon-garlic butter and garnish with the parsley before serving.

"Faux-Tato" Hash

Prep time: 10 minutes | Cook time: 12 minutes | Serves 4

1 pound (454 g) radishes, ends removed, quartered
¼ medium yellow onion, peeled and diced
½ medium green bell pepper, seeded and chopped

2 tablespoons salted butter, melted
½ teaspoon garlic powder
¼ teaspoon ground black pepper

1. In a large bowl, combine radishes, onion, and bell pepper. Toss with butter. 2. Sprinkle garlic powder and black pepper over mixture in bowl, then spoon into ungreased air fryer basket. 3. Adjust the temperature to 320°F (160°C) and air fry for 12 minutes. Shake basket halfway through cooking. Radishes will be tender when done. Serve warm.

Corn Croquettes

Prep time: 10 minutes | Cook time: 12 to 14 minutes | Serves 4

½ cup leftover mashed potatoes
2 cups corn kernels (if frozen, thawed, and well drained)
¼ teaspoon onion powder
⅛ teaspoon ground black

pepper
¼ teaspoon salt
½ cup panko bread crumbs
Oil for misting or cooking spray

1. Place the potatoes and half the corn in food processor and pulse until corn is well chopped. 2. Transfer mixture to large bowl and stir in remaining corn, onion powder, pepper and salt. 3. Shape mixture into 16 balls. 4. Roll balls in panko crumbs, mist with oil or cooking spray, and place in air fryer basket. 5. Air fry at 360°F (182°C) for 12 to 14 minutes, until golden brown and crispy.

Five-Spice Roasted Sweet Potatoes

Prep time: 10 minutes | Cook time: 12 minutes | Serves 4

½ teaspoon ground cinnamon
¼ teaspoon ground cumin
¼ teaspoon paprika
1 teaspoon chile powder
⅛ teaspoon turmeric
½ teaspoon salt (optional)

Freshly ground black pepper, to taste
2 large sweet potatoes, peeled and cut into ¾-inch cubes (about 3 cups)
1 tablespoon olive oil

1. In a large bowl, mix together cinnamon, cumin, paprika, chile powder, turmeric, salt, and pepper to taste. 2. Add potatoes and stir well. 3. Drizzle the seasoned potatoes with the olive oil and stir until evenly coated. 4. Place seasoned potatoes in a baking pan or an ovenproof dish that fits inside your air fryer basket. 5. Cook for 6 minutes at 390°F (199°C), stop, and stir well. 6. Cook for an additional 6 minutes.

Broccoli with Sesame Dressing

Prep time: 5 minutes | Cook time: 10 minutes | Serves 4

6 cups broccoli florets, cut into bite-size pieces
1 tablespoon olive oil
¼ teaspoon salt
2 tablespoons sesame seeds
2 tablespoons rice vinegar

2 tablespoons coconut aminos
2 tablespoons sesame oil
½ teaspoon Swerve
¼ teaspoon red pepper flakes (optional)

1. Preheat the air fryer to 400°F (204°C). 2. In a large bowl, toss the broccoli with the olive oil and salt until thoroughly coated. 3. Transfer the broccoli to the air fryer basket. Pausing halfway through the cooking time to shake the basket, air fry for 10 minutes until the stems are tender and the edges are beginning to crisp. 4. Meanwhile, in the same large bowl, whisk together the sesame seeds, vinegar, coconut aminos, sesame oil, Swerve, and red pepper flakes (if using). 5. Transfer the broccoli to the bowl and toss until thoroughly coated with the seasonings. Serve warm or at room temperature.

Caramelized Eggplant with Harissa Yogurt

Prep time: 10 minutes | Cook time: 15 minutes | Serves 2

1 medium eggplant (about ¾ pound / 340 g), cut crosswise into ½-inch-thick slices and quartered 2 tablespoons vegetable oil Kosher salt and freshly ground	black pepper, to taste ½ cup plain yogurt (not Greek) 2 tablespoons harissa paste 1 garlic clove, grated 2 teaspoons honey

1. In a bowl, toss together the eggplant and oil, season with salt and pepper, and toss to coat evenly. Transfer to the air fryer and air fry at 400°F (204°C), shaking the basket every 5 minutes, until the eggplant is caramelized and tender, about 15 minutes. 2. Meanwhile, in a small bowl, whisk together the yogurt, harissa, and garlic, then spread onto a serving plate. 3. Pile the warm eggplant over the yogurt and drizzle with the honey just before serving.

Asparagus Fries

Prep time: 15 minutes | Cook time: 5 to 7 minutes per batch | Serves 4

12 ounces (340 g) fresh asparagus spears with tough ends trimmed off 2 egg whites ¼ cup water	¾ cup panko bread crumbs ¼ cup grated Parmesan cheese, plus 2 tablespoons ¼ teaspoon salt Oil for misting or cooking spray

1. Preheat the air fryer to 390°F (199°C). 2. In a shallow dish, beat egg whites and water until slightly foamy. 3. In another shallow dish, combine panko, Parmesan, and salt. 4. Dip asparagus spears in egg, then roll in crumbs. Spray with oil or cooking spray. 5. Place a layer of asparagus in air fryer basket, leaving just a little space in between each spear. Stack another layer on top, crosswise. Air fry at 390°F (199°C) for 5 to 7 minutes, until crispy and golden brown. 6. Repeat to cook remaining asparagus.

Lemon-Thyme Asparagus

Prep time: 5 minutes | Cook time: 4 to 8 minutes | Serves 4

1 pound (454 g) asparagus, woody ends trimmed off 1 tablespoon avocado oil ½ teaspoon dried thyme or ½ tablespoon chopped fresh thyme Sea salt and freshly ground	black pepper, to taste 2 ounces (57 g) goat cheese, crumbled Zest and juice of 1 lemon Flaky sea salt, for serving (optional)

1. In a medium bowl, toss together the asparagus, avocado oil, and thyme, and season with sea salt and pepper. 2. Place the asparagus in the air fryer basket in a single layer. Set the air fryer to 400°F (204°C) and air fry for 4 to 8 minutes, to your desired doneness. 3. Transfer to a serving platter. Top with the goat cheese, lemon zest, and lemon juice. If desired, season with a pinch of flaky salt.

Spiced Honey-Walnut Carrots

Prep time: 5 minutes | Cook time: 12 minutes | Serves 6

1 pound (454 g) baby carrots 2 tablespoons olive oil ¼ cup raw honey	¼ teaspoon ground cinnamon ¼ cup black walnuts, chopped

1. Preheat the air fryer to 360°F (182°C). 2. In a large bowl, toss the baby carrots with olive oil, honey, and cinnamon until well coated. 3. Pour into the air fryer and roast for 6 minutes. Shake the basket, sprinkle the walnuts on top, and roast for 6 minutes more. 4. Remove the carrots from the air fryer and serve.

Green Bean Casserole

Prep time: 10 minutes | Cook time: 20 minutes | Serves 4

1 pound (454 g) fresh green beans, ends trimmed, strings removed, and chopped into 2-inch pieces 1 (8-ounce / 227-g) package sliced brown mushrooms ½ onion, sliced 1 clove garlic, minced	1 tablespoon olive oil ½ teaspoon salt ¼ teaspoon freshly ground black pepper 4 ounces (113 g) cream cheese ½ cup chicken stock ¼ teaspoon ground nutmeg ½ cup grated Cheddar cheese

1. Preheat the air fryer to 400°F (204°C). Coat a casserole dish with olive oil and set aside. 2. In a large bowl, combine the green beans, mushrooms, onion, garlic, olive oil, salt, and pepper. Toss until the vegetables are thoroughly coated with the oil and seasonings. 3. Transfer the mixture to the air fryer basket. Pausing halfway through the cooking time to shake the basket, air fry for 10 minutes until tender. 4. While the vegetables are cooking, in a 2-cup glass measuring cup, warm the cream cheese and chicken stock in the microwave on high for 1 to 2 minutes until the cream cheese is melted. Add the nutmeg and whisk until smooth. 5. Transfer the vegetables to the prepared casserole dish and pour the cream cheese mixture over the top. Top with the Cheddar cheese. Air fry for another 10 minutes until the cheese is melted and beginning to brown.

Rosemary-Roasted Red Potatoes

Prep time: 5 minutes | Cook time: 20 minutes | Serves 6

1 pound (454 g) red potatoes, quartered ¼ cup olive oil ½ teaspoon kosher salt	¼ teaspoon black pepper 1 garlic clove, minced 4 rosemary sprigs

1. Preheat the air fryer to 360°F (182°C). 2. In a large bowl, toss the potatoes with the olive oil, salt, pepper, and garlic until well coated. 3. Pour the potatoes into the air fryer basket and top with the sprigs of rosemary. 4. Roast for 10 minutes, then stir or toss the potatoes and roast for 10 minutes more. 5. Remove the rosemary sprigs and serve the potatoes. Season with additional salt and pepper, if needed.

Tingly Chili-Roasted Broccoli

Prep time: 5 minutes | Cook time: 10 minutes | Serves 2

12 ounces (340 g) broccoli
florets
2 tablespoons Asian hot chili oil
1 teaspoon ground Sichuan
peppercorns (or black pepper)

2 garlic cloves, finely chopped
1 (2-inch) piece fresh ginger,
peeled and finely chopped
Kosher salt and freshly ground
black pepper, to taste

1. In a bowl, toss together the broccoli, chili oil, Sichuan peppercorns, garlic, ginger, and salt and black pepper to taste. 2. Transfer to the air fryer and roast at 375°F (191°C), shaking the basket halfway through, until lightly charred and tender, about 10 minutes. Remove from the air fryer and serve warm.

Lemony Broccoli

Prep time: 10 minutes | Cook time: 9 to 14 minutes

per batch | Serves 4

1 large head broccoli, rinsed
and patted dry
2 teaspoons extra-virgin olive
oil

1 tablespoon freshly squeezed
lemon juice
Olive oil spray

1. Cut off the broccoli florets and separate them. You can use the stems, too; peel the stems and cut them into 1-inch chunks. 2. Insert the crisper plate into the basket and the basket into the unit. Preheat the unit by selecting AIR ROAST, setting the temperature to 390°F (199°C), and setting the time to 3 minutes. Select START/STOP to begin. 3. In a large bowl, toss together the broccoli, olive oil, and lemon juice until coated. 4. Once the unit is preheated, spray the crisper plate with olive oil. Working in batches, place half the broccoli into the basket. 5. Select AIR ROAST, set the temperature to 390°F (199°C), and set the time to 14 minutes. Select START/STOP to begin. 6. After 5 minutes, remove the basket and shake the broccoli. Reinsert the basket to resume cooking. Check the broccoli after 5 minutes. If it is crisp-tender and slightly brown around the edges, it is done. If not, resume cooking. 7. When the cooking is complete, transfer the broccoli to a serving bowl. Repeat steps 5 and 6 with the remaining broccoli. Serve immediately.

Air Fried Potatoes with Olives

Prep time: 15 minutes | Cook time: 40 minutes | Serves 1

1 medium russet potatoes,
scrubbed and peeled
1 teaspoon olive oil
¼ teaspoon onion powder
⅛ teaspoon salt

Dollop of butter
Dollop of cream cheese
1 tablespoon Kalamata olives
1 tablespoon chopped chives

1. Preheat the air fryer to 400°F (204°C). 2. In a bowl, coat the potatoes with the onion powder, salt, olive oil, and butter. 3. Transfer to the air fryer and air fry for 40 minutes, turning the potatoes over at the halfway point. 4. Take care when removing the potatoes from the air fryer and serve with the cream cheese, Kalamata olives and chives on top.

Easy Greek Briami (Ratatouille)

Prep time: 15 minutes | Cook time: 40 minutes | Serves 6

2 russet potatoes, cubed
½ cup Roma tomatoes, cubed
1 eggplant, cubed
1 zucchini, cubed
1 red onion, chopped
1 red bell pepper, chopped
2 garlic cloves, minced
1 teaspoon dried mint
1 teaspoon dried parsley

1 teaspoon dried oregano
½ teaspoon salt
½ teaspoon black pepper
¼ teaspoon red pepper flakes
⅓ cup olive oil
1 (8-ounce / 227-g) can tomato
paste
¼ cup vegetable broth
¼ cup water

1. Preheat the air fryer to 320°F(160°C). 2. In a large bowl, combine the potatoes, tomatoes, eggplant, zucchini, onion, bell pepper, garlic, mint, parsley, oregano, salt, black pepper, and red pepper flakes. 3. In a small bowl, mix together the olive oil, tomato paste, broth, and water. 4. Pour the oil-and-tomato-paste mixture over the vegetables and toss until everything is coated. 5. Pour the coated vegetables into the air fryer basket in an even layer and roast for 20 minutes. After 20 minutes, stir well and spread out again. Roast for an additional 10 minutes, then repeat the process and cook for another 10 minutes.

Corn on the Cob

Prep time: 5 minutes | Cook time: 12 to 15 minutes |

Serves 4

2 large ears fresh corn
Olive oil for misting

Salt, to taste (optional)

1. Shuck corn, remove silks, and wash. 2. Cut or break each ear in half crosswise. 3. Spray corn with olive oil. 4. Air fry at 390°F (199°C) for 12 to 15 minutes or until browned as much as you like. 5. Serve plain or with coarsely ground salt.

Fig, Chickpea, and Arugula Salad

Prep time: 15 minutes | Cook time: 20 minutes | Serves 4

8 fresh figs, halved
1½ cups cooked chickpeas
1 teaspoon crushed roasted
cumin seeds
4 tablespoons balsamic vinegar
2 tablespoons extra-virgin olive

oil, plus more for greasing
Salt and ground black pepper,
to taste
3 cups arugula rocket, washed
and dried

1. Preheat the air fryer to 375°F (191°C). 2. Cover the air fryer basket with aluminum foil and grease lightly with oil. Put the figs in the air fryer basket and air fry for 10 minutes. 3. In a bowl, combine the chickpeas and cumin seeds. 4. Remove the air fried figs from the air fryer and replace with the chickpeas. Air fry for 10 minutes. Leave to cool. 5. In the meantime, prepare the dressing. Mix the balsamic vinegar, olive oil, salt and pepper. 6. In a salad bowl, combine the arugula rocket with the cooled figs and chickpeas. 7. Toss with the sauce and serve.

Roasted Brussels Sprouts with Bacon

Prep time: 10 minutes | Cook time: 20 minutes | Serves 4

4 slices thick-cut bacon, chopped (about ¼ pound / 113 g)
1 pound (454 g) Brussels

sprouts, halved (or quartered if large)
Freshly ground black pepper, to taste

1. Preheat the air fryer to 380°F (193°C). 2. Air fry the bacon for 5 minutes, shaking the basket once or twice during the cooking time. 3. Add the Brussels sprouts to the basket and drizzle a little bacon fat from the bottom of the air fryer drawer into the basket. Toss the sprouts to coat with the bacon fat. Air fry for an additional 15 minutes, or until the Brussels sprouts are tender to a knifepoint. 4. Season with freshly ground black pepper.

Roasted Potatoes and Asparagus

Prep time: 5 minutes | Cook time: 23 minutes | Serves 4

4 medium potatoes
1 bunch asparagus
⅓ cup cottage cheese
⅓ cup low-fat crème fraiche

1 tablespoon wholegrain mustard
Salt and pepper, to taste
Cooking spray

1. Preheat the air fryer to 390°F (199°C). Spritz the air fryer basket with cooking spray. 2. Place the potatoes in the basket. Air fry the potatoes for 20 minutes. 3. Boil the asparagus in salted water for 3 minutes. 4. Remove the potatoes and mash them with rest of ingredients. Sprinkle with salt and pepper. 5. Serve immediately.

Hasselback Potatoes with Chive Pesto

Prep time: 10 minutes | Cook time: 40 minutes | Serves 2

2 medium russet potatoes
5 tablespoons olive oil
Kosher salt and freshly ground black pepper, to taste
¼ cup roughly chopped fresh chives
2 tablespoons packed fresh flat-

leaf parsley leaves
1 tablespoon chopped walnuts
1 tablespoon grated Parmesan cheese
1 teaspoon fresh lemon juice
1 small garlic clove, peeled
¼ cup sour cream

1. Place the potatoes on a cutting board and lay a chopstick or thin-handled wooden spoon to the side of each potato. Thinly slice the potatoes crosswise, letting the chopstick or spoon handle stop the blade of your knife, and stop ½ inch short of each end of the potato. Rub the potatoes with 1 tablespoon of the olive oil and season with salt and pepper. 2. Place the potatoes, cut-side up, in the air fryer and air fry at 375°F (191°C) until golden brown and crisp on the outside and tender inside, about 40 minutes, drizzling the insides with 1 tablespoon more olive oil and seasoning with more salt and pepper halfway through. 3. Meanwhile, in a small blender or food processor, combine the remaining 3 tablespoons olive oil, the chives, parsley, walnuts, Parmesan, lemon juice, and garlic and purée until smooth. Season the chive pesto with salt and pepper. 4. Remove the potatoes from the air fryer and transfer to plates. Drizzle the potatoes with the pesto, letting it drip down into the grooves, then dollop each with sour cream and serve hot.

Burger Bun for One

Prep time: 2 minutes | Cook time: 5 minutes | Serves 1

2 tablespoons salted butter, melted
¼ cup blanched finely ground almond flour

¼ teaspoon baking powder
⅛ teaspoon apple cider vinegar
1 large egg, whisked

1. Pour butter into an ungreased ramekin. Add flour, baking powder, and vinegar to ramekin and stir until combined. Add egg and stir until batter is mostly smooth. 2. Place ramekin into air fryer basket. Adjust the temperature to 350°F (177°C) and bake for 5 minutes. When done, the center will be firm and the top slightly browned. Let cool, about 5 minutes, then remove from ramekin and slice in half. Serve.

Fried Zucchini Salad

Prep time: 10 minutes | Cook time: 5 to 7 minutes | Serves 4

2 medium zucchini, thinly sliced
5 tablespoons olive oil, divided
¼ cup chopped fresh parsley
2 tablespoons chopped fresh mint

Zest and juice of ½ lemon
1 clove garlic, minced
¼ cup crumbled feta cheese
Freshly ground black pepper, to taste

1. Preheat the air fryer to 400°F (204°C). 2. In a large bowl, toss the zucchini slices with 1 tablespoon of the olive oil. 3. Working in batches if necessary, arrange the zucchini slices in an even layer in the air fryer basket. Pausing halfway through the cooking time to shake the basket, air fry for 5 to 7 minutes until soft and lightly browned on each side. 4. Meanwhile, in a small bowl, combine the remaining 4 tablespoons olive oil, parsley, mint, lemon zest, lemon juice, and garlic. 5. Arrange the zucchini on a plate and drizzle with the dressing. Sprinkle the feta and black pepper on top. Serve warm or at room temperature.

Rosemary New Potatoes

Prep time: 10 minutes | Cook time: 5 to 6 minutes | Serves 4

3 large red potatoes (enough to make 3 cups sliced)
¼ teaspoon ground rosemary
¼ teaspoon ground thyme

⅛ teaspoon salt
⅛ teaspoon ground black pepper
2 teaspoons extra-light olive oil

1. Preheat the air fryer to 330°F (166°C). 2. Place potatoes in large bowl and sprinkle with rosemary, thyme, salt, and pepper. 3. Stir with a spoon to distribute seasonings evenly. 4. Add oil to potatoes and stir again to coat well. 5. Air fry at 330°F (166°C) for 4 minutes. Stir and break apart any that have stuck together. 6. Cook an additional 1 to 2 minutes or until fork-tender.

Easy Rosemary Green Beans

Prep time: 5 minutes | Cook time: 5 minutes | Serves 1

1 tablespoon butter, melted	3 cloves garlic, minced
2 tablespoons rosemary	¾ cup chopped green beans
½ teaspoon salt	

1. Preheat the air fryer to 390ºF (199ºC). 2. Combine the melted butter with the rosemary, salt, and minced garlic. Toss in the green beans, coating them well. 3. Air fry for 5 minutes. 4. Serve immediately.

Bacon Potatoes and Green Beans

Prep time: 10 minutes | Cook time: 25 minutes | Serves 4

Oil, for spraying	beans
2 pounds (907 g) medium russet potatoes, quartered	1 teaspoon salt
¾ cup bacon bits	½ teaspoon freshly ground black pepper
10 ounces (283 g) fresh green	

1. Line the air fryer basket with parchment and spray lightly with oil. 2. Place the potatoes in the prepared basket. Top with the bacon bits and green beans. Sprinkle with the salt and black pepper and spray liberally with oil. 3. Air fry at 355ºF (179ºC) for 25 minutes, stirring after 12 minutes and spraying with oil, until the potatoes are easily pierced with a fork.

Parmesan-Thyme Butternut Squash

Prep time: 15 minutes | Cook time: 20 minutes | Serves 4

2½ cups butternut squash, cubed into 1-inch pieces (approximately 1 medium)	¼ teaspoon garlic powder
	¼ teaspoon black pepper
2 tablespoons olive oil	1 tablespoon fresh thyme
¼ teaspoon salt	¼ cup grated Parmesan

1. Preheat the air fryer to 360ºF(182ºC). 2. In a large bowl, combine the cubed squash with the olive oil, salt, garlic powder, pepper, and thyme until the squash is well coated. 3. Pour this mixture into the air fryer basket, and roast for 10 minutes. Stir and roast another 8 to 10 minutes more. 4. Remove the squash from the air fryer and toss with freshly grated Parmesan before serving.

Maple-Roasted Tomatoes

Prep time: 15 minutes | Cook time: 20 minutes | Serves 2

10 ounces (283 g) cherry tomatoes, halved	2 sprigs fresh thyme, stems removed
Kosher salt, to taste	1 garlic clove, minced
2 tablespoons maple syrup	Freshly ground black pepper
1 tablespoon vegetable oil	

1. Place the tomatoes in a colander and sprinkle liberally with salt. Let stand for 10 minutes to drain. 2. Transfer the tomatoes cut-side up to a cake pan, then drizzle with the maple syrup, followed by the oil. Sprinkle with the thyme leaves and garlic and season with pepper. Place the pan in the air fryer and roast at 325ºF (163ºC) until the tomatoes are soft, collapsed, and lightly caramelized on top, about 20 minutes. 3. Serve straight from the pan or transfer the tomatoes to a plate and drizzle with the juices from the pan to serve.

Curry Roasted Cauliflower

Prep time: 10 minutes | Cook time: 20 minutes | Serves 4

¼ cup olive oil	1 head cauliflower, cut into bite-size florets
2 teaspoons curry powder	
½ teaspoon salt	½ red onion, sliced
¼ teaspoon freshly ground black pepper	2 tablespoons freshly chopped parsley, for garnish (optional)

1. Preheat the air fryer to 400ºF (204ºC). 2. In a large bowl, combine the olive oil, curry powder, salt, and pepper. Add the cauliflower and onion. Toss gently until the vegetables are completely coated with the oil mixture. Transfer the vegetables to the basket of the air fryer. 3. Pausing about halfway through the cooking time to shake the basket, air fry for 20 minutes until the cauliflower is tender and beginning to brown. Top with the parsley, if desired, before serving.

Tofu Bites

Prep time: 15 minutes | Cook time: 30 minutes | Serves 4

1 packaged firm tofu, cubed and pressed to remove excess water	1 teaspoon hot sauce
	2 tablespoons sesame seeds
1 tablespoon soy sauce	1 teaspoon garlic powder
1 tablespoon ketchup	Salt and ground black pepper, to taste
1 tablespoon maple syrup	
½ teaspoon vinegar	Cooking spray
1 teaspoon liquid smoke	

1. Preheat the air fryer to 375ºF (191ºC). 2. Spritz a baking dish with cooking spray. 3. Combine all the ingredients to coat the tofu completely and allow the marinade to absorb for half an hour. 4. Transfer the tofu to the baking dish, then air fry for 15 minutes. Flip the tofu over and air fry for another 15 minutes on the other side. 5. Serve immediately.

Mediterranean Zucchini Boats

Prep time: 5 minutes | Cook time: 10 minutes | Serves 4

1 large zucchini, ends removed, halved lengthwise	¼ cup feta cheese
	1 tablespoon balsamic vinegar
6 grape tomatoes, quartered	1 tablespoon olive oil
¼ teaspoon salt	

1. Use a spoon to scoop out 2 tablespoons from center of each zucchini half, making just enough space to fill with tomatoes and feta. 2. Place tomatoes evenly in centers of zucchini halves and sprinkle with salt. Place into ungreased air fryer basket. Adjust the temperature to 350ºF (177ºC) and roast for 10 minutes. When done, zucchini will be tender. 3. Transfer boats to a serving tray and sprinkle with feta, then drizzle with vinegar and olive oil. Serve warm.

Parmesan Mushrooms

Prep time: 5 minutes | Cook time: 15 minutes | Serves 4

Oil, for spraying
1 pound (454 g) cremini mushrooms, stems trimmed
2 tablespoons olive oil
2 teaspoons granulated garlic
1 teaspoon dried onion soup mix
½ teaspoon salt
¼ teaspoon freshly ground black pepper
⅓ cup grated Parmesan cheese, divided

1. Line the air fryer basket with parchment and spray lightly with oil. 2. In a large bowl, toss the mushrooms with the olive oil, garlic, onion soup mix, salt, and black pepper until evenly coated. 3. Place the mushrooms in the prepared basket. 4. Roast at 370ºF (188ºC) for 13 minutes. 5. Sprinkle half of the cheese over the mushrooms and cook for another 2 minutes. 6. Transfer the mushrooms to a serving bowl, add the remaining Parmesan cheese, and toss until evenly coated. Serve immediately.

Tahini-Lemon Kale

Prep time: 5 minutes | Cook time: 15 minutes | Serves 2 to 4

¼ cup tahini
¼ cup fresh lemon juice
2 tablespoons olive oil
1 teaspoon sesame seeds
½ teaspoon garlic powder
¼ teaspoon cayenne pepper
4 cups packed torn kale leaves (stems and ribs removed and leaves torn into palm-size pieces; about 4 ounces / 113 g)
Kosher salt and freshly ground black pepper, to taste

1. In a large bowl, whisk together the tahini, lemon juice, olive oil, sesame seeds, garlic powder, and cayenne until smooth. Add the kale leaves, season with salt and black pepper, and toss in the dressing until completely coated. Transfer the kale leaves to a cake pan. 2. Place the pan in the air fryer and roast at 350ºF (177ºC), stirring every 5 minutes, until the kale is wilted and the top is lightly browned, about 15 minutes. Remove the pan from the air fryer and serve warm.

Hawaiian Brown Rice

Prep time: 10 minutes | Cook time: 12 to 16 minutes | Serves 4 to 6

¼ pound (113 g) ground sausage
1 teaspoon butter
¼ cup minced onion
¼ cup minced bell pepper
2 cups cooked brown rice
1 (8-ounce / 227-g) can crushed pineapple, drained

1. Shape sausage into 3 or 4 thin patties. Air fry at 390ºF (199ºC) for 6 to 8 minutes or until well done. Remove from air fryer, drain, and crumble. Set aside. 2. Place butter, onion, and bell pepper in baking pan. Roast at 390ºF (199ºC) for 1 minute and stir. Cook 3 to 4 minutes longer or just until vegetables are tender. 3. Add sausage, rice, and pineapple to vegetables and stir together. 4. Roast for 2 to 3 minutes, until heated through.

Scalloped Potatoes

Prep time: 5 minutes | Cook time: 20 minutes | Serves 4

2 cup sliced frozen potatoes, thawed
3 cloves garlic, minced
Pinch salt
Freshly ground black pepper, to taste
¾ cup heavy cream

1. Preheat the air fryer to 380ºF (193ºC). 2. Toss the potatoes with the garlic, salt, and black pepper in a baking pan until evenly coated. Pour the heavy cream over the top. 3. Place the baking pan in the air fryer basket and bake for 15 minutes, or until the potatoes are tender and top is golden brown. Check for doneness and bake for another 5 minutes as needed. 4. Serve hot.

Blackened Zucchini with Kimchi-Herb Sauce

Prep time: 10 minutes | Cook time: 15 minutes | Serves 2

2 medium zucchini, ends trimmed (about 6 ounces / 170 g each)
2 tablespoons olive oil
½ cup kimchi, finely chopped
¼ cup finely chopped fresh cilantro
¼ cup finely chopped fresh
flat-leaf parsley, plus more for garnish
2 tablespoons rice vinegar
2 teaspoons Asian chili-garlic sauce
1 teaspoon grated fresh ginger
Kosher salt and freshly ground black pepper, to taste

1. Brush the zucchini with half of the olive oil, place in the air fryer, and air fry at 400ºF (204ºC), turning halfway through, until lightly charred on the outside and tender, about 15 minutes. 2. Meanwhile, in a small bowl, combine the remaining 1 tablespoon olive oil, the kimchi, cilantro, parsley, vinegar, chili-garlic sauce, and ginger. 3. Once the zucchini is finished cooking, transfer it to a colander and let it cool for 5 minutes. Using your fingers, pinch and break the zucchini into bite-size pieces, letting them fall back into the colander. Season the zucchini with salt and pepper, toss to combine, then let sit a further 5 minutes to allow some of its liquid to drain. Pile the zucchini atop the kimchi sauce on a plate and sprinkle with more parsley to serve.

Zesty Fried Asparagus

Prep time: 3 minutes | Cook time: 10 minutes | Serves 4

Oil, for spraying
10 to 12 spears asparagus, trimmed
2 tablespoons olive oil
1 tablespoon granulated garlic
1 teaspoon chili powder
½ teaspoon ground cumin
¼ teaspoon salt

1. Line the air fryer basket with parchment and spray lightly with oil. 2. If the asparagus are too long to fit easily in the air fryer, cut them in half. 3. Place the asparagus, olive oil, garlic, chili powder, cumin, and salt in a zip-top plastic bag, seal, and toss until evenly coated. 4. Place the asparagus in the prepared basket. 5. Roast at 390ºF (199ºC) for 5 minutes, flip, and cook for another 5 minutes, or until bright green and firm but tender.

Green Peas with Mint

Prep time: 5 minutes | Cook time: 5 minutes | Serves 4

1 cup shredded lettuce
1 (10-ounce / 283-g) package
frozen green peas, thawed

1 tablespoon fresh mint,
shredded
1 teaspoon melted butter

1. Lay the shredded lettuce in the air fryer basket. 2. Toss together the peas, mint, and melted butter and spoon over the lettuce. 3. Air fry at 360°F (182°C) for 5 minutes, until peas are warm and lettuce wilts.

Ratatouille

**Prep time: 15 minutes | Cook time: 20 minutes |
Serves 2 to 3**

2 cups ¾-inch cubed peeled
eggplant
1 small red, yellow, or orange
bell pepper, stemmed, seeded,
and diced
1 cup cherry tomatoes
6 to 8 cloves garlic, peeled and

halved lengthwise
3 tablespoons olive oil
1 teaspoon dried oregano
½ teaspoon dried thyme
1 teaspoon kosher salt
½ teaspoon black pepper

1. In a medium bowl, combine the eggplant, bell pepper, tomatoes, garlic, oil, oregano, thyme, salt, and pepper. Toss to combine. 2. Place the vegetables in the air fryer basket. Set the air fryer to 400°F (204°C) for 20 minutes, or until the vegetables are crisp-tender.

Corn and Cilantro Salad

Prep time: 10 minutes | Cook time: 10 minutes | Serves 2

2 ears of corn, shucked (halved
crosswise if too large to fit in
your air fryer)
1 tablespoon unsalted butter, at
room temperature
1 teaspoon chili powder
¼ teaspoon garlic powder
Kosher salt and freshly ground
black pepper, to taste
1 cup lightly packed fresh

cilantro leaves
1 tablespoon sour cream
1 tablespoon mayonnaise
1 teaspoon adobo sauce (from
a can of chipotle peppers in
adobo sauce)
2 tablespoons crumbled queso
fresco
Lime wedges, for serving

1. Brush the corn all over with the butter, then sprinkle with the chili powder and garlic powder, and season with salt and pepper. Place the corn in the air fryer and air fry at 400°F (204°C), turning over halfway through, until the kernels are lightly charred and tender, about 10 minutes. 2. Transfer the ears to a cutting board, let stand 1 minute, then carefully cut the kernels off the cobs and move them to a bowl. Add the cilantro leaves and toss to combine (the cilantro leaves will wilt slightly). 3. In a small bowl, stir together the sour cream, mayonnaise, and adobo sauce. Divide the corn and cilantro among plates and spoon the adobo dressing over the top. Sprinkle with the queso fresco and serve with lime wedges on the side.

Buttery Mushrooms

Prep time: 10 minutes | Cook time: 10 minutes | Serves 4

8 ounces (227 g) cremini
mushrooms, halved
2 tablespoons salted butter,
melted

¼ teaspoon salt
¼ teaspoon ground black
pepper

1. In a medium bowl, toss mushrooms with butter, then sprinkle with salt and pepper. Place into ungreased air fryer basket. Adjust the temperature to 400°F (204°C) and air fry for 10 minutes, shaking the basket halfway through cooking. Mushrooms will be tender when done. Serve warm.

Kohlrabi Fries

**Prep time: 10 minutes | Cook time: 20 to 30 minutes
| Serves 4**

2 pounds (907 g) kohlrabi,
peeled and cut into ¼ to ½-inch
fries

2 tablespoons olive oil
Salt and freshly ground black
pepper, to taste

1. Preheat the air fryer to 400°F (204°C). 2. In a large bowl, combine the kohlrabi and olive oil. Season to taste with salt and black pepper. Toss gently until thoroughly coated. 3. Working in batches if necessary, spread the kohlrabi in a single layer in the air fryer basket. Pausing halfway through the cooking time to shake the basket, air fry for 20 to 30 minutes until the fries are lightly browned and crunchy.

Southwestern Roasted Corn

Prep time: 10 minutes | Cook time: 10 minutes | Serves 4

Corn:
1 ½ cups thawed frozen corn
kernels
1 cup diced yellow onion
1 cup mixed diced bell peppers
1 jalapeño, diced
1 tablespoon fresh lemon juice
1 teaspoon ground cumin

½ teaspoon ancho chile powder
½ teaspoon kosher salt
For Serving:
¼ cup queso fresco or feta
cheese
¼ cup chopped fresh cilantro
1 tablespoon fresh lemon juice

1. For the corn: In a large bowl, stir together the corn, onion, bell peppers, jalapeño, lemon juice, cumin, chile powder, and salt until well incorporated. 2. Pour the spiced vegetables into the air fryer basket. Set the air fryer to 375°F (191°C) for 10 minutes, stirring halfway through the cooking time. 3. Transfer the corn mixture to a serving bowl. Add the cheese, cilantro, and lemon juice and stir well to combine. Serve immediately.

Super Cheesy Gold Eggplant

Prep time: 15 minutes | Cook time: 30 minutes | Serves 4

1 medium eggplant, peeled and cut into ½-inch-thick rounds
1 teaspoon salt, plus more for seasoning
½ cup all-purpose flour
2 eggs
¾ cup Italian bread crumbs
2 tablespoons grated Parmesan cheese

Freshly ground black pepper, to taste
Cooking oil spray
¾ cup marinara sauce
½ cup shredded Parmesan cheese, divided
½ cup shredded Mozzarella cheese, divided

1. Blot the eggplant with paper towels to dry completely. You can also sprinkle with 1 teaspoon of salt to sweat out the moisture; if you do this, rinse the eggplant slices and blot dry again. 2. Place the flour in a shallow bowl. 3. In another shallow bowl, beat the eggs. 4. In a third shallow bowl, stir together the bread crumbs and grated Parmesan cheese and season with salt and pepper. 5. Dip each eggplant round in the flour, in the eggs, and into the bread crumbs to coat. 6. Insert the crisper plate into the basket and the basket into the unit. Preheat the unit by selecting AIR FRY, setting the temperature to 400°F (204°C), and setting the time to 3 minutes. Select START/STOP to begin. 7. Once the unit is preheated, spray the crisper plate and the basket with cooking oil. Working in batches, place the eggplant rounds into the basket. Do not stack them. Spray the eggplant with the cooking oil. 8. Select AIR FRY, set the temperature to 400°F (204°C), and set the time to 10 minutes. Select START/STOP to begin. 9. After 7 minutes, open the unit and top each round with 1 teaspoon of marinara sauce and ½ tablespoon each of shredded Parmesan and Mozzarella cheese. Resume cooking for 2 to 3 minutes until the cheese melts. 10. Repeat steps 5, 6, 7, 8, and 9 with the remaining eggplant. 11. When the cooking is complete, serve immediately.

Chapter 9 Vegetarian Mains

Basic Spaghetti Squash

Prep time: 10 minutes | Cook time: 45 minutes | Serves 2

½ large spaghetti squash
1 tablespoon coconut oil
2 tablespoons salted butter,

melted
½ teaspoon garlic powder
1 teaspoon dried parsley

1. Brush shell of spaghetti squash with coconut oil. Place the skin side down and brush the inside with butter. Sprinkle with garlic powder and parsley. 2. Place squash with the skin side down into the air fryer basket. 3. Adjust the temperature to 350°F (177°C) and air fry for 30 minutes. 4. Flip the squash so skin side is up and cook an additional 15 minutes or until fork tender. Serve warm.

Caprese Eggplant Stacks

Prep time: 5 minutes | Cook time: 12 minutes | Serves 4

1 medium eggplant, cut into
¼-inch slices
2 large tomatoes, cut into
¼-inch slices
4 ounces (113 g) fresh

Mozzarella, cut into ½-ounce /
14-g slices
2 tablespoons olive oil
¼ cup fresh basil, sliced

1. In a baking dish, place four slices of eggplant on the bottom. Place a slice of tomato on top of each eggplant round, then Mozzarella, then eggplant. Repeat as necessary. 2. Drizzle with olive oil. Cover dish with foil and place dish into the air fryer basket. 3. Adjust the temperature to 350°F (177°C) and bake for 12 minutes. 4. When done, eggplant will be tender. Garnish with fresh basil to serve.

Super Veg Rolls

Prep time: 20 minutes | Cook time: 10 minutes | Serves 6

2 potatoes, mashed
¼ cup peas
¼ cup mashed carrots
1 small cabbage, sliced
¼ cups beans

2 tablespoons sweetcorn
1 small onion, chopped
½ cup bread crumbs
1 packet spring roll sheets
½ cup cornstarch slurry

1. Preheat the air fryer to 390°F (199°C). 2. Boil all the vegetables in water over a low heat. Rinse and allow to dry. 3. Unroll the spring roll sheets and spoon equal amounts of vegetable onto the center of each one. Fold into spring rolls and coat each one with the slurry and bread crumbs. 4. Air fry the rolls in the preheated air fryer for 10 minutes. 5. Serve warm.

Broccoli-Cheese Fritters

Prep time: 5 minutes | Cook time: 20 to 25 minutes | Serves 4

1 cup broccoli florets
1 cup shredded Mozzarella
cheese
¾ cup almond flour
½ cup flaxseed meal, divided
2 teaspoons baking powder

1 teaspoon garlic powder
Salt and freshly ground black
pepper, to taste
2 eggs, lightly beaten
½ cup ranch dressing

1. Preheat the air fryer to 400°F (204°C). 2. In a food processor fitted with a metal blade, pulse the broccoli until very finely chopped. 3. Transfer the broccoli to a large bowl and add the Mozzarella, almond flour, ¼ cup of the flaxseed meal, baking powder, and garlic powder. Stir until thoroughly combined. Season to taste with salt and black pepper. Add the eggs and stir again to form a sticky dough. Shape the dough into 1¼-inch fritters. 4. Place the remaining ¼ cup flaxseed meal in a shallow bowl and roll the fritters in the meal to form an even coating. 5. Working in batches if necessary, arrange the fritters in a single layer in the basket of the air fryer and spray generously with olive oil. Pausing halfway through the cooking time to shake the basket, air fry for 20 to 25 minutes until the fritters are golden brown and crispy. Serve with the ranch dressing for dipping.

Baked Zucchini

Prep time: 10 minutes | Cook time: 8 minutes | Serves 4

2 tablespoons salted butter
¼ cup diced white onion
½ teaspoon minced garlic
½ cup heavy whipping cream
2 ounces (57 g) full-fat cream

cheese
1 cup shredded sharp Cheddar
cheese
2 medium zucchini, spiralized

1. In a large saucepan over medium heat, melt butter. Add onion and sauté until it begins to soften, 1 to 3 minutes. Add garlic and sauté for 30 seconds, then pour in cream and add cream cheese. 2. Remove the pan from heat and stir in Cheddar. Add the zucchini and toss in the sauce, then put into a round baking dish. Cover the dish with foil and place into the air fryer basket. 3. Adjust the temperature to 370°F (188°C) and set the timer for 8 minutes. 4. After 6 minutes remove the foil and let the top brown for remaining cooking time. Stir and serve.

Crispy Eggplant Slices with Parsley

Prep time: 5 minutes | Cook time: 10 to 12 minutes | Serves 4

1 cup flour
4 eggs
Salt, to taste
2 cups bread crumbs
1 teaspoon Italian seasoning

2 eggplants, sliced
2 garlic cloves, sliced
2 tablespoons chopped parsley
Cooking spray

1. Preheat the air fryer to 390ºF (199ºC). Spritz the air fryer basket with cooking spray. 2. On a plate, place the flour. In a shallow bowl, whisk the eggs with salt. In another shallow bowl, combine the bread crumbs and Italian seasoning. 3. Dredge the eggplant slices, one at a time, in the flour, then in the whisked eggs, finally in the bread crumb mixture to coat well. 4. Arrange the coated eggplant slices in the air fryer basket and air fry for 10 to 12 minutes until golden brown and crispy. Flip the eggplant slices halfway through the cooking time. 5. Transfer the eggplant slices to a plate and sprinkle the garlic and parsley on top before serving.

Italian Baked Egg and Veggies

Prep time: 10 minutes | Cook time: 10 minutes | Serves 2

2 tablespoons salted butter
1 small zucchini, sliced
lengthwise and quartered
½ medium green bell pepper,
seeded and diced
1 cup fresh spinach, chopped

1 medium Roma tomato, diced
2 large eggs
¼ teaspoon onion powder
¼ teaspoon garlic powder
½ teaspoon dried basil
¼ teaspoon dried oregano

1. Grease two ramekins with 1 tablespoon butter each. 2. In a large bowl, toss zucchini, bell pepper, spinach, and tomatoes. Divide the mixture in two and place half in each ramekin. 3. Crack an egg on top of each ramekin and sprinkle with onion powder, garlic powder, basil, and oregano. Place into the air fryer basket. 4. Adjust the temperature to 330ºF (166ºC) and bake for 10 minutes. 5. Serve immediately.

Teriyaki Cauliflower

Prep time: 5 minutes | Cook time: 14 minutes | Serves 4

½ cup soy sauce
⅓ cup water
1 tablespoon brown sugar
1 teaspoon sesame oil
1 teaspoon cornstarch

2 cloves garlic, chopped
½ teaspoon chili powder
1 big cauliflower head, cut into
florets

1. Preheat the air fryer to 340ºF (171ºC). 2. Make the teriyaki sauce: In a small bowl, whisk together the soy sauce, water, brown sugar, sesame oil, cornstarch, garlic, and chili powder until well combined. 3. Place the cauliflower florets in a large bowl and drizzle the top with the prepared teriyaki sauce and toss to coat well. 4. Put the cauliflower florets in the air fryer basket and air fry for 14 minutes, shaking the basket halfway through, or until the cauliflower is crisp-tender. 5. Let the cauliflower cool for 5 minutes before serving.

Cauliflower Steak with Gremolata

Prep time: 15 minutes | Cook time: 25 minutes | Serves 4

2 tablespoons olive oil
1 tablespoon Italian seasoning
1 large head cauliflower, outer
leaves removed and sliced
lengthwise through the core
into thick "steaks"
Salt and freshly ground black
pepper, to taste
¼ cup Parmesan cheese

Gremolata:
1 bunch Italian parsley (about 1
cup packed)
2 cloves garlic
Zest of 1 small lemon, plus 1 to
2 teaspoons lemon juice
½ cup olive oil
Salt and pepper, to taste

1. Preheat the air fryer to 400ºF (204ºC). 2. In a small bowl, combine the olive oil and Italian seasoning. Brush both sides of each cauliflower "steak" generously with the oil. Season to taste with salt and black pepper. 3. Working in batches if necessary, arrange the cauliflower in a single layer in the air fryer basket. Pausing halfway through the cooking time to turn the "steaks," air fry for 15 to 20 minutes until the cauliflower is tender and the edges begin to brown. Sprinkle with the Parmesan and air fry for 5 minutes longer. 4. To make the gremolata: In a food processor fitted with a metal blade, combine the parsley, garlic, and lemon zest and juice. With the motor running, add the olive oil in a steady stream until the mixture forms a bright green sauce. Season to taste with salt and black pepper. Serve the cauliflower steaks with the gremolata spooned over the top.

Roasted Spaghetti Squash

Prep time: 10 minutes | Cook time: 45 minutes | Serves 6

1 (4-pound / 1.8-kg) spaghetti
squash, halved and seeded
2 tablespoons coconut oil
4 tablespoons salted butter,

melted
1 teaspoon garlic powder
2 teaspoons dried parsley

1. Brush shell of spaghetti squash with coconut oil. Brush inside with butter. Sprinkle inside with garlic powder and parsley. 2. Place squash skin side down into ungreased air fryer basket, working in batches if needed. Adjust the temperature to 350ºF (177ºC) and set the timer for 30 minutes. When the timer beeps, flip squash and cook an additional 15 minutes until fork-tender. 3. Use a fork to remove spaghetti strands from shell and serve warm.

Eggplant and Zucchini Bites

Prep time: 30 minutes | Cook time: 30 minutes | Serves 8

2 teaspoons fresh mint leaves,
chopped
1½ teaspoons red pepper chili
flakes
2 tablespoons melted butter

1 pound (454 g) eggplant,
peeled and cubed
1 pound (454 g) zucchini,
peeled and cubed
3 tablespoons olive oil

1. Toss all the above ingredients in a large-sized mixing dish. 2. Roast the eggplant and zucchini bites for 30 minutes at 325ºF (163ºC) in your air fryer, turning once or twice. 3. Serve with a homemade dipping sauce.

Roasted Vegetables with Rice

Prep time: 5 minutes | Cook time: 12 minutes | Serves 4

2 teaspoons melted butter
1 cup chopped mushrooms
1 cup cooked rice
1 cup peas
1 carrot, chopped

1 red onion, chopped
1 garlic clove, minced
Salt and black pepper, to taste
2 hard-boiled eggs, grated
1 tablespoon soy sauce

1. Preheat the air fryer to 380ºF (193ºC). Coat a baking dish with melted butter. 2. Stir together the mushrooms, cooked rice, peas, carrot, onion, garlic, salt, and pepper in a large bowl until well mixed. 3. Pour the mixture into the prepared baking dish and transfer to the air fryer basket. 4. Roast in the preheated air fryer for 12 minutes until the vegetables are tender. 5. Divide the mixture among four plates. Serve warm with a sprinkle of grated eggs and a drizzle of soy sauce.

Broccoli Crust Pizza

Prep time: 15 minutes | Cook time: 12 minutes | Serves 4

3 cups riced broccoli, steamed and drained well
1 large egg
½ cup grated vegetarian Parmesan cheese

3 tablespoons low-carb Alfredo sauce
½ cup shredded Mozzarella cheese

1. In a large bowl, mix broccoli, egg, and Parmesan. 2. Cut a piece of parchment to fit your air fryer basket. Press out the pizza mixture to fit on the parchment, working in two batches if necessary. Place into the air fryer basket. 3. Adjust the temperature to 370ºF (188ºC) and air fry for 5 minutes. 4. The crust should be firm enough to flip. If not, add 2 additional minutes. Flip crust. 5. Top with Alfredo sauce and Mozzarella. Return to the air fryer basket and cook an additional 7 minutes or until cheese is golden and bubbling. Serve warm.

Fried Root Vegetable Medley with Thyme

Prep time: 10 minutes | Cook time: 22 minutes | Serves 4

2 carrots, sliced
2 potatoes, cut into chunks
1 rutabaga, cut into chunks
1 turnip, cut into chunks
1 beet, cut into chunks
8 shallots, halved

2 tablespoons olive oil
Salt and black pepper, to taste
2 tablespoons tomato pesto
2 tablespoons water
2 tablespoons chopped fresh thyme

1. Preheat the air fryer to 400ºF (204ºC). 2. Toss the carrots, potatoes, rutabaga, turnip, beet, shallots, olive oil, salt, and pepper in a large mixing bowl until the root vegetables are evenly coated. 3. Place the root vegetables in the air fryer basket and air fry for 12 minutes. Shake the basket and air fry for another 10 minutes until they are cooked to your preferred doneness. 4. Meanwhile, in a small bowl, whisk together the tomato pesto and water until smooth. 5. When ready, remove the root vegetables from the basket to a platter. Drizzle with the tomato pesto mixture and sprinkle with the thyme. Serve immediately.

Baked Turnip and Zucchini

Prep time: 5 minutes | Cook time: 15 to 20 minutes | Serves 4

3 turnips, sliced
1 large zucchini, sliced
1 large red onion, cut into rings

2 cloves garlic, crushed
1 tablespoon olive oil
Salt and black pepper, to taste

1. Preheat the air fryer to 330ºF (166ºC). 2. Put the turnips, zucchini, red onion, and garlic in a baking pan. Drizzle the olive oil over the top and sprinkle with the salt and pepper. 3. Place the baking pan in the preheated air fryer and bake for 15 to 20 minutes, or until the vegetables are tender. 4. Remove from the basket and serve on a plate.

Zucchini-Ricotta Tart

Prep time: 15 minutes | Cook time: 60 minutes | Serves 6

½ cup grated Parmesan cheese, divided
1½ cups almond flour
1 tablespoon coconut flour
½ teaspoon garlic powder
¾ teaspoon salt, divided
¼ cup unsalted butter, melted

1 zucchini, thinly sliced (about 2 cups)
1 cup ricotta cheese
3 eggs
2 tablespoons heavy cream
2 cloves garlic, minced
½ teaspoon dried tarragon

1. Preheat the air fryer to 330ºF (166ºC). Coat a round pan with olive oil and set aside. 2. In a large bowl, whisk ¼ cup of the Parmesan with the almond flour, coconut flour, garlic powder, and ¼ teaspoon of the salt. Stir in the melted butter until the dough resembles coarse crumbs. Press the dough firmly into the bottom and up the sides of the prepared pan. Air fry for 12 to 15 minutes until the crust begins to brown. Let cool to room temperature. 3. Meanwhile, place the zucchini in a colander and sprinkle with the remaining ½ teaspoon salt. Toss gently to distribute the salt and let sit for 30 minutes. Use paper towels to pat the zucchini dry. 4. In a large bowl, whisk together the ricotta, eggs, heavy cream, garlic, and tarragon. Gently stir in the zucchini slices. Pour the cheese mixture into the cooled crust and sprinkle with the remaining ¼ cup Parmesan. 5. Increase the air fryer to 350ºF (177ºC). Place the pan in the air fryer basket and air fry for 45 to 50 minutes, or until set and a tester inserted into the center of the tart comes out clean. Serve warm or at room temperature.

Crustless Spinach Cheese Pie

Prep time: 10 minutes | Cook time: 20 minutes | Serves 4

6 large eggs
¼ cup heavy whipping cream
1 cup frozen chopped spinach, drained

1 cup shredded sharp Cheddar cheese
¼ cup diced yellow onion

1. In a medium bowl, whisk eggs and add cream. Add remaining ingredients to bowl. 2. Pour into a round baking dish. Place into the air fryer basket. 3. Adjust the temperature to 320ºF (160ºC) and bake for 20 minutes. 4. Eggs will be firm and slightly browned when cooked. Serve immediately.

Black Bean and Tomato Chili

Prep time: 15 minutes | Cook time: 23 minutes | Serves 6

1 tablespoon olive oil	2 cans diced tomatoes
1 medium onion, diced	2 chipotle peppers, chopped
3 garlic cloves, minced	2 teaspoons cumin
1 cup vegetable broth	2 teaspoons chili powder
3 cans black beans, drained and	1 teaspoon dried oregano
rinsed	½ teaspoon salt

1. Over a medium heat, fry the garlic and onions in the olive oil for 3 minutes. 2. Add the remaining ingredients, stirring constantly and scraping the bottom to prevent sticking. 3. Preheat the air fryer to 400ºF (204ºC). 4. Take a dish and place the mixture inside. Put a sheet of aluminum foil on top. 5. Transfer to the air fryer and bake for 20 minutes. 6. When ready, plate up and serve immediately.

Garlicky Sesame Carrots

Prep time: 5 minutes | Cook time: 16 minutes |
Serves 4 to 6

1 pound (454 g) baby carrots	Freshly ground black pepper, to
1 tablespoon sesame oil	taste
½ teaspoon dried dill	6 cloves garlic, peeled
Pinch salt	3 tablespoons sesame seeds

1. Preheat the air fryer to 380ºF (193ºC). 2. In a medium bowl, drizzle the baby carrots with the sesame oil. Sprinkle with the dill, salt, and pepper and toss to coat well. 3. Place the baby carrots in the air fryer basket and roast for 8 minutes. 4. Remove the basket and stir in the garlic. Return the basket to the air fryer and roast for another 8 minutes, or until the carrots are lightly browned. 5. Serve sprinkled with the sesame seeds.

Garlic White Zucchini Rolls

Prep time: 20 minutes | Cook time: 20 minutes | Serves 4

2 medium zucchini	½ cup full-fat ricotta cheese
2 tablespoons unsalted butter	¼ teaspoon salt
¼ white onion, peeled and	½ teaspoon garlic powder
diced	¼ teaspoon dried oregano
½ teaspoon finely minced	2 cups spinach, chopped
roasted garlic	½ cup sliced baby portobello
¼ cup heavy cream	mushrooms
2 tablespoons vegetable broth	¾ cup shredded Mozzarella
⅛ teaspoon xanthan gum	cheese, divided

1. Using a mandoline or sharp knife, slice zucchini into long strips lengthwise. Place strips between paper towels to absorb moisture. Set aside. 2. In a medium saucepan over medium heat, melt butter. Add onion and sauté until fragrant. Add garlic and sauté 30 seconds. 3. Pour in heavy cream, broth, and xanthan gum. Turn off heat and whisk mixture until it begins to thicken, about 3 minutes. 4. In a medium bowl, add ricotta, salt, garlic powder, and oregano and mix well. Fold in spinach, mushrooms, and ½ cup Mozzarella. 5. Pour half of the sauce into a round baking pan. To assemble the rolls, place two strips of zucchini on a work surface. Spoon 2 tablespoons of ricotta mixture onto the slices and roll up. Place

seam side down on top of sauce. Repeat with remaining ingredients. 6. Pour remaining sauce over the rolls and sprinkle with remaining Mozzarella. Cover with foil and place into the air fryer basket. 7. Adjust the temperature to 350ºF (177ºC) and bake for 20 minutes. 8. In the last 5 minutes, remove the foil to brown the cheese. Serve immediately.

Lush Vegetables Roast

Prep time: 15 minutes | Cook time: 20 minutes | Serves 6

1⅓ cups small parsnips, peeled	1 tablespoon fresh thyme
and cubed	needles
1⅓ cups celery	1 tablespoon olive oil
2 red onions, sliced	Salt and ground black pepper,
1⅓ cups small butternut squash,	to taste
cut in half, deseeded and cubed	

1. Preheat the air fryer to 390ºF (199ºC). 2. Combine the cut vegetables with the thyme, olive oil, salt and pepper. 3. Put the vegetables in the basket and transfer the basket to the air fryer. 4. Roast for 20 minutes, stirring once throughout the roasting time, until the vegetables are nicely browned and cooked through. 5. Serve warm.

Mediterranean Pan Pizza

Prep time: 5 minutes | Cook time: 8 minutes | Serves 2

1 cup shredded Mozzarella	leaves
cheese	2 tablespoons chopped black
¼ medium red bell pepper,	olives
seeded and chopped	2 tablespoons crumbled feta
½ cup chopped fresh spinach	cheese

1. Sprinkle Mozzarella into an ungreased round nonstick baking dish in an even layer. Add remaining ingredients on top. 2. Place dish into air fryer basket. Adjust the temperature to 350ºF (177ºC) and bake for 8 minutes, checking halfway through to avoid burning. Top of pizza will be golden brown and the cheese melted when done. 3. Remove dish from fryer and let cool 5 minutes before slicing and serving.

Crispy Fried Okra with Chili

Prep time: 5 minutes | Cook time: 10 minutes | Serves 4

3 tablespoons sour cream	Salt and black pepper, to taste
2 tablespoons flour	1 pound (454 g) okra, halved
2 tablespoons semolina	Cooking spray
½ teaspoon red chili powder	

1. Preheat the air fryer to 400ºF (204ºC). Spray the air fryer basket with cooking spray. 2. In a shallow bowl, place the sour cream. In another shallow bowl, thoroughly combine the flour, semolina, red chili powder, salt, and pepper. 3. Dredge the okra in the sour cream, then roll in the flour mixture until evenly coated. 4. Arrange the okra in the air fryer basket and air fry for 10 minutes, flipping the okra halfway through, or until golden brown and crispy. 5. Cool for 5 minutes before serving.

Tangy Asparagus and Broccoli

Prep time: 25 minutes | Cook time: 22 minutes | Serves 4

½ pound (227 g) asparagus, cut into 1½-inch pieces
½ pound (227 g) broccoli, cut into 1½-inch pieces
2 tablespoons olive oil

Salt and white pepper, to taste
½ cup vegetable broth
2 tablespoons apple cider vinegar

1. Place the vegetables in a single layer in the lightly greased air fryer basket. Drizzle the olive oil over the vegetables. 2. Sprinkle with salt and white pepper. 3. Cook at 380°F (193°C) for 15 minutes, shaking the basket halfway through the cooking time. 4. Add ½ cup of vegetable broth to a saucepan; bring to a rapid boil and add the vinegar. Cook for 5 to 7 minutes or until the sauce has reduced by half. 5. Spoon the sauce over the warm vegetables and serve immediately. Bon appétit!

Vegetable Burgers

Prep time: 10 minutes | Cook time: 12 minutes | Serves 4

8 ounces (227 g) cremini mushrooms
2 large egg yolks
½ medium zucchini, trimmed and chopped
¼ cup peeled and chopped

yellow onion
1 clove garlic, peeled and finely minced
½ teaspoon salt
¼ teaspoon ground black pepper

1. Place all ingredients into a food processor and pulse twenty times until finely chopped and combined. 2. Separate mixture into four equal sections and press each into a burger shape. Place burgers into ungreased air fryer basket. Adjust the temperature to 375°F (191°C) and air fry for 12 minutes, turning burgers halfway through cooking. Burgers will be browned and firm when done. 3. Place burgers on a large plate and let cool 5 minutes before serving.

Basmati Risotto

Prep time: 10 minutes | Cook time: 30 minutes | Serves 2

1 onion, diced
1 small carrot, diced
2 cups vegetable broth, boiling
½ cup grated Cheddar cheese

1 clove garlic, minced
¾ cup long-grain basmati rice
1 tablespoon olive oil
1 tablespoon unsalted butter

1. Preheat the air fryer to 390°F (199°C). 2. Grease a baking tin with oil and stir in the butter, garlic, carrot, and onion. 3. Put the tin in the air fryer and bake for 4 minutes. 4. Pour in the rice and bake for a further 4 minutes, stirring three times throughout the baking time. 5. Turn the temperature down to 320°F (160°C). 6. Add the vegetable broth and give the dish a gentle stir. Bake for 22 minutes, leaving the air fryer uncovered. 7. Pour in the cheese, stir once more and serve.

Rice and Eggplant Bowl

Prep time: 15 minutes | Cook time: 10 minutes | Serves 4

¼ cup sliced cucumber
1 teaspoon salt
1 tablespoon sugar
7 tablespoons Japanese rice vinegar
3 medium eggplants, sliced
3 tablespoons sweet white miso

paste
1 tablespoon mirin rice wine
4 cups cooked sushi rice
4 spring onions
1 tablespoon toasted sesame seeds

1. Coat the cucumber slices with the rice wine vinegar, salt, and sugar. 2. Put a dish on top of the bowl to weight it down completely. 3. In a bowl, mix the eggplants, mirin rice wine, and miso paste. Allow to marinate for half an hour. 4. Preheat the air fryer to 400°F (204°C). 5. Put the eggplant slices in the air fryer and air fry for 10 minutes. 6. Fill the bottom of a serving bowl with rice and top with the eggplants and pickled cucumbers. 7. Add the spring onions and sesame seeds for garnish. Serve immediately.

Potato and Broccoli with Tofu Scramble

Prep time: 15 minutes | Cook time: 30 minutes | Serves 3

2½ cups chopped red potato
2 tablespoons olive oil, divided
1 block tofu, chopped finely
2 tablespoons tamari
1 teaspoon turmeric powder

½ teaspoon onion powder
½ teaspoon garlic powder
½ cup chopped onion
4 cups broccoli florets

1. Preheat the air fryer to 400°F (204°C). 2. Toss together the potatoes and 1 tablespoon of the olive oil. 3. Air fry the potatoes in a baking dish for 15 minutes, shaking once during the cooking time to ensure they fry evenly. 4. Combine the tofu, the remaining 1 tablespoon of the olive oil, turmeric, onion powder, tamari, and garlic powder together, stirring in the onions, followed by the broccoli. 5. Top the potatoes with the tofu mixture and air fry for an additional 15 minutes. Serve warm.

Gold Ravioli

Prep time: 10 minutes | Cook time: 6 minutes | Serves 4

½ cup panko bread crumbs
2 teaspoons nutritional yeast
1 teaspoon dried basil
1 teaspoon dried oregano
1 teaspoon garlic powder

Salt and ground black pepper, to taste
¼ cup aquafaba
8 ounces (227 g) ravioli
Cooking spray

1. Cover the air fryer basket with aluminum foil and coat with a light brushing of oil. 2. Preheat the air fryer to 400°F (204°C). Combine the panko bread crumbs, nutritional yeast, basil, oregano, and garlic powder. Sprinkle with salt and pepper to taste. 3. Put the aquafaba in a separate bowl. Dip the ravioli in the aquafaba before coating it in the panko mixture. Spritz with cooking spray and transfer to the air fryer. 4. Air fry for 6 minutes. Shake the air fryer basket halfway. 5. Serve hot.

Crispy Eggplant Rounds

Prep time: 15 minutes | Cook time: 10 minutes | Serves 4

1 large eggplant, ends trimmed, cut into ½-inch slices
½ teaspoon salt
2 ounces (57 g) Parmesan 100% cheese crisps, finely ground

½ teaspoon paprika
¼ teaspoon garlic powder
1 large egg

1. Sprinkle eggplant rounds with salt. Place rounds on a kitchen towel for 30 minutes to draw out excess water. Pat rounds dry. 2. In a medium bowl, mix cheese crisps, paprika, and garlic powder. In a separate medium bowl, whisk egg. Dip each eggplant round in egg, then gently press into cheese crisps to coat both sides. 3. Place eggplant rounds into ungreased air fryer basket. Adjust the temperature to 400ºF (204ºC) and air fry for 10 minutes, turning rounds halfway through cooking. Eggplant will be golden and crispy when done. Serve warm.

Chapter 10 Desserts

Chocolate Soufflés

Prep time: 5 minutes | Cook time: 14 minutes | Serves 2

Butter and sugar for greasing the ramekins
3 ounces (85 g) semi-sweet chocolate, chopped
¼ cup unsalted butter
2 eggs, yolks and white separated

3 tablespoons sugar
½ teaspoon pure vanilla extract
2 tablespoons all-purpose flour
Powdered sugar, for dusting the finished soufflés
Heavy cream, for serving

1. Butter and sugar two 6-ounce (170-g) ramekins. (Butter the ramekins and then coat the butter with sugar by shaking it around in the ramekin and dumping out any excess.) 2. Melt the chocolate and butter together, either in the microwave or in a double boiler. In a separate bowl, beat the egg yolks vigorously. Add the sugar and the vanilla extract and beat well again. Drizzle in the chocolate and butter, mixing well. Stir in the flour, combining until there are no lumps. 3. Preheat the air fryer to 330°F (166°C). 4. In a separate bowl, whisk the egg whites to soft peak stage (the point at which the whites can almost stand up on the end of your whisk). Fold the whipped egg whites into the chocolate mixture gently and in stages. 5. Transfer the batter carefully to the buttered ramekins, leaving about ½-inch at the top. (You may have a little extra batter, depending on how airy the batter is, so you might be able to squeeze out a third soufflé if you want to.) Place the ramekins into the air fryer basket and air fry for 14 minutes. The soufflés should have risen nicely and be brown on top. (Don't worry if the top gets a little dark, you'll be covering it with powdered sugar in the next step.) 6. Dust with powdered sugar and serve immediately with heavy cream to pour over the top at the table.

Graham Cracker Cheesecake

Prep time: 10 minutes | Cook time: 20 minutes | Serves 8

1 cup graham cracker crumbs
3 tablespoons butter, at room temperature
1½ (8-ounce / 227-g) packages cream cheese, at room temperature

⅓ cup sugar
2 eggs, beaten
1 tablespoon all-purpose flour
1 teaspoon vanilla extract
¼ cup chocolate syrup

1. In a small bowl, stir together the graham cracker crumbs and butter. Press the crust into the bottom of a 6-by-2-inch round baking pan and freeze to set while you prepare the filling. 2. In a medium bowl, stir together the cream cheese and sugar until mixed well. 3. One at a time, beat in the eggs. Add the flour and vanilla and stir to combine. 4. Transfer ⅔ cup of filling to a small bowl and stir in the chocolate syrup until combined. 5. Insert the crisper plate into the basket and the basket into the unit. Preheat the unit by selecting

BAKE, setting the temperature to 325°F (163°C), and setting the time to 3 minutes. Select START/STOP to begin. 6. Pour the vanilla filling into the pan with the crust. Drop the chocolate filling over the vanilla filling by the spoonful. With a clean butter knife stir the fillings in a zigzag pattern to marbleize them. Do not let the knife touch the crust. 7. Once the unit is preheated, place the pan into the basket. 8. Select BAKE, set the temperature to 325°F (163°C), and set the time to 20 minutes. Select START/STOP to begin. 9. When the cooking is done, the cheesecake should be just set. Cool on a wire rack for 1 hour. Refrigerate the cheesecake until firm before slicing.

S'mores

Prep time: 5 minutes | Cook time: 30 seconds |
Makes 8 s'mores

Oil, for spraying
8 graham cracker squares
2 (1½-ounce / 43-g) chocolate

bars
4 large marshmallows

1. Line the air fryer basket with parchment and spray lightly with oil. 2. Place 4 graham cracker squares in the prepared basket. 3. Break the chocolate bars in half and place 1 piece on top of each graham cracker. Top with 1 marshmallow. 4. Air fry at 370°F (188°C) for 30 seconds, or until the marshmallows are puffed and golden brown and slightly melted. 5. Top with the remaining graham cracker squares and serve.

Double Chocolate Brownies

Prep time: 5 minutes | Cook time: 15 to 20 minutes |
Serves 8

1 cup almond flour
½ cup unsweetened cocoa powder
½ teaspoon baking powder
⅓ cup Swerve
¼ teaspoon salt

½ cup unsalted butter, melted and cooled
3 eggs
1 teaspoon vanilla extract
2 tablespoons mini semisweet chocolate chips

1. Preheat the air fryer to 350°F (177°C). Line a cake pan with parchment paper and brush with oil. 2. In a large bowl, combine the almond flour, cocoa powder, baking powder, Swerve, and salt. Add the butter, eggs, and vanilla. Stir until thoroughly combined. (The batter will be thick.) Spread the batter into the prepared pan and scatter the chocolate chips on top. 3. Air fry for 15 to 20 minutes until the edges are set. (The center should still appear slightly undercooked.) Let cool completely before slicing. To store, cover and refrigerate the brownies for up to 3 days.

Pecan Butter Cookies

Prep time: 5 minutes | Cook time: 24 minutes |
Makes 12 cookies

1 cup chopped pecans
½ cup salted butter, melted
½ cup coconut flour

¾ cup erythritol, divided
1 teaspoon vanilla extract

1. In a food processor, blend together pecans, butter, flour, ½ cup erythritol, and vanilla 1 minute until a dough forms. 2. Form dough into twelve individual cookie balls, about 1 tablespoon each. 3. Cut three pieces of parchment to fit air fryer basket. Place four cookies on each ungreased parchment and place one piece parchment with cookies into air fryer basket. Adjust air fryer temperature to 325ºF (163ºC) and set the timer for 8 minutes. Repeat cooking with remaining batches. 4. When the timer goes off, allow cookies to cool 5 minutes on a large serving plate until cool enough to handle. While still warm, dust cookies with remaining erythritol. Allow to cool completely, about 15 minutes, before serving.

Apple Wedges with Apricots

Prep time: 5 minutes | Cook time: 15 to 18 minutes |
Serves 4

4 large apples, peeled and sliced into 8 wedges
2 tablespoons olive oil

½ cup dried apricots, chopped
1 to 2 tablespoons sugar
½ teaspoon ground cinnamon

1. Preheat the air fryer to 350ºF (180ºC). 2. Toss the apple wedges with the olive oil in a mixing bowl until well coated. 3. Place the apple wedges in the air fryer basket and air fry for 12 to 15 minutes. 4. Sprinkle with the dried apricots and air fry for another 3 minutes. 5. Meanwhile, thoroughly combine the sugar and cinnamon in a small bowl. 6. Remove the apple wedges from the basket to a plate. Serve sprinkled with the sugar mixture.

Hazelnut Butter Cookies

Prep time: 30 minutes | Cook time: 20 minutes |
Serves 10

4 tablespoons liquid monk fruit
½ cup hazelnuts, ground
1 stick butter, room temperature
2 cups almond flour

1 cup coconut flour
2 ounces (57 g) granulated Swerve
2 teaspoons ground cinnamon

1. Firstly, cream liquid monk fruit with butter until the mixture becomes fluffy. Sift in both types of flour. 2. Now, stir in the hazelnuts. Now, knead the mixture to form a dough; place in the refrigerator for about 35 minutes. 3. To finish, shape the prepared dough into the bite-sized balls; arrange them on a baking dish; flatten the balls using the back of a spoon. 4. Mix granulated Swerve with ground cinnamon. Press your cookies in the cinnamon mixture until they are completely covered. 5. Bake the cookies for 20 minutes at 310ºF (154ºC). 6. Leave them to cool for about 10 minutes before transferring them to a wire rack. Bon appétit!

Cardamom Custard

Prep time: 10 minutes | Cook time: 25 minutes | Serves 2

1 cup whole milk
1 large egg
2 tablespoons plus 1 teaspoon sugar

¼ teaspoon vanilla bean paste or pure vanilla extract
¼ teaspoon ground cardamom, plus more for sprinkling

1. In a medium bowl, beat together the milk, egg, sugar, vanilla, and cardamom. 2. Place two 8-ounce (227-g) ramekins in the air fryer basket. Divide the mixture between the ramekins. Sprinkle lightly with cardamom. Cover each ramekin tightly with aluminum foil. Set the air fryer to 350ºF (177ºC) for 25 minutes, or until a toothpick inserted in the center comes out clean. 3. Let the custards cool on a wire rack for 5 to 10 minutes. 4. Serve warm, or refrigerate until cold and serve chilled.

Pumpkin Spice Pecans

Prep time: 5 minutes | Cook time: 6 minutes | Serves 4

1 cup whole pecans
¼ cup granular erythritol
1 large egg white

½ teaspoon ground cinnamon
½ teaspoon pumpkin pie spice
½ teaspoon vanilla extract

1. Toss all ingredients in a large bowl until pecans are coated. Place into the air fryer basket. 2. Adjust the temperature to 300ºF (149ºC) and air fry for 6 minutes. 3. Toss two to three times during cooking. 4. Allow to cool completely. Store in an airtight container up to 3 days.

Rhubarb and Strawberry Crumble

Prep time: 10 minutes | Cook time: 12 to 17 minutes
| Serves 6

1½ cups sliced fresh strawberries
¾ cup sliced rhubarb
⅓ cup granulated sugar
⅔ cup quick-cooking oatmeal
½ cup whole-wheat pastry flour,

or all-purpose flour
¼ cup packed light brown sugar
½ teaspoon ground cinnamon
3 tablespoons unsalted butter, melted

1. Insert the crisper plate into the basket and the basket into the unit. Preheat the unit by selecting BAKE, setting the temperature to 375ºF (191ºC), and setting the time to 3 minutes. Select START/STOP to begin. 2. In a 6-by-2-inch round metal baking pan, combine the strawberries, rhubarb, and granulated sugar. 3. In a medium bowl, stir together the oatmeal, flour, brown sugar, and cinnamon. Stir the melted butter into this mixture until crumbly. Sprinkle the crumble mixture over the fruit. 4. Once the unit is preheated, place the pan into the basket. 5. Select BAKE, set the temperature to 375ºF (191ºC), and set the time to 17 minutes. Select START/STOP to begin. 6. After about 12 minutes, check the crumble. If the fruit is bubbling and the topping is golden brown, it is done. If not, resume cooking. 7. When the cooking is complete, serve warm.

Cherry Pie

Prep time: 15 minutes | Cook time: 35 minutes | Serves 6

All-purpose flour, for dusting	cherry pie filling
2 refrigerated piecrusts, at room temperature	1 egg
1 (12.5-ounce / 354-g) can	1 tablespoon water
	1 tablespoon sugar

1. Dust a work surface with flour and place the piecrust on it. Roll out the piecrust. Invert a shallow air fryer baking pan, or your own pie pan that fits inside the air fryer basket, on top of the dough. Trim the dough around the pan, making your cut ½ inch wider than the pan itself. 2. Repeat with the second piecrust but make the cut the same size as or slightly smaller than the pan. 3. Put the larger crust in the bottom of the baking pan. Don't stretch the dough. Gently press it into the pan. 4. Spoon in enough cherry pie filling to fill the crust. Do not overfill. 5. Using a knife or pizza cutter, cut the second piecrust into 1-inch-wide strips. Weave the strips in a lattice pattern over the top of the cherry pie filling. 6. Insert the crisper plate into the basket and the basket into the unit. Preheat the unit by selecting BAKE, setting the temperature to 325ºF (163ºC), and setting the time to 3 minutes. Select START/STOP to begin. 7. In a small bowl, whisk the egg and water. Gently brush the egg wash over the top of the pie. Sprinkle with the sugar and cover the pie with aluminum foil. 8. Once the unit is preheated, place the pie into the basket. 9. Select BAKE, set the temperature to 325ºF (163ºC), and set the time to 35 minutes. Select START/STOP to begin. 10. After 30 minutes, remove the foil and resume cooking for 3 to 5 minutes more. The finished pie should have a flaky golden brown crust and bubbling pie filling. 11. When the cooking is complete, serve warm. Refrigerate leftovers for a few days.

Pumpkin-Spice Bread Pudding

Prep time: 15 minutes | Cook time: 35 minutes | Serves 6

Bread Pudding:	baguette or crusty country bread
¾ cup heavy whipping cream	4 tablespoons (½ stick) unsalted
½ cup canned pumpkin	butter, melted
⅓ cup whole milk	Sauce:
⅓ cup sugar	⅓ cup pure maple syrup
1 large egg plus 1 yolk	1 tablespoon unsalted butter
½ teaspoon pumpkin pie spice	½ cup heavy whipping cream
⅛ teaspoon kosher salt	½ teaspoon pure vanilla extract
4 cups 1-inch cubed day-old	

1. For the bread pudding: In a medium bowl, combine the cream, pumpkin, milk, sugar, egg and yolk, pumpkin pie spice, and salt. Whisk until well combined. 2. In a large bowl, toss the bread cubes with the melted butter. Add the pumpkin mixture and gently toss until the ingredients are well combined. 3. Transfer the mixture to a baking pan. Place the pan in the air fryer basket. Set the fryer to 350ºF (177ºC) for 35 minutes, or until custard is set in the middle. 4. Meanwhile, for the sauce: In a small saucepan, combine the syrup and butter. Heat over medium heat, stirring, until the butter melts. Stir in the cream and simmer, stirring often, until the sauce has thickened, about 15 minutes. Stir in the vanilla. Remove the pudding from the air fryer. 5. Let the pudding stand for 10 minutes before serving with the warm sauce.

Vanilla and Cardamon Walnuts Tart

Prep time: 5 minutes | Cook time: 13 minutes | Serves 6

1 cup coconut milk	2 eggs
½ cup walnuts, ground	1 teaspoon vanilla essence
½ cup Swerve	¼ teaspoon ground cardamom
½ cup almond flour	¼ teaspoon ground cloves
½ stick butter, at room temperature	Cooking spray

1. Preheat the air fryer to 360ºF (182ºC). Coat a baking pan with cooking spray. 2. Combine all the ingredients except the oil in a large bowl and stir until well blended. Spoon the batter mixture into the baking pan. 3. Bake in the preheated air fryer for approximately 13 minutes. Check the tart for doneness: If a toothpick inserted into the center of the tart comes out clean, it's done. 4. Remove from the air fryer and place on a wire rack to cool. Serve immediately.

White Chocolate Cookies

Prep time: 5 minutes | Cook time: 11 minutes | Serves 10

8 ounces (227 g) unsweetened white chocolate	¾ cup granulated Swerve
2 eggs, well beaten	2 tablespoons coconut oil
¾ cup butter, at room temperature	⅓ teaspoon grated nutmeg
1⅔ cups almond flour	⅓ teaspoon ground allspice
½ cup coconut flour	⅓ teaspoon ground anise star
	¼ teaspoon fine sea salt

1. Preheat the air fryer to 350ºF (177ºC). Line the air fryer basket with parchment paper. 2. Combine all the ingredients in a mixing bowl and knead for about 3 to 4 minutes, or until a soft dough forms. Transfer to the refrigerator to chill for 20 minutes. 3. Make the cookies: Roll the dough into 1-inch balls and transfer to parchment-lined basket, spacing 2 inches apart. Flatten each with the back of a spoon. 4. Bake for about 11 minutes until the cookies are golden and firm to the touch. 5. Transfer to a wire rack and let the cookies cool completely. Serve immediately.

Almond-Roasted Pears

Prep time: 10 minutes | Cook time: 15 to 20 minutes | Serves 4

Yogurt Topping:	2 whole pears
1 container vanilla Greek yogurt (5 to 6 ounces / 142 to 170 g)	¼ cup crushed Biscoff cookies (approx. 4 cookies)
¼ teaspoon almond flavoring	1 tablespoon sliced almonds
	1 tablespoon butter

1. Stir almond flavoring into yogurt and set aside while preparing pears. 2. Halve each pear and spoon out the core. 3. Place pear halves in air fryer basket. 4. Stir together the cookie crumbs and almonds. Place a quarter of this mixture into the hollow of each pear half. 5. Cut butter into 4 pieces and place one piece on top of crumb mixture in each pear. 6. Roast at 360ºF (182ºC) for 15 to 20 minutes or until pears have cooked through but are still slightly firm. 7. Serve pears warm with a dollop of yogurt topping.

Coconut-Custard Pie

Prep time: 10 minutes | Cook time: 20 to 23 minutes | Serves 4

1 cup milk

¼ cup plus 2 tablespoons sugar

¼ cup biscuit baking mix

1 teaspoon vanilla

2 eggs

2 tablespoons melted butter

Cooking spray

½ cup shredded, sweetened coconut

1. Place all ingredients except coconut in a medium bowl. 2. Using a hand mixer, beat on high speed for 3 minutes. 3. Let sit for 5 minutes. 4. Preheat the air fryer to 330°F (166°C). 5. Spray a baking pan with cooking spray and place pan in air fryer basket. 6. Pour filling into pan and sprinkle coconut over top. 7. Cook pie at 330°F (166°C) for 20 to 23 minutes or until center sets.

Mini Cheesecake

Prep time: 10 minutes | Cook time: 15 minutes | Serves 2

½ cup walnuts

2 tablespoons salted butter

2 tablespoons granular erythritol

4 ounces (113 g) full-fat cream

cheese, softened

1 large egg

½ teaspoon vanilla extract

⅛ cup powdered erythritol

1. Place walnuts, butter, and granular erythritol in a food processor. Pulse until ingredients stick together and a dough forms. 2. Press dough into a springform pan then place the pan into the air fryer basket. 3. Adjust the temperature to 400°F (204°C) and bake for 5 minutes. 4. When done, remove the crust and let cool. 5. In a medium bowl, mix cream cheese with egg, vanilla extract, and powdered erythritol until smooth. 6. Spoon mixture on top of baked walnut crust and place into the air fryer basket. 7. Adjust the temperature to 300°F (149°C) and bake for 10 minutes. 8. Once done, chill for 2 hours before serving.

Molten Chocolate Almond Cakes

Prep time: 5 minutes | Cook time: 13 minutes | Serves 3

Butter and flour for the ramekins

4 ounces (113 g) bittersweet chocolate, chopped

½ cup (1 stick) unsalted butter

2 eggs

2 egg yolks

¼ cup sugar

½ teaspoon pure vanilla extract,

or almond extract

1 tablespoon all-purpose flour

3 tablespoons ground almonds

8 to 12 semisweet chocolate discs (or 4 chunks of chocolate)

Cocoa powder or powdered sugar, for dusting

Toasted almonds, coarsely chopped

1. Butter and flour three (6-ounce / 170-g) ramekins. (Butter the ramekins and then coat the butter with flour by shaking it around in the ramekin and dumping out any excess.) 2. Melt the chocolate and butter together, either in the microwave or in a double boiler. In a separate bowl, beat the eggs, egg yolks and sugar together until light and smooth. Add the vanilla extract. Whisk the chocolate mixture into the egg mixture. Stir in the flour and ground almonds.

3. Preheat the air fryer to 330°F (166°C). 4. Transfer the batter carefully to the buttered ramekins, filling halfway. Place two or three chocolate discs in the center of the batter and then fill the ramekins to ½-inch below the top with the remaining batter. Place the ramekins into the air fryer basket and air fry at 330°F (166°C) for 13 minutes. The sides of the cake should be set, but the centers should be slightly soft. Remove the ramekins from the air fryer and let the cakes sit for 5 minutes. (If you'd like the cake a little less molten, air fry for 14 minutes and let the cakes sit for 4 minutes.) 5. Run a butter knife around the edge of the ramekins and invert the cakes onto a plate. Lift the ramekin off the plate slowly and carefully so that the cake doesn't break. Dust with cocoa powder or powdered sugar and serve with a scoop of ice cream and some coarsely chopped toasted almonds.

Pecan Brownies

Prep time: 10 minutes | Cook time: 20 minutes | Serves 6

½ cup blanched finely ground almond flour

½ cup powdered erythritol

2 tablespoons unsweetened cocoa powder

½ teaspoon baking powder

¼ cup unsalted butter, softened

1 large egg

¼ cup chopped pecans

¼ cup low-carb, sugar-free chocolate chips

1. In a large bowl, mix almond flour, erythritol, cocoa powder, and baking powder. Stir in butter and egg. 2. Fold in pecans and chocolate chips. Scoop mixture into a round baking pan. Place pan into the air fryer basket. 3. Adjust the temperature to 300°F (149°C) and bake for 20 minutes. 4. When fully cooked a toothpick inserted in center will come out clean. Allow 20 minutes to fully cool and firm up.

Pears with Honey-Lemon Ricotta

Prep time: 10 minutes | Cook time: 8 minutes | Serves 4

2 large Bartlett pears

3 tablespoons butter, melted

3 tablespoons brown sugar

½ teaspoon ground ginger

¼ teaspoon ground cardamom

½ cup whole-milk ricotta

cheese

1 tablespoon honey, plus additional for drizzling

1 teaspoon pure almond extract

1 teaspoon pure lemon extract

1. Peel each pear and cut in half lengthwise. Use a melon baller to scoop out the core. Place the pear halves in a medium bowl, add the melted butter, and toss. Add the brown sugar, ginger, and cardamom; toss to coat. 2. Place the pear halves, cut side down, in the air fryer basket. Set the air fryer to 375°F (191°C) for 8 to 10 minutes, or until the pears are lightly browned and tender, but not mushy. 3. Meanwhile, in a medium bowl, combine the ricotta, honey, and almond and lemon extracts. Beat with an electric mixer on medium speed until the mixture is light and fluffy, about 1 minute. 4. To serve, divide the ricotta mixture among four small shallow bowls. Place a pear half, cut side up, on top of the cheese. Drizzle with additional honey and serve.

Chocolate Bread Pudding

Prep time: 10 minutes | Cook time: 10 to 12 minutes | Serves 4

Nonstick flour-infused baking spray	2 tablespoons cocoa powder
1 egg	3 tablespoons light brown sugar
1 egg yolk	3 tablespoons peanut butter
¾ cup chocolate milk	1 teaspoon vanilla extract
	5 slices firm white bread, cubed

1. Spray a 6-by-2-inch round baking pan with the baking spray. Set aside. 2. In a medium bowl, whisk the egg, egg yolk, chocolate milk, cocoa powder, brown sugar, peanut butter, and vanilla until thoroughly combined. Stir in the bread cubes and let soak for 10 minutes. Spoon this mixture into the prepared pan. 3. Insert the crisper plate into the basket and the basket into the unit. Preheat the unit by selecting BAKE, setting the temperature to 325°F (163°C), and setting the time to 3 minutes. Select START/STOP to begin. 4. Once the unit is preheated, place the pan into the basket. Select BAKE, set the temperature to 325°F (163°C), and set the time to 12 minutes. Select START/STOP to begin. 5. Check the pudding after about 10 minutes. It is done when it is firm to the touch. If not, resume cooking. 6. When the cooking is complete, let the pudding cool for 5 minutes. Serve warm.

Mixed Berry Hand Pies

Prep time: 5 minutes | Cook time: 30 minutes | Serves 4

¾ cup sugar	1 teaspoon water
½ teaspoon ground cinnamon	1 package refrigerated pie
1 tablespoon cornstarch	dough (or your own homemade
1 cup blueberries	pie dough)
1 cup blackberries	1 egg, beaten
1 cup raspberries, divided	

1. Combine the sugar, cinnamon, and cornstarch in a small saucepan. Add the blueberries, blackberries, and ½ cup of the raspberries. Toss the berries gently to coat them evenly. Add the teaspoon of water to the saucepan and turn the stovetop on to medium-high heat, stirring occasionally. Once the berries break down, release their juice and start to simmer (about 5 minutes), simmer for another couple of minutes and then transfer the mixture to a bowl, stir in the remaining ½ cup of raspberries and let it cool. 2. Preheat the air fryer to 370°F (188°C). 3. Cut the pie dough into four 5-inch circles and four 6-inch circles. 4. Spread the 6-inch circles on a flat surface. Divide the berry filling between all four circles. Brush the perimeter of the dough circles with a little water. Place the 5-inch circles on top of the filling and press the perimeter of the dough circles together to seal. Roll the edges of the bottom circle up over the top circle to make a crust around the filling. Press a fork around the crust to make decorative indentations and to seal the crust shut. Brush the pies with egg wash and sprinkle a little sugar on top. Poke a small hole in the center of each pie with a paring knife to vent the dough. 5. Air fry two pies at a time. Brush or spray the air fryer basket with oil and place the pies into the basket. Air fry for 9 minutes. Turn the pies over and air fry for another 6 minutes. Serve warm or at room temperature.

Blackberry Cobbler

Prep time: 15 minutes | Cook time: 25 to 30 minutes | Serves 6

3 cups fresh or frozen blackberries	8 tablespoons (1 stick) butter, melted
1¾ cups sugar, divided	1 cup self-rising flour
1 teaspoon vanilla extract	1 to 2 tablespoons oil

1. In a medium bowl, stir together the blackberries, 1 cup of sugar, and vanilla. 2. In another medium bowl, stir together the melted butter, remaining ¾ cup of sugar, and flour until a dough forms. 3. Spritz a baking pan with oil. Add the blackberry mixture. Crumble the flour mixture over the fruit. Cover the pan with aluminum foil. 4. Preheat the air fryer to 350°F (177°C). 5. Place the covered pan in the air fryer basket. Cook for 20 to 25 minutes until the filling is thickened. 6. Uncover the pan and cook for 5 minutes more, depending on how juicy and browned you like your cobbler. Let sit for 5 minutes before serving.

Bourbon Bread Pudding

Prep time: 10 minutes | Cook time: 20 minutes | Serves 4

3 slices whole grain bread, cubed	½ teaspoons vanilla extract
1 large egg	¼ cup maple syrup, divided
1 cup whole milk	½ teaspoons ground cinnamon
2 tablespoons bourbon	2 teaspoons sparkling sugar

1. Preheat the air fryer to 270°F (132°C). 2. Spray a baking pan with nonstick cooking spray, then place the bread cubes in the pan. 3. In a medium bowl, whisk together the egg, milk, bourbon, vanilla extract, 3 tablespoons of maple syrup, and cinnamon. Pour the egg mixture over the bread and press down with a spatula to coat all the bread, then sprinkle the sparkling sugar on top and bake for 20 minutes. 4. Remove the pudding from the air fryer and allow to cool in the pan on a wire rack for 10 minutes. Drizzle the remaining 1 tablespoon of maple syrup on top. Slice and serve warm.

Zucchini Bread

Prep time: 10 minutes | Cook time: 40 minutes | Serves 12

2 cups coconut flour	1 teaspoon vanilla extract
2 teaspoons baking powder	3 eggs, beaten
¾ cup erythritol	1 zucchini, grated
½ cup coconut oil, melted	1 teaspoon ground cinnamon
1 teaspoon apple cider vinegar	

1. In the mixing bowl, mix coconut flour with baking powder, erythritol, coconut oil, apple cider vinegar, vanilla extract, eggs, zucchini, and ground cinnamon. 2. Transfer the mixture into the air fryer basket and flatten it in the shape of the bread. 3. Cook the bread at 350°F (177°C) for 40 minutes.

Protein Powder Doughnut Holes

Prep time: 25 minutes | Cook time: 6 minutes |
Makes 12 holes

½ cup blanched finely ground almond flour	½ teaspoon baking powder
½ cup low-carb vanilla protein powder	1 large egg
	5 tablespoons unsalted butter, melted
½ cup granular erythritol	½ teaspoon vanilla extract

1. Mix all ingredients in a large bowl. Place into the freezer for 20 minutes. 2. Wet your hands with water and roll the dough into twelve balls. 3. Cut a piece of parchment to fit your air fryer basket. Working in batches as necessary, place doughnut holes into the air fryer basket on top of parchment. 4. Adjust the temperature to 380°F (193°C) and air fry for 6 minutes. 5. Flip doughnut holes halfway through the cooking time. 6. Let cool completely before serving.

Mixed Berries with Pecan Streusel Topping

Prep time: 5 minutes | Cook time: 17 minutes | Serves 3

½ cup mixed berries	2 tablespoons chopped walnuts
Cooking spray	3 tablespoons granulated Swerve
Topping:	
1 egg, beaten	2 tablespoons cold salted butter, cut into pieces
3 tablespoons almonds, slivered	
3 tablespoons chopped pecans	½ teaspoon ground cinnamon

1. Preheat the air fryer to 340°F (171°C). Lightly spray a baking dish with cooking spray. 2. Make the topping: In a medium bowl, stir together the beaten egg, nuts, Swerve, butter, and cinnamon until well blended. 3. Put the mixed berries in the bottom of the baking dish and spread the topping over the top. 4. Bake in the preheated air fryer for 17 minutes, or until the fruit is bubbly and topping is golden brown. 5. Allow to cool for 5 to 10 minutes before serving.

Pumpkin Cookie with Cream Cheese Frosting

Prep time: 10 minutes | Cook time: 7 minutes | Serves 6

½ cup blanched finely ground almond flour	½ teaspoon pumpkin pie spice
½ cup powdered erythritol, divided	2 tablespoons pure pumpkin purée
2 tablespoons butter, softened	½ teaspoon ground cinnamon, divided
1 large egg	¼ cup low-carb, sugar-free chocolate chips
½ teaspoon unflavored gelatin	
½ teaspoon baking powder	3 ounces (85 g) full-fat cream cheese, softened
½ teaspoon vanilla extract	

1. In a large bowl, mix almond flour and ¼ cup erythritol. Stir in butter, egg, and gelatin until combined. 2. Stir in baking powder, vanilla, pumpkin pie spice, pumpkin purée, and ¼ teaspoon cinnamon, then fold in chocolate chips. 3. Pour batter into a round baking pan. Place pan into the air fryer basket. 4. Adjust the temperature to 300°F (149°C) and bake for 7 minutes. 5. When fully cooked, the top will be golden brown and a toothpick inserted in center will come out clean. Let cool at least 20 minutes. 6. To make the frosting: mix cream cheese, remaining ¼ teaspoon cinnamon, and remaining ¼ cup erythritol in a large bowl. Using an electric mixer, beat until it becomes fluffy. Spread onto the cooled cookie. Garnish with additional cinnamon if desired.

Old-Fashioned Fudge Pie

Prep time: 15 minutes | Cook time: 25 to 30 minutes | Serves 8

1½ cups sugar	butter, melted
⅓ cup unsweetened cocoa powder	1½ teaspoons vanilla extract
½ cup self-rising flour	1 (9-inch) unbaked piecrust
3 large eggs, unbeaten	¼ cup confectioners' sugar (optional)
12 tablespoons (1½ sticks)	

1. In a medium bowl, stir together the sugar, cocoa powder, and flour. Stir in the eggs and melted butter. Stir in the vanilla. 2. Preheat the air fryer to 350°F (177°C). 3. Pour the chocolate filing into the crust. 4. Cook for 25 to 30 minutes, stirring every 10 minutes, until a knife inserted into the middle comes out clean. Let sit for 5 minutes before dusting with confectioners' sugar (if using) to serve.

Lush Chocolate Chip Cookies

Prep time: 7 minutes | Cook time: 9 minutes | Serves 4

3 tablespoons butter, at room temperature	chocolate
	¼ teaspoon baking soda
⅓ cup plus 1 tablespoon light brown sugar	½ teaspoon vanilla extract
	¾ cup semisweet chocolate chips
1 egg yolk	
½ cup all-purpose flour	Nonstick flour-infused baking spray
2 tablespoons ground white	

1. In medium bowl, beat together the butter and brown sugar until fluffy. Stir in the egg yolk. 2. Add the flour, white chocolate, baking soda, and vanilla and mix well. Stir in the chocolate chips. 3. Line a 6-by-2-inch round baking pan with parchment paper. Spray the parchment paper with flour-infused baking spray. 4. Insert the crisper plate into the basket and the basket into the unit. Preheat the unit by selecting BAKE, setting the temperature to 300°F (149°C), and setting the time to 3 minutes. Select START/STOP to begin. 5. Spread the batter into the prepared pan, leaving a ½-inch border on all sides. 6. Once the unit is preheated, place the pan into the basket. 7. Select BAKE, set the temperature to 300°F (149°C), and set the time to 9 minutes. Select START/STOP to begin. 8. When the cooking is complete, the cookie should be light brown and just barely set. Remove the pan from the basket and let cool for 10 minutes. Remove the cookie from the pan, remove the parchment paper, and let cool completely on a wire rack.

Dark Brownies

Prep time: 10 minutes | Cook time: 11 to 13 minutes | Serves 4

1 egg	¼ cup cocoa
½ cup granulated sugar	Cooking spray
¼ teaspoon salt	Optional:
½ teaspoon vanilla	Vanilla ice cream
¼ cup butter, melted	Caramel sauce
¼ cup flour, plus 2 tablespoons	Whipped cream

1. Beat together egg, sugar, salt, and vanilla until light. 2. Add melted butter and mix well. 3. Stir in flour and cocoa. 4. Spray a baking pan lightly with cooking spray. 5. Spread batter in pan and bake at 330ºF (166ºC) for 11 to 13 minutes. Cool and cut into 4 large squares or 16 small brownie bites.

Kentucky Chocolate Nut Pie

Prep time: 20 minutes | Cook time: 25 minutes | Serves 8

2 large eggs, beaten	pecans
⅓ cup butter, melted	1 cup milk chocolate chips
1 cup sugar	2 tablespoons bourbon
½ cup all-purpose flour	1 (9-inch) unbaked piecrust
1½ cups coarsely chopped	

1. In a large bowl, stir together the eggs and melted butter. Add the sugar and flour and stir until combined. Stir in the pecans, chocolate chips, and bourbon until well mixed. 2. Using a fork, prick holes in the bottom and sides of the pie crust. Pour the pie filling into the crust. 3. Preheat the air fryer to 350ºF (177ºC). 4. Cook for 25 minutes, or until a knife inserted into the middle of the pie comes out clean. Let set for 5 minutes before serving.

Luscious Coconut Pie

Prep time: 5 minutes | Cook time: 45 minutes | Serves 6

1 cup plus ¼ cup unsweetened shredded coconut, divided	1½ teaspoons vanilla extract
2 eggs	¼ teaspoon salt
1½ cups almond milk	2 tablespoons powdered Swerve (optional)
½ cup granulated Swerve	½ cup sugar-free whipped topping (optional)
½ cup coconut flour	
¼ cup unsalted butter, melted	

1. Spread ¼ cup of the coconut in the bottom of a pie plate and place in the air fryer basket. Set the air fryer to 350ºF (177ºC) and air fry the coconut while the air fryer preheats, about 5 minutes, until golden brown. Transfer the coconut to a small bowl and set aside for garnish. Brush the pie plate with oil and set aside. 2. In a large bowl, combine the remaining 1 cup shredded coconut, eggs, milk, granulated Swerve, coconut flour, butter, vanilla, and salt. Whisk until smooth. Pour the batter into the prepared pie plate and air fry for 40 to 45 minutes, or until a toothpick inserted into the center of the pie comes out clean. (Check halfway through the baking time and rotate the pan, if necessary, for even baking.) 3. Remove the pie from the air fryer and place on a baking rack to cool completely. Garnish with the reserved toasted coconut and the powdered Swerve or sugar-free whipped topping, if desired. Cover and refrigerate leftover pie for up to 3 days.

Almond Butter Cookie Balls

Prep time: 5 minutes | Cook time: 10 minutes | Makes 10 balls

1 cup almond butter	¼ cup shredded unsweetened coconut
1 large egg	
1 teaspoon vanilla extract	¼ cup low-carb, sugar-free chocolate chips
¼ cup low-carb protein powder	
¼ cup powdered erythritol	½ teaspoon ground cinnamon

1. In a large bowl, mix almond butter and egg. Add in vanilla, protein powder, and erythritol. 2. Fold in coconut, chocolate chips, and cinnamon. Roll into 1-inch balls. Place balls into a round baking pan and put into the air fryer basket. 3. Adjust the temperature to 320ºF (160ºC) and bake for 10 minutes. 4. Allow to cool completely. Store in an airtight container in the refrigerator up to 4 days.

Apple Dutch Baby

Prep time: 30 minutes | Cook time: 16 minutes | Serves 2 to 3

Batter:	Apples:
2 large eggs	2 tablespoon butter
¼ cup all-purpose flour	4 tablespoons granulated sugar
¼ teaspoon baking powder	¼ teaspoon ground cinnamon
1½ teaspoons granulated sugar	¼ teaspoon ground nutmeg
Pinch kosher salt	1 small tart apple (such as
½ cup whole milk	Granny Smith), peeled, cored,
1 tablespoon butter, melted	and sliced
½ teaspoon pure vanilla extract	Vanilla ice cream (optional), for
¼ teaspoon ground nutmeg	serving

1. For the batter: In a medium bowl, combine the eggs, flour, baking powder, sugar, and salt. Whisk lightly. While whisking continuously, slowly pour in the milk. Whisk in the melted butter, vanilla, and nutmeg. Let the batter stand for 30 minutes. (You can also cover and refrigerate overnight.) 2. For the apples: Place the butter in a baking pan. Place the pan in the air fryer basket. Set the air fryer to 400ºF (204ºC) for 2 minutes. In a small bowl, combine 2 tablespoons of the sugar with the cinnamon and nutmeg and stir until well combined. 3. When the pan is hot and the butter is melted, brush some butter up the sides of the pan. Sprinkle the spiced sugar mixture over the butter. Arrange the apple slices in the pan in a single layer and sprinkle the remaining 2 tablespoons sugar over the apples. Set the air fryer to 400ºF (204ºC) to 2 minutes, or until the mixture bubbles. 4. Gently pour the batter over the apples. Set the air fryer to 350ºF (177ºC) for 12 minutes, or until the pancake is golden brown around the edges, the center is cooked through, and a toothpick emerges clean. 5. Serve immediately with ice cream, if desired.

Butter and Chocolate Chip Cookies

Prep time: 20 minutes | Cook time: 11 minutes | Serves 8

1 stick butter, at room temperature
1¼ cups Swerve
¼ cup chunky peanut butter
1 teaspoon vanilla paste
1 fine almond flour
⅔ cup coconut flour
⅓ cup cocoa powder, unsweetened
1 ½ teaspoons baking powder
¼ teaspoon ground cinnamon
¼ teaspoon ginger
½ cup chocolate chips, unsweetened

1. In a mixing dish, beat the butter and Swerve until creamy and uniform. Stir in the peanut butter and vanilla. 2. In another mixing dish, thoroughly combine the flour, cocoa powder, baking powder, cinnamon, and ginger. 3. Add the flour mixture to the peanut butter mixture; mix to combine well. Afterwards, fold in the chocolate chips. Drop by large spoonfuls onto a parchment-lined air fryer basket. Bake at 365°F (185°C) for 11 minutes or until golden brown on the top. Bon appétit!

Pecan and Cherry Stuffed Apples

Prep time: 10 minutes | Cook time: 20 minutes | Serves 4

4 apples (about 1¼ pounds / 567 g)
¼ cup chopped pecans
⅓ cup dried tart cherries
1 tablespoon melted butter
3 tablespoons brown sugar
¼ teaspoon allspice
Pinch salt
Ice cream, for serving

1. Cut off top ½ inch from each apple; reserve tops. With a melon baller, core through stem ends without breaking through the bottom. (Do not trim bases.) 2. Preheat the air fryer to 350°F (177°C). Combine pecans, cherries, butter, brown sugar, allspice, and a pinch of salt. Stuff mixture into the hollow centers of the apples. Cover with apple tops. Put in the air fryer basket, using tongs. Air fry for 20 to 25 minutes, or just until tender. 3. Serve warm with ice cream.

Coconut Muffins

Prep time: 5 minutes | Cook time: 25 minutes | Serves 5

½ cup coconut flour
2 tablespoons cocoa powder
3 tablespoons erythritol
1 teaspoon baking powder
2 tablespoons coconut oil
2 eggs, beaten
½ cup coconut shred

1. In the mixing bowl, mix all ingredients. 2. Then pour the mixture into the molds of the muffin and transfer in the air fryer basket. 3. Cook the muffins at 350°F (177°C) for 25 minutes.

Vanilla Scones

Prep time: 20 minutes | Cook time: 10 minutes | Serves 6

4 ounces (113 g) coconut flour
½ teaspoon baking powder
1 teaspoon apple cider vinegar
2 teaspoons mascarpone
¼ cup heavy cream
1 teaspoon vanilla extract
1 tablespoon erythritol
Cooking spray

1. In the mixing bowl, mix coconut flour with baking powder, apple cider vinegar, mascarpone, heavy cream, vanilla extract, and erythritol. 2. Knead the dough and cut into scones. 3. Then put them in the air fryer basket and sprinkle with cooking spray. 4. Cook the vanilla scones at 365°F (185°C) for 10 minutes.

Simple Pineapple Sticks

Prep time: 5 minutes | Cook time: 10 minutes | Serves 4

½ fresh pineapple, cut into sticks
¼ cup desiccated coconut

1. Preheat the air fryer to 400°F (204°C). 2. Coat the pineapple sticks in the desiccated coconut and put each one in the air fryer basket. 3. Air fry for 10 minutes. 4. Serve immediately

Appendix 1: Measurement Conversion Chart

MEASUREMENT CONVERSION CHART

VOLUME EQUIVALENTS(DRY)

US STANDARD	METRIC (APPROXIMATE)
1/8 teaspoon	0.5 mL
1/4 teaspoon	1 mL
1/2 teaspoon	2 mL
3/4 teaspoon	4 mL
1 teaspoon	5 mL
1 tablespoon	15 mL
1/4 cup	59 mL
1/2 cup	118 mL
3/4 cup	177 mL
1 cup	235 mL
2 cups	475 mL
3 cups	700 mL
4 cups	1 L

VOLUME EQUIVALENTS(LIQUID)

US STANDARD	US STANDARD (OUNCES)	METRIC (APPROXIMATE)
2 tablespoons	1 fl.oz.	30 mL
1/4 cup	2 fl.oz.	60 mL
1/2 cup	4 fl.oz.	120 mL
1 cup	8 fl.oz.	240 mL
1 1/2 cup	12 fl.oz.	355 mL
2 cups or 1 pint	16 fl.oz.	475 mL
4 cups or 1 quart	32 fl.oz.	1 L
1 gallon	128 fl.oz.	4 L

WEIGHT EQUIVALENTS

US STANDARD	METRIC (APPROXIMATE)
1 ounce	28 g
2 ounces	57 g
5 ounces	142 g
10 ounces	284 g
15 ounces	425 g
16 ounces (1 pound)	455 g
1.5 pounds	680 g
2 pounds	907 g

TEMPERATURES EQUIVALENTS

FAHRENHEIT(F)	CELSIUS(C) (APPROXIMATE)
225 °F	107 °C
250 °F	120 °C
275 °F	135 °C
300 °F	150 °C
325 °F	160 °C
350 °F	180 °C
375 °F	190 °C
400 °F	205 °C
425 °F	220 °C
450 °F	235 °C
475 °F	245 °C
500 °F	260 °C

Appendix 2: Air Fryer Cooking Chart

Air Fryer Cooking Chart

Beef

Item	Temp (°F)	Time (mins)	Item	Temp (°F)	Time (mins)
Beef Eye Round Roast (4 lbs.)	400 °F	45 to 55	Meatballs (1-inch)	370 °F	7
Burger Patty (4 oz.)	370 °F	16 to 20	Meatballs (3-inch)	380 °F	10
Filet Mignon (8 oz.)	400 °F	18	Ribeye, bone-in (1-inch, 8 oz)	400 °F	10 to 15
Flank Steak (1.5 lbs.)	400 °F	12	Sirloin steaks (1-inch, 12 oz)	400 °F	9 to 14
Flank Steak (2 lbs.)	400 °F	20 to 28			

Chicken

Item	Temp (°F)	Time (mins)	Item	Temp (°F)	Time (mins)
Breasts, bone in (1 ¼ lb.)	370 °F	25	Legs, bone-in (1 ¾ lb.)	380 °F	30
Breasts, boneless (4 oz)	380 °F	12	Thighs, boneless (1 ½ lb.)	380 °F	18 to 20
Drumsticks (2 ½ lb.)	370 °F	20	Wings (2 lb.)	400 °F	12
Game Hen (halved 2 lb.)	390 °F	20	Whole Chicken	360 °F	75
Thighs, bone-in (2 lb.)	380 °F	22	Tenders	360 °F	8 to 10

Pork & Lamb

Item	Temp (°F)	Time (mins)	Item	Temp (°F)	Time (mins)
Bacon (regular)	400 °F	5 to 7	Pork Tenderloin	370 °F	15
Bacon (thick cut)	400 °F	6 to 10	Sausages	380 °F	15
Pork Loin (2 lb.)	360 °F	55	Lamb Loin Chops (1-inch thick)	400 °F	8 to 12
Pork Chops, bone in (1-inch, 6.5 oz)	400 °F	12	Rack of Lamb (1.5 – 2 lb.)	380 °F	22

Fish & Seafood

Item	Temp (°F)	Time (mins)	Item	Temp (°F)	Time (mins)
Calamari (8 oz)	400 °F	4	Tuna Steak	400 °F	7 to 10
Fish Fillet (1-inch, 8 oz)	400 °F	10	Scallops	400 °F	5 to 7
Salmon, fillet (6 oz)	380 °F	12	Shrimp	400 °F	5
Swordfish steak	400 °F	10			

Air Fryer Cooking Chart

Vegetables					
INGREDIENT	AMOUNT	PREPARATION	OIL	TEMP	COOK TIME
Asparagus	2 bunches	Cut in half, trim stems	2 Tbsp	420°F	12-15 mins
Beets	1½ lbs	Peel, cut in ½-inch cubes	1Tbsp	390°F	28-30 mins
Bell peppers (for roasting)	4 peppers	Cut in quarters, remove seeds	1Tbsp	400°F	15-20 mins
Broccoli	1 large head	Cut in 1-2-inch florets	1Tbsp	400°F	15-20 mins
Brussels sprouts	1lb	Cut in half, remove stems	1Tbsp	425°F	15-20 mins
Carrots	1lb	Peel, cut in ¼-inch rounds	1 Tbsp	425°F	10-15 mins
Cauliflower	1 head	Cut in 1-2-inch florets	2 Tbsp	400°F	20-22 mins
Corn on the cob	7 ears	Whole ears, remove husks	1 Tbps	400°F	14-17 mins
Green beans	1 bag (12 oz)	Trim	1 Tbps	420°F	18-20 mins
Kale (for chips)	4 oz	Tear into pieces,remove stems	None	325°F	5-8 mins
Mushrooms	16 oz	Rinse, slice thinly	1 Tbps	390°F	25-30 mins
Potatoes, russet	1½ lbs	Cut in 1-inch wedges	1 Tbps	390°F	25-30 mins
Potatoes, russet	1lb	Hand-cut fries, soak 30 mins in cold water, then pat dry	½ -3 Tbps	400°F	25-28 mins
Potatoes, sweet	1lb	Hand-cut fries, soak 30 mins in cold water, then pat dry	1 Tbps	400°F	25-28 mins
Zucchini	1lb	Cut in eighths lengthwise, then cut in half	1 Tbps	400°F	15-20 mins

Made in the USA
Las Vegas, NV
26 January 2024

84951215R00059